The Limits of State Power & Private Rights

This book tackles a complex area of law, social policy and social work, providing a comprehensive analysis of the theoretical, practical and legal boundaries of State power following safeguarding and child protection referrals in England. The book examines the history, rationale and implications of the current position, concluding that the balance of power is weighted in favour of the State.

The Limits of State Power & Private Rights is ground-breaking in its approach to the subject and its detailed, critical analysis. Traditionally the subject matter of the book is considered within a welfare framework. The analysis in this book argues that a policing agenda is embedded within policy but without appropriate safeguards and controls, creating potentially irreconcilable tension described by the author as the 'welfare/policing dichotomy'.

This book is of importance to academics, lawyers, social workers, policy makers, practitioners and service users. The book is written so as to be accessible to a multidisciplinary audience, but is sufficiently detailed so as to be suitable for specialists and non-specialists alike in this subject area. The chapters include introductory and contextual sections as well as doctrinal, theoretical and socio-legal analysis. Although the focus is on the English system, the book is equally applicable to the many worldwide jurisdictions adopting the Anglo/American 'child rights'-based framework of child protection. It is also of use as a comparative work in countries where a family support-based system is practiced.

Dr Lauren Devine is an Associate Professor of Law, University of the West of England. A Barrister with research interests in State powers, private rights and child protection, Lauren is Principal Investigator of the Economic and Social Research Council-funded project 'Rethinking Child Protection Strategy'.

The Limits of State Power & Private Rights

Exploring Child Protection & Safeguarding Referrals and Assessments

Lauren Devine

Routledge
Taylor & Francis Group

LONDON AND NEW YORK

First published 2017
by Routledge
2 Park Square, Milton Park, Abingdon, Oxon OX14 4RN

and by Routledge
711 Third Avenue, New York, NY 10017

Routledge is an imprint of the Taylor & Francis Group, an informa business

British Library Cataloguing in Publication Data
A catalogue record for this book is available
from the British Library

Library of Congress Cataloging in Publication Data
Names: Devine, Lauren, (Law teacher)
Title: The limits of state power & private rights : exploring child
protection & safeguarding referrals and assessments / Lauren Devine.
Other titles: Limits of state power and private rights
Description: New York, NY : Routledge, 2017. | Includes bibliographical
references and index.
Identifiers: LCCN 2016046640 | ISBN 9781138782266 (hbk) |
ISBN 9781315767048 (ebk)
Subjects: LCSH: Children--Legal status, laws, etc.--Great Britain. |
Children's rights--Great Britain. | Civil rights--Great Britain. | Guardian
and ward--Great Britain.
Classification: LCC KD735 .D49 2017 | DDC 342.4108/772--dc23LC
record available at https://lccn.loc.gov/2016046640

ISBN: 9781138782266 (hbk)
ISBN: 9781315767048 (ebk)

Typeset in Galliard
by Sunrise Setting Ltd, Brixham, UK

MIX
Paper from
responsible sources
FSC
www.fsc.org   FSC® C013604   Printed and bound by CPI Group (UK) Ltd, Croydon, CR0 4YY

For Poppy, Jacob and Tom

Contents

List of figures

List of tables

Table of cases

Preface

The idea for this book originated in Birmingham when I was completing my doctorate under the supervision of Professors Sally Lloyd-Bostock and Sonia Harris-Short. I was interested in the broad concept of the limits of State powers and private rights, and had watched with interest the development of surveillance and data sharing in relation to child protection and safeguarding. Although it was not a widely held view at the time, I felt there was an interesting situation developing where the technological means of surveillance and data collection had outstripped protections for citizens, creating a potential imbalance in systems of State interventions.

During the data collection stage of my doctorate the Children Act 2004 came into force. This not only changed my focus in order to embrace the new legislation and the implications of 'safeguarding', but I found myself researching an untested area. In this new framework it was unclear where the boundaries of surveillance and intervention would lie, or the extent to which it was permissible for the State to non-consensually or coercively interfere into private family life. However, by the time my doctorate was complete concerns about the blurring of consensual boundaries and expansion of State power in relation to child protection and safeguarding had become well understood.

Developing my work into a book presented new challenges in bringing together the theoretical and applied elements of my research. In 2014 I was awarded an Economic and Social Research Council (ESRC) Transformative Research grant to lead the project 'Rethinking Child Protection Strategy'[1] enabling development of many ideas in the book. The funding enabled research into more detailed and diverse aspects of the child protection and safeguarding system than had been possible for the doctorate, including identifying that, despite the increasing trend of referrals, there is a lack of proportionate increase in child abuse detection. This additional research also provided the opportunity for detailed discussion of the possibilities for a new, rebalanced policy direction in this field.

Note

1 Grant number: ES/M000990/1.

Acknowledgements

This book would not have been possible without the support and insights provided by people I have been privileged to work with during the writing of the manuscript. I was extremely fortunate to have been offered the opportunity to develop my ideas about child protection and safeguarding during the completion of my doctorate under the supervision of Professors Sally Lloyd-Bostock and Sonia Harris-Short. Their encouragement, inspiration and belief in my idea to write about the balance between State powers and private rights in child protection and safeguarding made my doctorate, and this book, possible. I would also like to thank Penny Mullen, who kindly offered her advice on my statistical analysis, and my external doctoral examiners Professor John Eekelaar and Dr Lynne Wrennall, who gave invaluable comment and insights. The list of thanks would not be complete without acknowledging the eclectic input and support of Stephen Parker, Ben Cooke and Rob Upjohn. I would also like to thank Poppy and Jacob for their patience.

Introduction

Exploring the issue: State power and private rights

The most appropriate way to address the problem of child abuse is an important question. It is generally accepted that governments in developed societies have a role to play. The precise nature of that role has been addressed in different ways worldwide albeit with some core similarities. The approach in England is unusual, and worth detailed consideration. Over the past three decades there have been major policy changes expanding the State's role, and a significant change to the rationale for intervening into children's lives. This has led to an increase in State powers and corresponding erosion of parental autonomy.

The Children Act 1989 introduced the modern legislative framework in England, placing a duty upon local authorities to investigate reasonable suspicions of significant harm to children (s.47), and to assess need in cases where children and their families wanted help (s.17). The 1997–2010 Labour administration changed the landscape of the State's role via policy change and new legislation without changing this enabling legislation. The public inquiry into the death of Victoria Climbié[1] and the Green Paper *Every Child Matters*[2] paved the way for the expansion of the role of the local authority and other State agencies involved in child welfare: agencies working with children were mandated to report cases of suspected 'safeguarding concerns' under s.11 Children Act 2004. This was much wider than cases of suspected child abuse. An 'early intervention' response to low-level 'concerns' was implemented on the basis that it would prevent family problems becoming child abuse. The policy also intended to steer children in a direction that would lead to them becoming productive members of society once they reached adulthood. The aim was to invest in the future generation because they were important as a future workforce, not simply to improve children's lives whilst they were still children. The reduction of child abuse for welfare reasons was to be only one rationale for State intervention into private family life.

To implement the Labour Government's policies there have been major changes to the way in which the suspicion of child abuse and safeguarding concerns are responded to. There is a robust framework of State powers, many of which invade the privacy and interrupt the autonomy of private family life, including in cases which fall below the statutory threshold in s.47 of 'reasonable suspicion of significant harm'. This prompts an important question: what is the appropriate balance between the powers of the State and the private rights of citizens, including children, to question and prevent unwanted or unwarranted intrusion and interference?

When the Children Act 1989 was enacted it was envisaged that cases of need under s.17 would be dealt with consensually under Part III of the Act, and that cases of suspected significant harm would be investigated non-consensually (if necessary) by s.47 under Part V. The intention was to ensure that coercive interferences with parental autonomy would only occur where it was necessary. The enactment of the Children Act 2004 and subsequent policy changes has placed all children and families under an unprecedented level of surveillance. This was coupled with a mandate to agencies with whom children have contact to report 'safeguarding concerns', including 'signs' of unexpected behaviour in children, or identification of pre-determined risk factors in the family demographic. As a consequence, an increasing number of families are reported to local authorities each year, the vast majority of whom are not reported as a result of suspected child abuse.[3] The need to respect the autonomy of families has consequently become a low priority partly because the adverse consequences of England's approach understandably are less prominent than high profile child abuse fatalities. Prevalence estimates published by the NSPCC[4] reinforce a drive towards a public perception that there is a high level of undetected child abuse which in turn supports the argument for increasingly intrusive and coercive interventions at a low level.

In situations where a child is being systematically and deliberately harmed by their parents the argument for the State to intervene is strong. Welfare arguments setting out that it is not acceptable in a civilised society to leave children at the mercy of abusive parents will invariably prioritise the need for the State to be empowered to intervene in such situations. In these cases, the question of parental 'rights' is secondary to the duty placed upon the State to at least investigate the situation. However, the vast majority of cases that are referred to local authorities are not cases where systematic and deliberate abuse is found to be occurring. Where there is significant harm it may be at least partly attributable to the family's situation in circumstances where parents may not be intending to harm the child but poverty, lack of adequate housing, health issues, substance abuse or a lack of understanding about what constitutes appropriate child care may be causing an untenable situation. These situations are very different in nature to the rare cases where parents have a deliberate desire to inflict harm.

Whilst the justification for investigating and removing a child from deliberately abusive parents may be relatively clear cut, the justification for investigating and removing a child from inadequate or poorly supported parents is less so. Under the current framework there is provision for support, but at a certain point the same local authority responsible for providing that support can also decide to take action to apply to the court for an order to remove a child from their family. Consequently, once a family is referred they may find themselves escalated into a process which requires social workers to assess whether a family may need services within an inflexible framework designed to deal with cases of significant harm.

The welfare/policing dichotomy in such cases is not easily reconciled. The intention and aim of this book is therefore to bring the question of the appropriate balance of State powers and private rights into a more prominent position.

Central themes and structure of the book

The first half of the book considers the evolution of the social, political and legal position. The middle part of the book focusses attention on the discourses that influenced the development of the current situation and identifies the dominant discourse. Welfare discourse informs the historic development of the need for the State to have a duty. This duty extends to the requirement to make inquiries to establish what is happening in cases of reasonably suspected significant harm. The assumption is that action can then be taken to protect the child. This part of the book considers the Labour Government's use of the existing welfare-informed framework to introduce surveillance and policing models to ensure social compliance. The final chapters consider the consequences of the mixed welfare/policing model, concluding with a tentative suggestion for a revised system. The thread that runs throughout the book is an examination of whether there is an appropriate balance between State powers and private rights.

The first two chapters provide an overview explaining how the modern situation has developed. They explain how the issue of children's welfare was identified as a question for government, rather than a problem that must be resolved (or not) within individual families without the State having either a role or a responsibility. It is now firmly entrenched in England (and in many other jurisdictions) that the State does have a role, with much of the modern system being developed in the twentieth and early twenty-first century. The recognition of the need for the State to have a formal role and responsibility and the reasons for it are considered in Chapter 1. This chapter sets out the history in England of the emergence of child welfare policies and more latterly policies of family policing. The focus in Chapter 2 is a close examination of the nature and scope of child abuse. What amounts to child abuse is an important question. Identifying behaviours and characteristics that should and should not be considered to amount to child abuse is important, as is the recognition of 'grey areas'. This chapter explores the notion that societal, legal and policy understanding of the meaning of 'child abuse' may differ.

Chapter 3 is concerned with the way in which families are identified for referral to local authority children's social care departments (social services). It describes the rise in surveillance of all families in order to target those considered to exhibit signs or characteristics deemed 'risky'. Those families are referred with or without their consent. When described as a system of surveillance and policing, it becomes apparent that all families are subject to mass surveillance via their day to day interactions with State agencies. This is leading to an unprecedented mass of data being collected, stored and shared. Children who grow up and become parents will now have a 'data double', or historic official record that is increasingly linked to a social profile amounting to a type of risk score. Chapter 4 examines the response to referrals, looking in detail at the assessment process. The modern position post-Munro[5] is set out together with the Public Law Outline Guide 2014.[6] The process by which an assessment occurs is considered with special attention given to the divides between lawful consensual assessment and lawful non-consensual assessment. The blurring of the boundary between the two and the lack of advance warning and appropriate advice and information for parents is argued to create a quasi-consensual situation which is potentially subject to legal challenge.

Chapter 5 places the issues raised in Chapters 3 and 4 into a theoretical framework to provide insights about the nature and power of State processes such as child protection and safeguarding. The processes, described as schema, are reconstructed showing how a family progresses inexorably through stages of a surveillance/policing process, constructed in a way so as to make it very difficult for a family to extract itself. Attempts to subvert the schema do not work: the framework prevails and, once it has started, lack of evidence does not stop the process until there is a point at which the schema allows decision making. A striking element of this examination is the fact that, despite this framework of State power to investigate and assess the increasing number of families referred year on year, there is no corresponding increase in the proportion of child abuse detected or addressed.[7]

Chapter 6 provides a detailed examination of the extent to which law and policy provides protection for children and parents: is the balance between State power and private rights adequate? This chapter considers the question from the perspective of a case where a child is being abused, and also from the perspective of a case where a child is not being abused but rather is a child in need, where the referral could be unfounded (for example mistaken, malicious or over-zealous), or where there is insufficient information or evidence to suggest there is need, risk or actual abuse. The final part of this chapter develops the latter scenario and considers the system's impact on such families. This examination includes the question of potential and actual harm to families caused by State processes. In a welfare context such harms may be inexplicable as welfare discourse perceives the system through the lens of the child at the centre of a system which is there to cater to their need for services or protection. In this discourse the child is the 'client'. However, in a policing context, the evidence that harms exist is easily understood. The 'service users', including the child, may not be consensual parties to a process that escalates them into increasingly coercive stages of intense surveillance from which they may not be able to extricate themselves. In genuine cases of significant harm there is a strong argument that this is justified. But this experience is not restricted to these extreme cases. Examination via welfare and policing lenses enables imbalances between State powers and private rights to be identified.

Having identified harms, the question of remedies is the final piece of the puzzle. Although State powers are stronger than private rights in the process, the balance between State powers and private rights may still be argued to be appropriate if there are adequate remedies available for those harmed by the exercise of them. Chapter 7 discusses the available remedies, establishing that there is no specific remedy, but that a number of avenues exist for potential redress. This chapter draws these remedies together and provides a systematic analysis of their nature, scope and adequacy. The evidence presented in this chapter enables conclusions to be drawn about the weight of State power, and the limits of private rights.

The final chapter, Chapter 8, suggests a new model that takes into account the issues discussed in the earlier chapters. The new model is suggested as a starting point for discussion, not as a definitive means of resolving all of the problems. To some extent, the framework set out in Chapter 8 already exists as there is a drift towards 'multi-agency' approaches. However, the approach suggested here re-establishes protective boundaries between them. The key difference in this suggestion is to disentangle the 'welfare/policing dichotomy'.[8] This dichotomy potentially causes a major conflict between families and social workers and pollutes the role of social workers as providers of professional family support. In the suggested framework the need to address actual cases of abuse is acknowledged and a means of doing so is provided, albeit with a different emphasis.

Notes

1 Lord Laming (2003) *The Victoria Climbié Inquiry Report*, HC 570, 24 June 2003. Online at: www.publications.parliament.uk/pa/cm200203/cmselect/cmhealth/570/570.pdf (Accessed 1 January 2016).

2 The Chief Secretary to the Treasury (2003) *Every Child Matters: Green Paper Presented to Parliament by the Chief Secretary to the Treasury*, Cm 5860, TSO, London.

3 For example see: Devine, L. and Parker, S. (2015) *Rethinking Child Protection Strategy: Learning from Trends*, Working Paper, Centre for Legal Research, Bristol Law School, UWE, Bristol, p. 5. Online at: http://eprints.uwe.ac.uk/25258/ (Accessed 28 February 2016); and Devine, L. (2015) 'Considering Social Work Assessment of Families', *Journal of Social Welfare & Family Law* 37(1): 70–83. Online at: http://dx.doi.org/10.1080/09649069.2015.998005 (Accessed 28 February 2016).

4 For example see: Cawson, P., Wattam, C., Brooker, S. and Kelly, G. (2000) *Child Maltreatment in the United Kingdom: A Study of the Prevalence of Child Abuse and Neglect*, NSPCC, London; and Radford, L., Corral, S., Bradley, C., Fisher, H., Bassett, C., Howat, N. and Collishaw, S. (2011) 'Child Abuse and Neglect in the UK Today', NSPCC. Online at: www.nspcc.org.uk/Inform/research/findings/child_abuse_neglect_research_PDF_wdf84181.pdf (Accessed 25 November 2011).

5 Munro, E. (2011) *The Munro Review of Child Protection: Final Report, A Child Centred System*, Cm 8062, Department for Education, HMSO, London. Online at www.official-documents.gov.uk/document/cm80/8062/8062.pdf (Accessed 4 May 2016).

6 The latest version of the PLO (2014) can now be found in the Family Procedure Rules at: Ministry of Justice (2014) *Practice Direction 12a – Care, Supervision and Other Part 4 Proceedings: Guide to Case Management*. Online at: www.justice.gov.uk/courts/procedure-rules/family/practice_directions/pd_part_12a#para (Accessed 25 February 2016). This replaces the earlier PLO document used before the Family Procedure Rules were introduced and came into force on 6 April 2011. See original PLO at: Ministry of Justice (2008) *The Public Law Outline Guide to Case Management in Public Law Proceedings*, TSO, London.

Online at: www.familylaw.co.uk/system/uploads/attachments/0000/2168/public_law_outline.pdf (Accessed 25 January 2016).

7 See: Devine, L. and Parker, S. (2015) 'Rethinking Child Protection Strategy: Learning from Trends', Working Paper, Centre for Legal Research, Bristol Law School, UWE, Bristol, p. 19. Online at: http://eprints.uwe.ac.uk/25258/ (Accessed 28 February 2016).

8 Devine, L. (2015) 'Considering Social Work Assessment of Families', *Journal of Social Welfare & Family Law* 37(1): 70–83. Online at: http://dx.doi.org/10.1080/09649069.2015.998005 (Accessed 28 February 2016), p. 71.

1 Development of the State's role
Child welfare and family policing

The State's developing role in children's welfare: good intentions and opposing narratives

The State has an important role in supporting child welfare. Most developed countries have social welfare provisions in place including measures to relieve poverty and related problems such as lack of adequate housing, and to provide health care and education. Additional social services extend to direct provisions intended to ensure that children do not suffer maltreatment or neglect. The modern role of the State in England and elsewhere (although the focus of this book and its data applies to England) has developed as a response to major developments in relation to child welfare which took place during the twentieth century. These developments reformed the way in which children and families are treated if they are unable to supply their own needs and include the provision of some services which are universal, and the provision of others which are rationed.

Health care and education are universal services in England. Eligibility for State benefits and social housing are rationed. The provision of direct social work family services and interventions are also rationed services, accessed via referral and assessment. Whilst the use of referral and assessment to check eligibility for rationed services may appear unproblematic, the system is complex. Families who want to access services may find themselves considered 'risky' or 'abusive' in addition to 'needy'. Families who do not want to access services may also find themselves referred, either because someone else believes they have a need for services or because a child in the family is considered to be suffering or at risk of suffering significant harm.

To add to the complexity, the legal framework operates to protect the child, not to consider the child in the context of their families' needs or provide protection for parents. The multidisciplinary nature of the system has led to two concurrent narrative strands which seem largely unaffected by the existence of the other: welfare and policing discourses have developed creating two broad narratives in relation to the role of the State in providing welfare services to children, and the connected role of policing parents. These narratives can be summarised as considering that:

- that mass surveillance of children and their families, followed by targeted social work intervention, is justified because it aims to protect children from abuse; or

- that it is not justified as it largely fails to achieve its aim to protect children from abuse, and harms families who are not abusing their children through unnecessary interference.

Most commentators adopt a position falling somewhere in between these two competing schools of thought. The origins of these narratives can be traced via the development of child welfare principles, the ideology of public responsibility for protecting children from abuse, the arguments in favour of State surveillance and interference into private family life, the counter-narrative highlighting the erosion of privacy and the rise of the e-Government agenda. The introduction of parental responsibility in the Children Act 1989 provides legal context.

The development of child welfare principles

The notion that parents should not have complete autonomy over their children derives from a belief that the State should take some responsibility for protecting children from serious maltreatment within families. This ideology developed from an emergence of the concept of welfare and of children's rights, which ran counter to the historical discourse of children as possessions of parents, originally fathers and more latterly both fathers and mothers.

Historically, children whose parents could or would not care for them had few options. Children were predominantly the responsibility of families rather than the responsibility of the State. The development of laws which created some State responsibility for children's welfare traces a slow erosion of parental autonomy and an initially reluctant assumption of State responsibility in limited circumstances. This assumption of responsibility primarily derives from the discourse of poverty and delinquency as well as, more recently, the broad concept of child abuse.

In the sixteenth century, the Poor Laws, enacted between 1536 and 1601, obliged parishes to support and train orphans where ordered to do so by a court.[1] Where children had living parents, responsibility for children vested in the parents, rather than the State. It was some considerable time before the assumption of responsibility by the State expanded. By the mid-eighteenth century a jurisdiction had evolved that looked to address the problem of child welfare via protection.[2] In the late eighteenth century and the early part of the nineteenth, movements such as The Philanthropic Society for the Prevention of Crime and the Reform of the Criminal Poor came into existence. Such societies were concerned with ensuring that the social order was maintained, and with the prevention of crime. Thus, child welfare was linked with crime prevention. The mid-nineteenth century saw the first legislative restriction of paternal rights at the suit of the mother and the State. This was brought about by Caroline Norton's campaign, begun in 1838.[3] Following separation from her husband she found her access to her three children restricted. She contributed to the introduction of what eventually became the Custody of Infants Act 1839[4] which encouraged mothers to apply for custody or access. This Act, for the first time in British law, denied the absolute nature of the father's rights at common law. In practice, however, courts continued to uphold paternal rights, although a court could make such order 'as it think fit'.[5]

The Custody of Infants Act 1873[6] made two main changes, removing the mother's adultery as a bar to her obtaining custody of her children, and legitimising separation deeds giving custody to mothers, although they remained unenforceable unless they were deemed to be for the benefit of the infant. This is an early example of 'best interests'. A similar test remains in respect of modern contact and residence Orders in respect of children[7] as these orders are made in accordance with the welfare principle,[8] whereby the child's welfare must be the paramount concern in judicial decision making.[9]

The subsequent Custody of Infants Act 1839 not only challenged male autonomy within family life, but introduced the concept of decisions concerning children whose parents were alive being decided by courts. This took absolute power away from families, which tended to be patriarchal, and began a discourse whereby judicial mechanisms took over certain decisions concerning children. This was not necessarily informed by concern for children's welfare, however, as it was instigated by the issue of parents' rights as opposed to welfare concerns. The notion of children as a group with their own welfare rights developed later in the nineteenth century: for example the Infant Custody Act 1873 changed the direction of the 1839 Act by indicating that the correct principle for deciding custody was the needs of the child rather than the rights of either parent. This introduced the idea of children as a group with rights distinct from those of their parents.

The concept of wardship also emerged as a means of transferring power away from parents. Wardship has its origins in the feudal system and 'is largely a creature of common law'.[10] It developed from the principle of *parens patriae* whereby it was the Sovereign's prerogative to have care of those who could not look after themselves, and to delegate this prerogative to the court.[11] Any person could make the High Court the guardian of any child within its jurisdiction. Leave of the court was needed in relation to any important step in the child's life and the court could make and enforce any order or direction in relation to the child if it was consistent with the principle that the first and paramount consideration was the welfare of the child.[12] An application to the court could be made by 'any person . . . by issuing proceedings for the purpose'.[13] This gave *locus standi* to any applicant wanting to invoke the power of the court in relation to a child on the grounds of 'welfare'. The only limit upon this was procedural; on issuing the summons the applicant must state his or her interest in or relationship to the child. Where the interest or relationship was unclear the registrar had discretion to decide the application was an abuse of process and could either dismiss the summons or refer it to a judge.[14]

The widening of the categories of interested parties was consistent with the idea that the welfare of children should be of concern to society rather than of concern only to the child's immediate family. The common law framework of wardship enabled interested applicants to bring children to the attention of the State via a court application and enabled the State to take responsibility through exercise of the court's powers. This was an important milestone in the development of the concept that children's welfare is of concern to non-family members, the State and the courts. As well as referring children to the courts, society also took an active philanthropic interest in children's welfare from the end of the nineteenth century. Societies began to be formed for the purpose of encouraging the raising of children without cruelty, and many parts of Europe began to develop early welfare states. The discourses of poverty, cruelty and welfare developed together as it was argued that poverty led to child neglect.

These modern welfare arguments developed in democratic capitalist countries where it was argued the poor should be assisted by the more fortunate, and also through a sense of public responsibility demonstrated by public assistance. Flora and Heidenheimer observe that the welfare state has arisen as a response to two fundamental developments: the formation of national States and their transformation into mass democracies since the French Revolution, and the growth of capitalism that became the dominant mode of production after the Industrial Revolution.[15] They observe that the growth of the modern welfare state can be understood as organised around three regulating, organising structures.[16] This structure was not, however, understood or described as 'welfare' in the UK until the 1940s[17] where it developed as: 'the antithesis of the old poor law situations in which "welfare" recipients, the paupers, lost their personal freedom and their right to vote because social dependency implied the sacrifice of citizenship rights'.[18]

Long before the concept of the welfare state, the National Society for the Prevention of Cruelty to Children (NSPCC), modelled on the Royal Society for the Prevention of Cruelty to Animals (RSPCA), was founded in 1884. The Custody of Infants Act 1873 followed by the Prevention of Cruelty to and Protection of Children Act 1889[19] were the first legislative attempts at State protection of children as they embodied the notion of child welfare in the sense of 'protection' in statute for the first time. Under the Prevention of Cruelty to and Protection of Children Act 1889 a punishment for ill-treatment and neglect of children could be imposed if an adult: '[w]ilfully ill-treats, neglects, abandons, or exposes such child, or causes or procures such child to be ill-treated, neglected, abandoned or exposed, in a manner likely to cause such child unnecessary suffering, or injury to its health'.[20] A child could then be brought before the court and committed to the care of a relative or another 'fit person'.[21]

The Victorian era saw the moral training of children as important to prevent crime, thereby maintaining social order. This was seen as primarily the function of the parents, with the State interfering only when parents became unable to care for their children, or when they exhibited criminal behaviour towards their children. As well as provision for protecting children from parents convicted of the type of cruelty described above, the Industrial Schools Act 1866[22] enabled courts to commit children to industrial schools until the age of 18 in certain circumstances, including circumstances where they did not have any 'proper guardianship or visible means of subsistence'.[23] The mixing of children deemed to require protection (the abused) with those deemed to require correction (the delinquent) derived from this notion of moral training as paramount to society's wellbeing.

Such State policies were not without unintended consequences and it is well documented that children encountered harsh conditions in State institutions. However, some children subject to private arrangements for care fared no better. Consequently, despite harsh State conditions, the emergence of fatalities in relation to informal fostering arrangements led to public perception that the State should play a more active role in regulating arrangements relating to children. The case of Margaret Waters in 1870 concerned a foster mother who was executed following the death of one of the neglected infants in her care, causing: 'a wave of public consternation and prompted the infant life protection movement to press for legislative change to regulate private boarding out'.[24] But only minor changes were made in the Prevention of Cruelty to Children Act 1904,[25] which involved transferring responsibility for offences against children from the Poor Law Guardians to local authorities. Dingwall *et al.* (1984) consider that:

> children were the focus for action because of the threat which inadequate moral socialization represented to the social order, although this does not preclude all concern for their physical well-being . . . If one concentrates on legal development what is striking is the apparent disappearance of concern of child victims, with the short-lived exception of events around the passage of the Children Act 1948.[26]

The development of State principles for the protection of children

The recognition of children as a group separate and distinct from their parents is a relatively recent development (in legal terms), evolving for just over a century.[27] During the twentieth century the concept of children as a group in need of specific protection gathered momentum. This development, although altruistic in principle, is not without controversy. Historically, there has been a sense that a child lacking a family would therefore lack moral and social responsibility. Reflecting this, the Children and Young Persons Act 1933[28] considers child victims of abuse and young offenders to be in the same category. Dingwall *et al.* (1984)[29] describe this as the assimilation of: 'child victims to the category of state offenders'.[30] It took serious child abuse scandals, including a desperately sad case involving children who were already in the care of the State, to raise public and political awareness of the plight of maltreated children as a general social concern. The Children Act 1948[31] was introduced three years after the Dennis O'Neill scandal.[32] Dennis O'Neill died whilst in the care of the State following physical abuse by his foster father. This raised public awareness of the vulnerability of children in the care of the State as well as in the care of their parents. In relation to children who were not living with their parents a key provision of the 1948 Act was to require local authorities, where it was consistent with the welfare of the child, to try to ensure that when a child had been received into the care of a local authority the care of the child should be taken over either by a 'parent or guardian', or 'a relative or friend of his'.[33] This was a decisive shift away from the policy of trying to sever all connections between children in State care (formerly 'Poor Law children') and their home environments. The Act also rearranged child care services after the break-up of the Poor Law.

There have been more than seventy public inquiries since the implementation of the Children Act 1948. These have been carried out in circumstances where, despite social services involvement, a child has died as a result of abuse within the family or within State care.[34] The remit has been to focus on single cases and individual failings as they occur. Most have identified perceived social work failures, mainly in communication and record keeping, causing many to question their efficacy. As early as 1975, for example, the British Association of Social Workers described inquiries as: 'a pointless exercise, serving mainly to scapegoat social workers'.[35] Each inquiry's findings became the precursor of national or local policies designed to prevent further child deaths as a result of failures of social services. The question of whether this was possible or successful was not addressed, but a theory of risk assessment in relation to preventing child deaths as a result of parental abuse emerged as a result.

The notion that children in families who already had 'contact' of varying degrees with social services could somehow be saved from behaviours which proved to be fatal created a theory of risk prediction in relation to child welfare. The common theme in many of these inquiries was the belief that increased State powers and less concern for parents' rights would solve the problem of child fatalities at the hands of their parents. From this theme a discourse emerged, located in the prevention of harm to children as justifying the erosion of parental rights to privacy and autonomy.[36]

By the late 1960s, the concept that neglected children were analogous to delinquents was redefined, and offending children were seen as a product of neglect. This same period saw the model of abused children alter: children were seen as victims of their circumstance, rather than delinquents in need of correction. The Children and Young Persons (Amendment) Act 1952[37] removed the requirement in the 1933 Act that in order to be pronounced an 'unfit person' under 'child protection' legislation a person had to be convicted of cruelty. This Act also placed an obligation on Children's Departments to pursue enquiries if allegations of child abuse were made to them; a precursor to s.47 Children Act 1989.

By 1961, the NSPCC considered itself to be principally concerned with issues of neglect rather than cruelty. It felt that: 'most of that neglect springs from poor home and families whose immaturity makes parenthood in its fullest sense impossible'.[38] The Children and Young Persons Act 1969[39] and the Child Care Act 1980[40] were the statutes in force immediately prior to the Children Act 1989. The new Act was described by Sir Geoffrey Howe as: 'the most comprehensive and far reaching reform of this branch of the law ever introduced'.[41] It was considered to meet a perceived need for a comprehensive and integrated statutory framework to ensure the welfare of children. It covered virtually all areas of law relating to the care and upbringing of children, together with the social services to be made available to families.[42] It came into force in 1991 and is still the main statutory enabler of consensual and non-consensual surveillance and interference into private family life. The Act places on local authorities an absolute duty to investigate cases of reasonably suspected child abuse. S.47 states that:

> Where a local authority–
>
> a) is informed that a child who lives, or is found, in their area–
>   i) is the subject of an emergency protection order; or
>   ii) is in police protection; or
>   iii) has contravened a ban imposed by a curfew notice imposed within the meaning of Chapter 1 of Part 1 of the Crime and Disorder Act 1998; or
> b) has reasonable cause to suspect that a child who lives, or is found, in their area is suffering, or is likely to suffer, significant harm, the authority shall make, or cause to be made, such enquiries as they consider necessary to enable them to decide whether they should take any action to safeguard or promote the child's welfare.[43]

Definitions are widely construed. S.31(9) Children Act 1989 states that:

> 'Harm' means ill treatment or the impairment of health or development; 'development' means physical, intellectual, emotional, social or behavioural development; 'health' means physical or mental health; and 'ill treatment' includes sexual abuse and forms of ill-treatment which are not physical.

S.31(10) Children Act 1989 qualified the standard to be that of a 'similar' child. It states:

> Where the question of whether harm suffered by a child is significant turns on the child's health and development, his health or development shall be compared with that which could reasonably be expected of a similar child.

The Children Act 1989 was the result of a long consultation process, which continued during its passage through Parliament[44] and was introduced following an Interdepartmental Working Party set up by the Department of Health and Social Security to review child care law. The Working Party was set up as a response to a recommendation in the *Second Report from the House of Commons Social Services Committee, 1983–1984 on Children in Care*.[45]

The Law Commission Family Law team conducted a review which included twelve informal consultation papers during 1984 and 1985, and a Report to Ministers in September 1985, which was published as a further consultation document. This was followed by the government White Paper, *The Law Relating to Child Care and Family Services*[46] in January 1987. These were concerned with public law provision in respect of child welfare, namely the services to be provided for children and their families, and the procedures designed to interfere into private family life when child abuse was suspected.

At the same time, the Law Commission was reviewing private law on the allocation of responsibility between parents and other individuals. In this context, the Law Commission published Working Papers on Guardianship;[47] Custody;[48] Care, Supervision and Interim Orders in Custody Proceedings;[49] and Wards of Court.[50] The papers on Guardianship, Custody and Care, Supervision and Interim Orders in Custody Proceedings resulted in the Law Commission's *Review of Child Care Law, Guardianship and Custody*,[51] published in July 1988. Annexed to the Report was a Bill to give effect to the Law Commission's recommendations and to the government's proposals on care proceedings.[52] The Bill was adopted by the government and expanded to cover almost all civil law relating to children, with the exception of adoption and education, although it did regulate private schools.[53] The Bill was introduced in the House of Lords in the 1988–9 Session, and received Royal Assent on 16 November 1989.

By this time, the result of the *Report of the Inquiry into Child Abuse in Cleveland in 1987* by Lady Justice Butler-Sloss and her colleagues had been published.[54] This Report was produced following the Secretary of State for Social Services' order for a public inquiry, made on 9 July 1987 pursuant to s.84 National Health Service Act 1977[55] and s.76 Child Care Act 1980. Its remit was to review what had happened to families in Cleveland following medical opinion that many children had been sexually abused: 121 children were removed from their families before it was decided in the majority of cases there was no reliable evidence that sexual abuse had occurred.

The focus of the report was to consider the difficult issue of the appropriate social work response to suspicions of child abuse. One of the Report's main findings was that intervention could itself be damaging to families.[56] Corby *et al.* (2001) report that:

> the key significant factor about Cleveland was its concern about what the inquiry panel saw as overzealous intrusion into family life. It posted a warning that there was a limit to the forms of action to be taken in regard to protecting children.[57]

The Report together with other public enquiry findings, particularly those inquiring into the deaths of children 'known to social services' contributed to the view that adequate measures should be put in place in order to protect children from abuse.[58] This was to happen together with consideration of precisely how families were to be protected from unnecessary intrusion. Both needed to happen in the context of the best interests of the child.

Following these concerns about over-interference, the discourse advocating surveillance and interference took precedence and was strengthened by further legislation,[59] and further high profile child fatalities.[60] This seemed to reinforce the argument that increased surveillance and interference was the correct preventative approach.

Moving from parental autonomy to parental responsibility

The notion that parenthood is a matter of responsibility rather than rights is a central plank of the Children Act 1989. The emphasis in the Act on parental responsibility laid the foundation for more extensive State surveillance by moving the focus away from parental rights and parental autonomy. Ensuring parents upheld their responsibilities required a means of policing parents, together with a means of intervening where parents were suspected of failing to achieve the threshold of acceptable behaviour towards their children.

This change occurred because the Law Commission found that existing statutes relating to children contained phrases emphasising the powers that parents had over their children in conjunction with mention of their duties. These terms were considered outdated and misleading and were therefore removed in the Children Act 1989. The Law Commission recommended the introduction of 'parental responsibility', which would replace any other terms. The role of a parent was to be understood solely in terms of their responsibilities, not their rights. Whilst this was intended to be a step forward in relation to freeing children from outdated notions of 'ownership' by their parents (particularly fathers) it did not acknowledge a balance was needed to prevent a position where children were to be protected from their parents at the expense of support for balanced family functioning. It was felt that the change would simply reflect the reality of being a parent and that such a change would make little difference in substance. It was intended to reflect the everyday reality of being a parent and emphasise the responsibility of all who are in that position.[61] The government accepted the recommendation. It was stated by Lord Mackay LC upon the introduction of the Bill for its second reading that the concept of parental responsibility:

> emphasises that the days when a child should be regarded as a possession of his parent – indeed when in the past they had a right to his services and to sue on their loss – are now buried forever. The overwhelming purpose of parenthood is the responsibility of caring for and raising the child to be a properly developed adult both physically and morally.[62]

This was consistent with judicial reasoning, for example the House of Lords emphasised in *Gillick v West Norfolk and Wisbech Area Health Authority*[63] that parental power to control a child exists not for the benefit of the parent but for the benefit of the child. This decision was in line with the rising idea of children's rights, and this same concept was to be applied to a local authority when a child came into its care. It was not considered that this would also give rise to an increase in State paternalism in respect of private family life as, amongst other changes, the Act was considered to: 'realign the balance between families and the state so as to protect families from unwarranted state interference'.[64] This may have been the intention. However, there has been an enormous increase in the amount of State interference into family life since its introduction. Policies setting out how local authorities will police parents in relation to the satisfactory discharge of their responsibilities towards children have increased the level of surveillance and intervention. There is consequently a tension between parents, who have a duty to discharge their responsibilities towards children, and local authorities who have a duty to police parents to ensure that they do so. Parental failures to discharge their responsibility can, in turn, create a failure in the statutory duty of a local authority to discharge its own responsibilities. This chain of responsibility creates tension between the right to privacy and the right to police. The Children Act 1989 may have aimed to balance the competing interests between the State and citizens in cases of suspected child abuse by making the threshold for interference 'reasonable cause to suspect'[65] but it may not be possible in practice to adequately reconcile these competing interests.

Westlake and Pearson observe that to compound the tension between the State's duty and the parents' responsibility, parental responsibility as a concept has been subject to considerable redefinition and interpretation in analysis of the Children Act 1989 and other current policies on children and families.[66] Fox-Harding concludes that the legislation creates contradictions:

> Analysts of the Children Act have exposed the contradictions embodied in the legislation . . . between, on the one hand, the principles of a paternalist coercive state which has a role in surveillance and inspection and . . . the 'duties and obligations' of parenting, and on the other, a . . . non-interventionist role for the state.[67]

The position is far from satisfactory. The practical difficulties for the State in relation to predicting the possibility of likely 'significant harm' means that local authorities have the dilemma of deciding whether the State should interfere or not into private family life, based on the concept of a 'reasonable suspicion'. This conflict stems from the ways in which parental responsibility may be defined: should it be seen as a statutory obligation placed on parents to behave dutifully towards their children, or do parents rightfully have responsibility for child care, autonomous from State control? Westlake and Pearson state that the latter position can be interpreted as meaning: 'either that parental rights are genuinely considered paramount, or that the state absolves itself of responsibilities using the rhetoric of parents' rights'.[68]

In theory, the notion of parental autonomy is upheld by the Children Act 1989 as the State should not interfere unless services are requested by a family or there is 'reasonable cause to suspect' the risk of 'significant harm'.[69] However, the categories of coercive and non-coercive intervention have proved to be less separate than originally conceptualised.

Under the Act it was not only children deemed to be at risk of abuse whose families attracted social work attention. Pursuant to s.17, Part III Children Act 1989, children who were deemed to be 'in need' were to be targets for consensual services. The intention was to reduce the need for coercive State interference by enabling support for struggling families. Only a few years later it emerged in *Child Protection Messages from Research*[70] there was evidence of social work practice of deliberately placing non-abusing families through the s.47[71] 'child protection' procedures detailed in *Working Together to Safeguard Children*.[72] This was occurring in order that services could be obtained for 'children in need' where they were not provided under s.17.[73] This review triggered the refocussing debate which aimed to rebalance social work with families away from a child protection focus.[74]

The refocussing debate

The Children Act 1989 separated out two discrete categories of children on whose behalf the State would conduct assessments and/or investigations.[75] S.17 assessments considered whether a child was in need of services. Referrals for this type of assessment could arise through illness, disability, educational needs and for a variety of situations that did not assume parental failings. S.47 was intended to investigate cases of suspected child abuse with a view to establishing whether a child was at risk of significant harm if the State did not intervene to take steps to prevent this harm from occurring. As noted above, these different categories were separated in the Children Act 1989 into inclusion in Parts III and V respectively.[76]

The Children Act 1989 created firm categorisation and separation of children into being 'at risk' or 'in need'. As children and families may have changing, escalating, diminishing or complex circumstances the process of early separation and categorisation were considered problematic. During the early 1990s, debate and investigation took place to consider whether this division was working and, if not, what should be done. The Conservative Government commissioned a series of research papers on the functioning of the Children Act 1989. In 1995 these were published as *Child Protection: Messages from Research*.[77] Its conclusions were *inter alia* that social work was now focussed almost exclusively upon risk and investigation of suspected abuse to the exclusion of assessing and providing services to children in need.

This was perceived as problematic. *Messages from Research* highlighted that 'long-term difficulties seldom follow from a single abusive event'[78] and suggested children needed to be considered within their wider environment. It challenged the prevailing discourse of 'child protection'[79] and reframed the concept of the 'dangerous family' in child protection work into a more complex concept of a family with a variety of needs that could be identified and addressed at an early stage via a comprehensive, holistic assessment and support services.[80] *Messages from Research* thus introduced a discourse advocating 'refocusing' of 'child protection' policy and practice.[81] However, concern over categorisation continued to be a point of concern which some years later was reiterated by Lord Laming:

> Throughout the inquiry, I repeatedly heard evidence which caused me great concern about the way in which social services departments interpret their responsibilities under sections 17 and 47 of the Children Act 1989 . . . [The] approach to the use of sections 17 and 47 can only be described as dangerous.[82]

The refocussing debate signalled the rise of early intervention strategies. This involved State intervention into family life before problems became abuse, thus moving away from s.47 investigations as a social work response to referral. In practical terms this involved a prioritization of s.17 and Part III of the Children Act 1989.[83] Development of this debate coincided with the new Labour Government in 1997 and their 'explicit family policy'[84] aimed at 'supporting' and 'working in partnership with families' on a multi-level basis to 'reduce child poverty, build stronger communities and reduce crime'.[85]

This represented part of a wider debate that was taking place at the same time about child development with emphasis on 'early prevention' strategies.[86] A range of criminological studies had argued that family influences and factors were linked to increased risks of offending as a result of a link between early problematic childhood behavioural problems and poor parenting.[87] Parton notes this debate drew on risk discourse which indicated that certain:

> clusters of risk factors predicted a range of different problems encountered by young people in children's circumstance and environments and overlapping personal and environmental risk factors had been identified not only for drug abuse, criminal behaviour and violence but also for educational failure, unsafe sexual behaviour and poor mental health.[88]

Prevention, Parton argues, became important not 'simply to combat risks but also to enhance the opportunities for child development via maximizing protective factors and processes'.[89] This ideology underpins the modern assessment framework which is continually being developed and expanded. These changes are not without controversy as they increasingly extend surveillance to all families, and extend interventions to not only those families who fit into the categories of ss.47 or 17 but a wider group fitting into broad categories conceived by the Department of Health in *Every Child Matters*.[90] This expanding concept is termed 'safeguarding'.

Safeguarding and early intervention

When the Labour Government came to power in 1997 its policy agenda included addressing social exclusion and the problem of crime and crucially the 'causes of crime'.[91] The government's 'explicit family policy'[92] concentrated on assessments and services that it considered were 'supporting' and 'working in partnership with families' to reduce child poverty, build stronger communities and reduce crime.[93] As part of its policies, the Labour Government established a series of projects aimed at reducing social exclusion. The focus shifted from emphasis on services intended to be coercive and to 'encourage passivity'[94] to those intended to 'encourage individual responsibility and active positive risk taking'.[95] Practices that focussed narrowly on child protection were replaced by increased focus towards practices supporting a preventative and holistic approach.[96]

Much of this coincided with provision for children in need, and most of the provision was set up in the form of external organisations and within the voluntary sector.[97] The rolling out of Labour's policies overtook the refocussing debate; for example Parton argues that: 'debates prompted by *Messages from Research* have been overtaken by other more wide-ranging policies and priorities being introduced by New Labour concerned with supporting the family, parenting and early interventions'.[98] One of the key examples was Labour's Sure Start programme. This programme aimed to 'improve the health, well-being and life chances of families and children before and from birth, working in partnership with mainstream agencies to provide integrated services'.[99] Broadhurst *et al.* describe it as 'a flagship policy for the tackling of social exclusion through improving the life chances of children'.[100] However, they observe the policy is based on a 'neoliberal agenda and a confusing and contradictory social inclusion agenda that has resulted in increased regulation and surveillance of poor families'.[101] Interestingly, they conclude that the Sure Start policy is 'in the final analysis, "mother blaming"'.[102] This analysis is supported by Clarke who observed:

> Poor mothers whose behaviour does not conform to the norms promoted by this [Sure Start] ideology and who come under scrutiny from the state are easily constructed as exhibiting pathological behaviour resulting from a combination of ignorance and moral deviance.[103]

The use by parents, particularly mothers, of State services such as Sure Start operates as a mechanism for increased surveillance of them. This enables the assessment of parenting against the State's criteria for safeguarding and implementation of early intervention policies. These programmes are designed to address deviation from State norms. A lack of conformity (breach of an implied social contract) may trigger a referral, leading a family into tutelage (to remedy the breach). Compliant parents who co-operate with assessments can return to a position where they are considered to be upholding their part of the contract, whereas non-compliant parents may be subject to increased levels of coercive tutelage until they comply. This has led to an increasing expectation that parental compliance is essential once social work involvement is triggered. This compliance is highly valued, described as parents 'working with' social workers. It is an increasingly essential prerequisite for parents to be able to demonstrate this before they are able to extricate themselves from the process of social work involvement.[104]

Research findings support this. For example, social work assessments were found by Holland to be heavily reliant upon the assessment of the personalities and social skills of the parents; parental co-operation with the local authority was assessed on the basis of perceived co-operation with the assessment.[105] Social workers highly rated a parent's willingness and ability to provide a plausible explanation for concerns or to accept the concerns leading to the referral. Holland found that parents who were able to demonstrate compliance and acceptance were all reunited with their children whereas parents who were seen as passive and inarticulate were unlikely to be reunited with their children. Woodcock drew similar conclusions, observing that social work assessments were based heavily on the perceived personality traits of parents as opposed to the events leading to the referral.[106] The introduction of the Public Law Outline 2014[107] sets out a compliance model which parents must follow if the local authority decides to escalate matters beyond assessment. This model relies on parental co-operation with social work requirements and does not leave room for dispute resolution at an early stage.

Conclusion: the modern categorisation of levels of surveillance and interference

It is evident that the modern role of the State has developed to an extent far beyond that envisaged when the Children Act 1989 was enacted. Over time the use of surveillance and interference into private life via assessment has increased. The 'price' of rationed social services is the giving up of privacy and submission to extensive intrusion into family life. However, the use of universal services also requires the giving up of personal data. In England, primary interventions provide a few universally available services such as health care, including antenatal care and health visiting. In return, data is collected about the service users. Amongst other reasons for the data collection, this may trigger a referral to a children's social care department for social work assessment.

The assessment process that occurs following referral is designed to assess what, if any, level of intervention is appropriate. These levels of intervention are categorised (by Bromfield and Holzer, 2008) as primary, secondary, tertiary or quaternary.[108] They are ranked according to their increasingly coercive nature. This extends far beyond the categories envisaged in the Children Act 1989 under Parts III and V which very clearly separated the two 'arms' of intervention into those which are consensual under s.17, and those which are non-consensual under s.47. Consequently, instead of swiftly investigating abuse claims to either substantiate or eliminate them families are drawn into a high level of investigation and loss of privacy simply to obtain 'services'. Hunter identifies this model as one derived from public health: 'In the public health module of disease prevention, preventative interventions are described as either primary, secondary or tertiary interventions.'[109] Bromfield and Holzer (2008) describe this public health model as separating interference into discrete levels; Hardiker *et al.* elaborated the usual three-fold levels in relation to intervention services by adding a quaternary level, optimising the prospects for children where family problems have resulted in their placement in substitute care.[110] Table 1.1 explains these four levels.[111]

This separation of interventions into four discrete levels was included in the *Every Child Matters* Green Paper.[112] Parton notes that:

> while the Green Paper was informed by the Laming Report, it was primarily concerned with bringing together the government's proposals for reforming children's services which it had been developing for a number of years but with a much broader remit than previously. For, rather than being entitled

Table 1.1 Intervention levels

Levels of intervention	Details
Primary/universal interventions (self-regulation)	These interventions providing support and education are offered to everyone. This level aims to take universal action to promote conditions ensuring problems do not arise
Secondary interventions (supported regulation)	These interventions are targeted at families in need. They provide additional support or help to alleviate identified problems and to prevent escalation, focussing on individuals or families who are considered to be high risk, but may not yet have problems
Tertiary interventions (coercive regulation)	These interventions involve coercive statutory care and protection services. They provide services where abuse and neglect have already occurred, targeting individuals or families who are known to have problems in order to minimise their adverse effects.
Quaternary interventions (non-rehabilitative regulation)	These interventions are not intended to be rehabilitative and involve permanent separation of parent and child, for example through the removal of the child into State care or the adoption of the child.

'Children at Risk' as originally envisaged, the Green Paper was entitled *Every Child Matters*. This was not to say the Green Paper was not centrally concerned with 'risk', clearly it was, but framed in such a way that any child, at some point in their life, could be seen as vulnerable to some form of risk. The government therefore deemed it necessary that *all children* were potentially covered by the proposals.[113]

These separations, encapsulating policies of escalating and fluctuating levels of need form part of the reconceptualisation of how referrals are understood and processed through the schema of assessment. A referral to a children's social care department is not necessarily an allegation of child abuse, and may be intended by the referrer to be an expression of concern, a request for services or a request for advice, help and support. The categorisation of referrals is undertaken not by the referrer but by the local authority, and the assessment process through which all referrals are intended to be fed is intended to enable a local authority to decide how to categorise a family. It is therefore the social work response to a referral that is important rather than the intention of the referrer. The holistic assessment framework in both the *Framework for the Assessment of Children in Need*[114] and *Working Together*[115] set out the comprehensive nature of the assessment, designed to situate issues that pass the thresholds for State involvement in the wider context of the family and its internal and external functionality. It is described in the *Framework for the Assessment of Children in Need* as:

> a conceptual map which can be used to understand what is happening to all children in whatever circumstances they may be growing up. For most children referred or whose families seek help, the issues of concern will be relatively straightforward, parents will be clear about requiring assistance and the impact on the child will not be difficult to identify. For a smaller number of children, the causes for concern will be serious and complex and the relationship between their needs, their parents' responses and the circumstances in which they are living, less straightforward.[116]

This expansion was intended to reduce child abuse and neglect. An important question is whether the development and expansion of the concept of interventions has achieved this aim. The question is complex, the answer even more so. Finding a satisfactory answer requires examination of how child abuse is defined, measured and predicted under this increasingly intrusive model of rationed early intervention services.

Notes

1 For a detailed discussion of the development of welfare in relation to children and the Poor Laws see generally Pinchbeck, I. and Hewitt, M., *Children in English Society*, 2 vols: (1969) *From Tudor Times to the Eighteenth Century*, and (1973) *From the Eighteenth Century to the Children Act 1948*, Routledge, London; Henriques, U. (1967) 'Bastardy and the New Poor Law', *Past and Present* 37: 103–29; Nutt, T. (2006) 'Bastardy' in: Levene, A., King, S., Tomkins, A. and Nutt, T. (eds) *Narratives of the Poor in Eighteenth-Century Britain*, Vol. I (5 vols), Pickering and Chatto, London; Nutt, T. (2005) 'The Paradox and Problems of Illegitimate Paternity in Old Poor Law Essex' in: Levene, A., Nutt, T. and Williams, S. (eds) *Illegitimacy in Britain, 1700–1920*, Palgrave Macmillan, Basingstoke.

2 See for example the discussion in: Lowe, N. and White, R.A.H. (1979) *Wards of Court*, Butterworths, London.

3 Sir Thomas Talfourd, MP for Reading, introduced the *Custody of Infants Bill* on Mrs Norton's behalf following her pamphlet *The Natural Claim of a Mother to the Custody of her Children as affected by the Common Law Rights of the Father*. After initial rejection by the House of Lords and Mrs Norton's further pamphlet a *Plain Letter to the Lord Chancellor on the Law of Custody of Infants* it passed at the second attempt. For further examples of Caroline Norton's views see: Norton, C. (1855) *A Letter to the Queen on Lord Chancellor Cranworth's Marriage and Divorce Bill*, Longmans, London. Online at: http://digital.library. upenn.edu/women/norton/alttq/alttq.html (Accessed 1 February 2016).

4 c.54.

5 Matrimonial Causes Act 1857 (20 and 21 Vict. c.85), s.35.

6 c.12.

7 Under s.8 Children Act 1989 c.41.

8 S.1(1) Children Act 1989 c.41.

9 'Welfare' is not defined. The Children and Family Court Advisory and Support Service (CAFCASS), i.e. State-appointed assessors prepare reports making

recommendations in contested cases. The recommendations are CAFCASS's opinion as to the outcome that best fits the child's best interests.

10 Law Commission (1987) *Working Paper No. 101: Family Law Review of Child Care Law, Wards of Court*, HMSO, London, Part I, para. 1.4(a), p. 2.
11 Ibid., part II, para. 2.3, p. 10.
12 Ibid., para. 2.2, p. 9.
13 Ibid.
14 Ibid., para. 2.5, p. 11 and *Practice Direction* [1967] 1 WLR 623.
15 Flora, P. and Heidenheimer, A. (eds) (1982) *The Development of Welfare States in Europe and America*, Transaction Books, New Brunswick, p. 22.
16 Markets, associations and State bureaucracy. Ibid., p. 40.
17 Ibid., p. 20.
18 Ibid.
19 c.44.
20 S.1 Protection of Cruelty to and Protection of Children Act 1990 c.44.
21 Ibid., ss.5(1) and (2).
22 c.118.
23 S.1(b).
24 Eekelaar, J. and McLean, M. (eds) (1994) *A Reader on Family Law*, Oxford University Press, Oxford, p. 293.
25 c.15.
26 Dingwall, R., Eekelaar, J. and Murray, T. (1984) 'Childhood as a Social Problem: A Survey of the History of Legal Regulation', *Journal of Law and Society* 2(2): 207–32 (Summer): 221.
27 Freeman, M. and Veerman, P. (1992) *The Ideologies of Children's Rights*, Martinus Nijhoff Publishers, The Netherlands.
28 c.12.
29 Dingwall *et al.* (n. 26).
30 Ibid., 223.
31 c.43.
32 See the public inquiry report: Sir William Monckton (1945) *Report by Sir William Monckton KCMG KCVO MC KC on the Circumstances which led to the Boarding Out of Dennis and Terence O'Neill at Bank Farm, Minsterly and the Steps Taken to Supervise their Welfare*, Cmd 6636, Home Office, HMSO, London and mentioned for example in: Cretney, S. (2005) *Family Law in the Twentieth Century*, Oxford University Press, Oxford; Cretney, S. (1997) 'The Children Act 1948: Lessons for Today?', *Child & Family Law Quarterly* 359. Although not academic texts, Terence O'Neil, younger brother of Dennis O'Neil has written two books about their experiences in relation to State care, leading up to Dennis's death and the subsequent criminal trial of their foster parents: O'Neill, T. (2000) *A Place Called Hope* (2nd edn), Educational Printing Services, Blackburn; and O'Neill, T. (2010) *Someone to Love Us*, HarperCollins, London. The second book was originally aptly called 'never again', but the title was changed by the publishers.
33 Children Act 1948 c.43, ss.1(3)(a) and (b), as originally enacted. See for example in relation to the rationale for the key provisions of the Act the discussion in: Hansard (1948) *House of Lords Debate*, 9 March: Vol. 154, Cols 531–614.
34 This was noted by the: Select Committee on Health (2002) *Sixth Report*, para. 7. This report considered non-accidental death and injury to children. Online at: www.publications.parliament.uk/pa/cm200203/cmselect/cmhealth/570/57004.htm (Accessed 1 February 2016).
35 Hopkins, G. (2007) 'What Have We Learned? Child Death Scandals since 1944', 10 January, *Community Care Website*. Online at: www.communitycare.co.uk

/Articles/2007/01/11/102713/What-have-we-learned-Child-death-scandals-since-1944.htm (Accessed 1 February 2016).

36 This theme is also emerging in Serious Case Reviews, the most recent of note being the review into the death of Khyra Ishaq in Birmingham of which one focus was the mother's refusal to consent to assessment. See: Radford, J. (2010) *Serious Case Review Under Chapter VIII 'Working Together to Safeguard Children' In respect of the Death of a Child Case Number 14*, Birmingham Safeguarding Children Board. Online at: http://northumberlandlscb.proceduresonline.com/pdfs/kyhra_ishaq_scr.pdf (Accessed 1 May 2016).

37 c.50.

38 Allen, A. and Morton, A. (1961) *This is Your Child: The Story of the National Society for the Prevention of Cruelty to Children*, Routledge, London, p. 72.

39 c.54.

40 c.5.

41 Hansard (1989) *House of Commons Debate*, 26 October: Vol. 158, Col. 1075.

42 Regulated by the Adoption Act 1976 c.36, repealed by the Adoption and Children Act 2002 c.38 and the Children Act 1989 c.41.

43 Children Act 1989 c.41, s.47. Note there is no subsequent duty on the local authority to do anything following the investigation.

44 White, R., Carr, P. and Low, N. (1990) *A Guide to the Children Act 1989*, Butterworths, London.

45 House of Commons Social Services Committee (1984) *Second Report: Session 1983–1984: Children in Care*, HMSO, London.

46 Department of Health and Social Security (1987) *The Law Relating to Child Care and Family Services*, White Paper, Cm 62, HMSO, London.

47 Law Commission (1986) *Family Law: Review of Child Law (Guardianship)* Working Paper 91, HMSO, London.

48 Law Commission (1986) *Family Law: Review of Child Law (Custody)*, Working Paper 96, HMSO, London.

49 Law Commission (1987) *Family Law: Review of Child Law (Care, Supervision and Interim Orders in Custody Proceedings)*, Working Paper 100, HMSO, London.

50 Law Commission (1987) *Family Law: Review of Child Law (Wards of Court)*, Working Paper 101, HMSO, London.

51 Law Commission (1988) *Review of Child Care Law: Guardianship and Custody*, No. 172, HMSO, London.

52 House of Commons Social Services Committee (1989) *Children Bill: Second Report Together with the Proceedings of the Committee*, Bill No. 178, HMSO, London.

53 The Adoption and Children Act 2002 regulates adoption, and the Education Act 1998 regulates education.

54 Dame Elizabeth Butler-Sloss (1988) *Report of the Inquiry into Child Abuse in Cleveland 1987*, Cm 412, HMSO, London.

55 c.49.

56 Butler-Sloss (n. 54) paras 2.1–2.65.

57 Corby, B., Doig, A. and Roberts, V. (2001) *Public Inquiries into Abuse of Children in Residential Care*, Jessica Kingsley Publishers, London, p. 43.

58 Corby *et al.* (Ibid., Appendix 1, p. 199) cite 77 reports between 1945 and 1989, starting with Dennis and Terence O'Neill, all concerning children who were or had been in residential care. In relation to reports concerning under-interference see particularly the inquiries into the deaths of Dennis O'Neill, Maria Colwell, Jasmine Beckford and Tyra Henry in: Monckton (n. 32); Department of Health (1974) *Report of the Committee of Inquiry in to the Care and Supervision Provided in Relation to Maria Colwell*, HMSO, London; Blom-Cooper, L. (1985) *A Child in Trust: The Report of the Panel of Inquiry into the Circumstances*

Surrounding the Death of Jasmine Beckford, HMSO, London; and Sedley, S. (1987) *Whose Child? The Report of the Panel Appointed to Inquire into the Death of Tyra Henry*, HMSO, London. These can be compared with inquiries into what happened in Cleveland and in the Orkneys, which are concerned with issues of over-interference. See Butler-Sloss, E. (n. 54); and Lord Clyde (1992) *The Report of the Enquiry Into The Removal of Children From Orkney in February 1991*, HMSO, Edinburgh.

59 Children Act 2004 c.31.
60 For example, the deaths of Peter Connolly on 3 August 2007 and Khyra Ishaq on 17 May 2008.
61 Law Commission (1988) *Review of Child Care Law: Guardianship and Custody*, No. 172, HMSO, London.
62 Hansard (1988) *House of Lords Debate*, 6 December: Vol. 502, Col. 490.
63 *Gillick v West Norfolk and Wisbech Area Health Authority* [1986] AC 112.
64 Allsop, P. (1990) 'Children Act 1989 "Introduction and General Note" "Major Changes"', in *Current Law Statutes Annotated 1989*, Vol. 4, Sweet and Maxwell, London, pp. 41–6.
65 S.47 Children Act 1989 c.41.
66 Westlake, D. and Pearson, M. (1997) 'Child Protection and Health Promotion: Whose Responsibility?', *Journal of Social Welfare and Family Law* 19(2): 139–58.
67 Fox-Harding, L. (1991) 'The Children Act 1989 in Context: Four Perspectives in Child Care Law and Policy', *Journal of Social Welfare and Family Law* 13(3): 140.
68 Westlake and Pearson (n. 66), 141.
69 S.47 Children Act 1989 c.41.
70 Department of Health (1995) *Child Protection: Messages from Research*, HMSO, London, p. 27.
71 Children Act 1989 c.41.
72 Department of Health (1999) *Working Together to Safeguard Children*, TSO, London, p. 42.
73 Children Act 1989 c.41.
74 Devine, L. (2015) 'Considering Social Work Assessment of Families', *Journal of Social Welfare and Family Law* 37(1): 70–83. Online at: http://dx.doi.org/10.1080/09649069.2015.998005 (Accessed 28 February 2016).
75 S.47, child at risk of significant harm, and s.17, child in need of services.
76 Part III was intended to be non-coercive as it concerned 'Local Authority Support for Children and Families', whereas Part V concerned 'Protection of Children'.
77 Department of Health (n. 70).
78 Ibid.
79 Ibid., the socio-medical model of child abuse.
80 Ibid., p. 54.
81 See for example the discussion in: Parton, N. (2008) 'The "Change for Children" Programme in England: Towards the Preventive–Surveillance State', *Journal of Law and Society* 35(1): 166–87 (March), at 169–70.
82 Lord Laming (2003) *The Victoria Climbié Inquiry Report*, HC 570, pp. 364–5. Online at: www.publications.parliament.uk/pa/cm200203/cmselect/cmhealth/570/570.pdf (Accessed 1 January 2016).
83 Part III is the part of the Children Act 1989 that is concerned with consensual intervention and non-coercive practices.
84 Skinner, C. (2003) 'New Labour and Family Policy' in: Bell, M. and Wilson, K. (eds) *The Practitioners Guide to Working with Families*, Palgrave Macmillan, Basingstoke, p. 19.

85 Ibid., pp. 19–24.
86 Parton (n. 81), 172.
87 See for example: Graham, J. and Utting, D. (1996) 'Families, Schools and Criminality Prevention' in: Bennett, T. (ed.) *Preventing Crime and Disorder: Targeting Strategies and Responsibilities*, University of Cambridge, Cambridge, p. 88; West, D.J. (1996) *Delinquency: Its Roots, Careers and Prospects*, Heinemann, Oxford; Farrington, D.P. (1996) *Understanding and Preventing Youth Crime*, Joseph Rowntree Foundation, York.
88 Parton (n. 81), 173.
89 Ibid.
90 The Chief Secretary to the Treasury (2003) *Every Child Matters*, Cm 5860, TSO, London; HM Government (2005) *Every Child Matters*, Vol. 1, TSO, London HC 40-I; HM Government (2005) *Every Child Matters*, Vol. 2, TSO, London, HC 40-II.
91 See note 90. The 'causes of crime' had already been linked to adverse childhood factors.
92 Skinner (n. 84), p. 19.
93 Ibid., pp. 19–24.
94 Parton (n. 81), 175.
95 Ibid.
96 See for example: Beecham, J. and Sinclair, I. (2007) *Costs and Outcomes in Children's Social Care*, DfES, London; and Garbers, C., Tunstill, J., Allnock, D. and Akhurst, S. (2006) 'Facilitating Access to Services for Children and Families: Lessons from Sure Start Local Programmes', *Child and Family Social Work* 11(4): 287–96.
97 Jordan, B. and Jordan, C. (2000) *Social Work and the Third Way*, Sage, London, pp. 71–82; Skinner (n. 84), pp. 34–6.
98 Parton, N. (2002) 'Protecting Children: A Socio-Historical Analysis' in: Wilson, K. and James, A. (eds) *The Child Protection Handbook* (2nd edn), Bailliere Tindall, London, p. 24.
99 Carpenter, J., Brown, S. and Griffin, M. (2007) 'Prevention in Integrated Children's Services: The Impact of Sure Start on Referrals to Social Services and Child Protection Registrations', *Child Abuse Review* 16: 17–31, 18.
100 Broadhurst, K., Mason, C. and Grover, C. (2007) 'Sure Start and the "re-authorisation" of Section 47 Child Protection Practices', *Critical Social Policy* 27(4): 443–61, 443.
101 Ibid., 454.
102 Ibid., 453.
103 Clarke, K. (2006) 'Childhood, Parenting and Early Intervention: A Critical Examination of the Sure Start National Programme', *Critical Social Policy* 26(4): 699–721, 701.
104 See requirements of the stages of the Public Law Outline 2014 in: Children and Families Act 2014, also referred to as PD12A or Practice Direction 12a. See: Ministry of Justice (MoJ) (2014) 'Practice Direction 12a – Care, Supervision and Other Part 4 Proceedings: Guide To Case Management', 16 May. Online at: www.justice.gov.uk/courts/procedure-rules/family/practice_directions/pd_part_12a (Accessed 13 June 2015).
105 Holland, S. (2000) 'The Assessment Relationship: Interactions Between Social Workers and Parents on Child Protection', *British Journal of Social Work* 30: 149–63.
106 Woodcock. J. (2003) 'The Social Work Assessment of Parenting: An Exploration', *British Journal of Social Work* 33: 87–106.
107 See n. 104 above.

108 For example see the discussion in: Bromfield, L. and Holzer, P. (2008) *A National Approach for Child Protection: Project Report*, Australian Institute of Family Studies, Melbourne, pp. 53–5; and Hunter, C. (2011) *Defining the Public Health Module for the Child Welfare Services Context*, Resource Sheet 11, Australian Institute of Family Studies, Melbourne.

109 Hunter, C. (2011), p. 1.

110 Bromfield and Holzer (n. 108), pp. 53–5. Hardiker, P., Exton, K. and Baker, M. (1996) 'The Prevention of Child Abuse: A Framework for Analysing Services' in: *Childhood Matters: Report of the National Commission of Inquiry into the Prevention of Child Abuse*, Vol. 2, TSO, London.

111 Based on the explanations provided in Bromfield and Holzer (n. 108), pp. 53–5 and Hardiker *et al.* (n. 110). The Department of Health (2000) *Framework for the Assessment of Children in Need and their Families*, TSO, London, Appendix 2, p. 90, reproduces Hardiker's model of levels of intervention, from: Hardiker P, Exton, K. and Barker, M. (1999) 'Children Still in Need, Indeed: Prevention Across Five Decades' in: Stevenson, O. (ed.) *Childhood Welfare in the UK*, Blackwell Science Ltd, Oxford.

112 The Chief Secretary to the Treasury (n. 90); and HM Government (n. 90), Vols 1 and 2.

113 Parton (n. 81), 178.

114 Department of Health (n. 111), Appendix A, p. 89.

115 HM Government (2010) *Working Together to Safeguard Children: A Guide to Inter-Agency Working to Safeguard and Promote the Welfare of Children*, TSO, London.

116 Department of Health (n. 111), para. 2.25, p. 26.

2 Defining and measuring the problem

Defining child abuse

Although the law refers specifically to 'reasonable suspicion of significant harm' as a trigger for non-consensual investigation under s.47 Children Act 1989, the statutory guidance, welfarist literature and the public's perception tend to refer to 'child abuse', which does not have a clear, universally agreed meaning. Consequently there is no consensus of the parameters of behaviour that can be described as child abuse. This is fundamental to understanding the uncertainty that surrounds child protection and safeguarding procedures and practice. Definitions tend to be vague and wide ranging, partly so as not to preclude any additions to behaviours considered abusive.[1] For example the following is the World Health Organisation's definition of child abuse:[2]

Preamble to the definition

Child Abuse has serious physical and psychosocial consequences which adversely affect health. It refers to any act or failure to act that violates the rights of the child that endangers his or her optimum health, survival and development.

Awareness of cultural factors must remain high as they influence all aspects from the occurrence and definition through its treatment and successful prevention. Any intervention, to be successful whether for data gathering, prevention or even increasing public awareness, must take into consideration the cultural environment in which it is to occur. Background or baseline conditions beyond the control of families or caretakers, such as poverty, inaccessible health care, inadequate nutrition, unavailability of education can be contributing factors to child abuse. Social upheaval and instability, conflict and war may also contribute to increases in child abuse and neglect.

General definition

Child abuse or maltreatment constitutes all forms of physical and/or emotional ill-treatment, sexual abuse, neglect or negligent treatment or commercial or other exploitation, resulting in actual or potential harm to the child's health, survival, development or dignity in the context of a relationship of responsibility, trust or power.

Physical abuse

Physical abuse of a child is that which results in actual or potential physical harm from an interaction or lack of an interaction, which is reasonably within the control of a parent or person in a position of responsibility, power or trust. There may be single or repeated incidents.

Emotional abuse

Emotional abuse includes the failure to provide a developmentally appropriate, supportive environment, including the availability of a primary attachment figure, so that the child can develop a stable and full range of emotional and social competencies commensurate with her or his personal potentials and in the context of the society in which the child dwells. There may also be acts towards the child that cause or have a high probability of causing harm to the child's health or physical, mental, spiritual, moral or social development. These acts must be reasonably within the control of the parent or person in a relationship of responsibility, trust or power. Acts include restriction of movement, patterns of belittling, denigrating, scapegoating, threatening, scaring, discriminating, ridiculing or other non-physical forms of hostile or rejecting treatment.

Neglect and negligent treatment

Neglect is the failure to provide for the development of the child in all spheres: health, education, emotional development, nutrition, shelter, and safe living conditions, in the context of resources reasonably available to the family or caretakers and causes or has a high probability of causing harm to the child's health or physical, mental, spiritual, moral or social development. This includes the failure to properly supervise and protect children from harm as much as is feasible.

Sexual abuse

Child sexual abuse is the involvement of a child in sexual activity that he or she does not fully comprehend, is unable to give informed consent to, or for which the child is not developmentally prepared and cannot give consent, or that violate the laws or social taboos of society. Child sexual abuse is evidenced by this activity between a child and an adult or another child who by age or development is in a relationship of responsibility, trust or power, the activity being intended to gratify or satisfy the needs of the other person. This may include but is not limited to:

- The inducement or coercion of a child to engage in any unlawful sexual activity.
- The exploitative use of child in prostitution or other unlawful sexual practices.
- The exploitative use of children in pornographic performances and materials.

Exploitation

Commercial or other exploitation of a child refers to use of the child in work or other activities for the benefit of others. This includes, but is not limited to, child labour and child prostitution. These activities are to the detriment of the child's physical or mental health, education, or spiritual, moral or social-emotional development.[3]

Under this definition, almost any parental behaviour could be construed as child abuse, particularly if taken out of context. Indeed the World Health Organisation concluded that no behaviour should be excluded.[4] The emotional abuse category is particularly notable for its uncertainty, particularly as a result of the operational problem of deciding what is 'reasonable'.

Cultural norms and values also create confusion, an issue which is being tackled more robustly since the mainstream recognition of cultural practices such as FGM (female genital mutilation). This highlighted the issue that acceptable parenting practice in one culture may be considered unacceptable elsewhere. The practice known as female circumcision in the 1980s was renamed FGM in the millennium. It is not considered to be abuse in parts of the world where it is still widespread, although it is a criminal offence in England.[5] This is an extreme example of cultural differences in normative parental behaviour towards children and it is emphatically not suggested that this practice is acceptable. However, there are many less extreme cultural variations in parenting styles and practices challenging definitions of child abuse as something that can be universally understood.[6] Time-specific norms and values also alter views on what is considered acceptable parenting. The most notable in England is the changing view towards corporal punishment; what was once commonplace parenting practice is now widely considered to be abuse.[7]

The government suggests child abuse fits into discrete categories,[8] but historically had to concede there is a category of 'other' and at one time included a category of 'grave concern'.[9] This sorting technique does little to resolve the uncertainty. Although some behaviour would clearly fall into one specific category, others may span more than one. Neglect, for example, may overlap with physical and emotional abuse. Within the government's categories precise behaviours are not defined, leaving issues with the question of categorisation unresolved. Nevertheless it is a system that requires a decision about categorisation to be made at an early stage. It is misleading to assume that each category occurs independently. Table 2.1 explains the government's changing categories.[10] The categories reflect the changes in attitudes over the years and the relative importance of behaviours considered abusive.

Despite the changing categories it is clear that at any point in time there will be certain behaviours that would be generally accepted as constituting child abuse. Examples might be serious non-accidental physical injury or rape. Severe and extreme behaviours would tend to extend beyond variations in parenting styles, also amounting to a criminal offence if they were inflicted on anyone, whether adult or child. For example, if a parent deliberately injures a child by breaking a bone it will amount to an offence under the Offences against the Person Act 1861.[11]

Defining and measuring the problem 31

Table 2.1 Official categories of child abuse

1988	2000		2005–9	2010–14
Neglect, physical abuse and sexual abuse	Neglect only	Neglect, physical injury and sexual abuse	Neglect	Neglect
Neglect and physical abuse	Physical injury only	Neglect and physical injury	Physical abuse	Physical abuse
Neglect and sexual abuse	Sexual abuse only	Neglect and sexual abuse	Sexual abuse	Sexual abuse
Physical abuse and sexual abuse	Emotional abuse only	Physical injury and sexual abuse	Emotional abuse	
Neglect (only)	Multiple categories	Neglect alone	Multiple/not recommended by *Working Together*	Emotional abuse
Physical abuse (only)	Other	Physical injury alone		Multiple
Sexual abuse (only)		Sexual abuse alone		Missing/ unknown or missing/ indeterminate
Emotional abuse (only)		Emotional abuse alone		
Grave concern		Categories not recommended by *Working Together*		
		No category available (transfer pending conferencing)		

It would not be difficult to argue that such an act is an act of child abuse. Less serious behaviours constituting child abuse, however, may change over time. The more severe the behaviour the more likely it is to be unambiguously accepted as abuse. The majority of problems, therefore, fall in situations where behaviour is less extreme but may be causing harm. It becomes more difficult, however, when issues such as the recently criminalised emotional abuse are considered.[12] Emotional abuse forms the largest category of child abuse allegations made in England after neglect, also a difficult category to define.[13] These most difficult categories have the largest number of referrals and have the largest number of cases filtered back out at an early stage. The uncertainty of where the boundaries lie in relation to emotional neglect and its subjective nature make this category particularly contentious.

When the Children Act 1989 was enacted there were very different views about acceptable parenting practices. The majority of parents in the 1980s would have been children in the 1950s and 1960s with different norms of parenting behaviour. By 2004 when the Children Act 2004[14] was enacted there was once again a different cultural outlook. Between 1989 and 2004 a significantly larger number of single parents changed the demographic profile of families.[15] This has created further uncertainty in relation to whether a parenting style is child abuse or an acceptable variation in parental style.[16]

If there is no clear definition of child abuse it puts parents and families into a precarious and uncertain position. The scandals of serious child maltreatment that precipitated the Children Act 1989 involved acts of physical and sexual maltreatment, most resulting in death.[17] The behaviours that may have been envisaged under the 'significant harm' definition in s.47[18] imply a level of damage to a child that is far higher than the type of concerns frequently referred into the modern system. The harm that would be the subject of investigation envisaged when the Children Act 1989 was drafted was informed by the extreme cases prompting public inquiries and behaviours that are clearly unacceptable.[19] These cases demonstrated that children could suffer severe, systematic and deliberate maltreatment. In such cases parents and carers did not welcome intervention, sometimes going to great lengths to prevent the child from being seen by anyone outside the family. It is notable, however, that some of these cases concerned children who were already in local authority care.[20]

Issues of measuring the prevalence of, and predicting, child abuse

The discussion concerning uncertainty over what amounts to child abuse highlights problems over how to measure it. If the problem that State intervention is expected to solve lacks defined parameters, and the interpretation of the categories are subjective and are subject to change, it is difficult to measure how prevalent a problem child abuse is in modern society. It is also difficult to measure whether the amount of child abuse is reducing, increasing or staying the same if there are regular categorisation changes and no central, consistent system of data collection and analysis.

Child abuse is not of itself a crime although it includes acts which are clearly criminal offences. Its meaning is understood in different ways depending upon the culture and time in which it is located. This creates difficulties of defining its meaning and parameters in relation to research into its prevalence. If there is uncertainty over its parameters, and an alteration over time in acceptable parenting styles, attempts to measure its prevalence are fraught with difficulty. Adding to this complexity is the expansion of intervention policies at the secondary stage (low-level targeted intervention) which aim to head off problems and thus reduce child abuse. This level of intervention is also accessed via assessment, resulting in referrals covering a much wider category than suspected significant harm.

The NSPCC has produced influential studies seeking to show both prevalence and factors necessary to predict risk and prevent abuse. The two issues are inextricably linked as the NSPCC took the data from their prevalence studies and used it to demonstrate how they believed future risk could be predicted. The studies were conducted by Creighton,[21] Cawson *et al.*[22] and Radford *et al.*[23] Creighton aimed to track the prevalence of child abuse then moved to consider risk indicators.[24] Creighton summarises her prevalence findings in relation to the NSPCC in a chapter of the same book that summarises Browne and Saqi's risk prediction findings.[25] The rise in popularity of risk prediction and early intervention in England can be traced to these origins. Following Creighton's studies Cawson *et al.* undertook their prevalence study on behalf of the NSPCC.[26] The more recent publication by the NSPCC of the Radford *et al.*[27] study also claims to measure prevalence and adopts a similar methodology.

From the early 1970s via Creighton's studies the NSPCC attempted to measure the incidence of child abuse via data collected through the Child Abuse Registers.[28] Problems of constructing a reliable methodology were apparent from the outset. Creighton recognises that 'previous estimates of the incidence of child abuse vary widely'.[29] For example, Creighton reports that the Select Committee on Violence in the Family in 1977[30] used Oliver *et al.*'s figure of 3,500 children under the age of four abused each year.[31] Their criterion for measuring abuse involved counting only children who were 'seriously injured' although what amounted to a 'serious injury' was not adequately defined. As an illustration of the methodological problems in measuring child abuse Creighton mentions that in the USA estimates range from 6,600[32] to 60,000, a huge range.[33]

Creighton also acknowledges that there is a difference between what she terms 'actual abuse' and 'reported abuse'.[34] Although there clearly is a difference between the two, Creighton does not engage in more detail with the problem of verification in respect of 'reported abuse' or the verification of 'actual abuse'. Creighton assumes that a 'reported case' is a 'real case' and that there are other, 'unreported cases' that if able to be quantified would give an aggregate, accurate figure for 'abused children'. It is thus assumed that 'actual abuse' is measured via reporting the suspicion of it, and does not need any further verification.

Creighton considers that 'the gap between the number of reported cases and the number of actual cases is likely to be narrowed by an increase in the public's and in professional knowledge about the problem and a sympathetic response to it.[35] The only research used by Creighton to support this proposition is that previous research has used self-reporting as a means to try to ascertain if there is a higher incidence of child abuse than is shown by the reported cases.[36]

Conversely, malicious and unfounded allegations are acknowledged by Creighton. Her solution is to suggest that 'it is essential that all reported cases receive a thorough investigation before being accepted as abuse'.[37] However, even assuming that a consensus could be reached about what constitutes a 'thorough investigation', there is no reliable measure to indicate whether such an investigation would be able to give such a finding or otherwise. The known problems of substantiation and reliability, and harm caused to families by such investigation, are not considered. Creighton concludes that:

> Child Abuse Registers provide the most reliable measure of the number of children identified and reported as abused in any area. On the basis of the reported rate of abuse derived from the research an estimate of the national incidence of abuse to children in England and Wales can be derived.[38]

This research was produced for the NSPCC in 1988. Until 1986 child sexual abuse was acknowledged to exist but was not accepted as a category of child abuse in its own right.[39] Emotional abuse, failure to thrive and neglect were attracting numbers of recorded cases 'too small to permit a reliable extrapolation'.[40] Therefore the conclusions were based upon cases of 'physical abuse' and early categorisations of 'sexual abuse'. This is consistent with the original intention in s.47 Children Act 1989 which applied to 'significant harm' and was prompted by the findings of public inquiries into child deaths, particularly the death of Maria Colwell.[41]

Prevalence: measuring of the amount of child abuse in England

Once it concluded its eighteen-year study, the NSPCC launched its Full Stop campaign in March 1999. Its objective was 'ending cruelty to children within a generation'.[42] Having indicated that the tools necessary to predict child abuse were available via risk assessment using risk characteristics gained from characteristics of families of children on the register, the NSPCC refocussed upon prevalence to suggest target numbers of abuse detection and prevention.

The *Cawson Report* was self-reported as the 'most authoritative prevalence study of child abuse ever to have been conducted in the United Kingdom'.[43] The *Radford Study* is the follow-up report on prevalence. At the time of the *Cawson Report* the NSPCC stated that it 'intends to repeat the study within ten years and that will enable us [the NSPCC] to chart changes in the treatment of children and young people over a period of time'.[44] The objective of the study was to 'provide us [the NSPCC] with a benchmark against which to assess the success of our campaign to end cruelty'.[45]

The *Cawson Report* was published by the NSPCC. In 2002 the NSPCC submitted parts of it for peer review[46] and in 2004 parts of it were rewritten with May-Chahal. The resubmitted parts were published.[47] It highlighted the operational problems of identifying child abuse parameters and the resultant problems of measuring its prevalence.[48] The peer-reviewed paper drew attention to the indeterminacy of definitions of 'child abuse', and placed the original report's findings in an international context. It restated the view of the original *Cawson Report* that prevalence in the UK was unacceptably high, and observed that the findings suggested that there was a need for a more informed public debate about what standards for treating children were acceptable.[49]

The study used a postcode sample of people between the ages of 18 and 24. The male response was scaled up to match the female response. Market researchers conducted interviews. Computer-generated interview questions and answers were also used.[50] The questions about childhood experiences were designed to generate responses from which the interviewers could code whether abuse had occurred. The conclusion did not match the perception of the interviewees in all cases: even where the interviewees did not consider they were 'abused' some were categorised as such. The article presents a summary of the questions and responses and produces percentages from each category.[51]

The discussion concludes that the study:

> demonstrates that, despite the existence of a developed child protection system over the last two decades in the UK, child maltreatment prevalence remains unacceptably high. There is a need for a more informed public debate about acceptable standards for the treatment of children. Respondents' attitudinal clarity about what were the unacceptable ways to treat children was not always consistent with ratings of the ways they assessed their own treatment.[52]

The latter part of this conclusion is validly inferred from the data. If there is no consensus over what constitutes 'acceptable standards for the treatment of children', is a falling below the standard suggested by Cawson *et al.* evidence of child abuse? This is a different research question outside the scope of the study. The study highlights that:

- there is no consensus over what child abuse is or where on a scale of events acts would have to fall before being reliably categorised as abuse; and
- there is a large disparity over respondents' perception of child abuse, the NSPCC's perception of child abuse and events reported as child abuse.

There are problems, however, with drawing any firm conclusions about prevalence or incidence from the study. The key reasons for this are:

- The data has been collected from events that occurred up to twenty-four years prior to publication of the study. The study states the respondents had no clear memories below 5 years of age and were up to 24 years old so the recollections refer to events up to nineteen years prior to the interviews. The study took a further five years for parts to be peer reviewed and published.
- There is no data collected of experience below the age of 5 years.
- There are no third party observations or verification of the recollections. There is consequently no means of checking whether the memories are generally objectively supported, or otherwise. This is particularly relevant as few of the recollections were subject to external scrutiny or investigation.

- There is no checking mechanism to screen for invalid, misremembered, forgotten (omitted) or falsified data. The recollections may be intentionally or unintentionally false, mistaken or exaggerated. Respondents may unconsciously respond to cues from interviewers or questions that suggest certain responses.
- There is no data collection from any other source or any attempt to triangulate results to increase reliability. For example, the parents were not interviewed nor was anyone else who would have been involved with the young adults as children. This has restricted the quality of the data to subjective recollections.
- No reason is given for the disparity between the recollected events and the lack of reporting of events that may have been abusive. There could be a number of reasons for this but one that cannot be discounted is that events are distorted or were simply not considered by anyone at the time to be incidents of child abuse. However, it may also be that events were deliberately unreported and if that is the case then further investigation as to the reasons for this could be undertaken.
- Of the reported events, there is a tapering effect where ultimately only eight respondents spoke to a social worker but there is no indication of what happened subsequently. There are several possible explanations for this ranging from a decision that the reported events did not merit investigation in more than eight cases or that the child protection procedures were not sufficiently rigorous to progress such cases through the system. Without further investigation it is not possible to draw an inference from the data.
- In relation to reliability of data, without any stringent methodology designed to check its reliability and its confidence limits, the data must be treated with caution rather than as giving rise to statistical conclusions.
- It is unclear what is being measured. There may be a difference in classification between, for example, an isolated violent or neglectful event that does not re-occur and a continuing situation.
- Due to the retrospective nature of the data collected the result is the application of new standards to historical situations based on childhood memories. Acceptable standards of parenting would have changed during the long period covered by the study. By the time the study was published the data related to a period between eighteen and twenty-four years previous to its impact. It is speculative to infer that the numbers categorised in the study are representative of what is occurring now.
- A sample obtained by inviting responses from the general population in relation to a specific area of research may not yield a representative sample. The disparity between male and female adjusted by a scaling up provides an *estimate* over a wider sample.
- No confidence limits are calculated for the data.

Although Cawson set out to estimate the 'prevalence of child abuse',[53] the data cannot be described as supplying accurate prevalence numbers. They could more accurately be described as an estimate of incidence numbers.

Regardless, the media reported widely that the NSPCC as part of its Full Stop campaign identified that 10 per cent of children in the whole population are abused.[54] In additional to the issues noted above, there was no clarification that the events classified as child abuse in the study were not all as severe as depicted in the NSPCC Full Stop television advertisements. The adverts suggested serious and possibly fatal acts of violence, sexual abuse and neglect.[55] The media reporting of serious, fatal cases did not assist in presenting a less dramatic view, which is more representative of the majority of cases.[56]

The NSPCC's follow-up report, the *Radford Study*, reported a reduction in the number of 'abused' children across the different categories. The executive summary gives an overview of the findings which show where categories of abuse have reduced. Some of the findings reflect the changes in what would be considered acceptable parenting practices. For example, there is a decline in what is described as 'harsh emotional and physical punishment' which is likely be reflective of society's changing views towards punishment. However, it is difficult to conclude whether child abuse has actually reduced, or indeed what the prevalence is or was. The study uses a similar methodology to Cawson *et al.*[57] The study is thus also an estimate of incidence.

The executive summary to the *Radford Study* reported that:

> We found levels of parental neglect to be very similar, with 9.4% reporting some form of neglect in 1998 compared with 9.9% in 2009. There was, however, a general decline in reported experiences of harsh emotional and physical punishment, and a decline in some experiences of physical and sexual violence.
>
> The prevalence of physical violence reduced significantly from 13.1% in 1998 to 9.8% in 2009. The 18–24s in 2009 who reported physical [ill] treatment/discipline at home, school or elsewhere were also less likely to report that this had happened regularly during childhood.
>
> The experience of prolonged verbal aggression at home, school or elsewhere also reduced significantly over time (from 14.5% in 1998 to 6% in 2009).
>
> The results for sexual abuse should be interpreted with caution, as composites from both studies were created to compare coercive sexual activity, but they do indicate a decline in forced or coercive sexual activity since 1998 and a relatively constant level of underage sexual activity. The comparison of coerced sexual acts under age 16 shows a reduction from 6.8% in 1998 to 5% in 2009.[58]

It does appear that there have been some changes in parental treatment of children based on the reports that young adults give of their treatment as children. These studies provide useful and valuable information about how young adults remember their treatment as children, and how that treatment can be categorised differently by the participants and the researchers, but they do not resolve the issue of the meaning and scope of child abuse or calculate its prevalence.

Measuring the outcome

Until this point this chapter has been concerned with the problems of measuring child abuse. The remainder of the chapter looks more closely at the difficulties of measuring the response to it. The main problem with any attempt at evaluation is the uncertainty about the scale and nature of the problem. Without a clear idea of the numbers involved it is difficult to measure how effective any solution is. To compound the issue, the rise in popularity since the 1980s of the idea that child abuse can be predicted (risk prediction) has introduced an extra layer in relation to government response to suspected significant harm (or the risk of it) and the success or otherwise of the responses.

Risk prediction: can child abuse be predicted and prevented?

The attempt by the NSPCC from the mid-1970s to collect non-consensual data via the 'at risk' registers[59] and consider the factors contributing to a family's registration is arguably a contributory factor in the increased government drive for routine data to be collected about every family. In 1992 Creighton's research for the NSPCC furthered this aim.[60] Her report marked the conclusion of the eighteen-year Register research. Described as an 'epidemiological study' it considered the 'nature of child abuse in order that children could be better protected and abuse prevented'.[61] Selected characteristics of the children on the Register and their families were included from a list of characteristics the NSPCC considered relevant for measurement.

Eighteen years previously, in the first report of the Register research it was noted that 'on the basis of the observed correlations, epidemiological studies can lead to the formulation of hypotheses about causal relations and these can be examined further in detailed studies of smaller populations'.[62] The total population of the concluding study followed the same methodology and considered 'all cases from a defined area and reported by a range of professionals and agencies'.[63]

The research aim was to 'contribute to a greater understanding of the *causes* of child abuse'.[64] In order to attempt to do this, eighteen years of information about families accused of causing non-accidental injury to their children, and families accused of the wider and more vague term 'abusing' them, was passed by government agencies to the NSPCC for research purposes. There was no consent or knowledge given by the data subjects, who had no opportunity to give their views on whether the data was accurate. Consequently the data was assumed to be correct. No consideration was given to the possibility of incorrect conclusions within the system or the problem of false allegations, or genuinely meant but mistaken concerns.

The data requested[65] by the NPSCC was intended to enable trends to be identified showing risk indicators in relation to families who abuse their children. The information returned to the NSPCC was matched against statistical averages, intended to represent the whole population, obtained from government census statistics. This resulted in some demographic characteristics of families showing as above the population average in the study group of 'abusing families'. The inference drawn from this was that the characteristics[66] identified as above the overall population average meant that parents with any of these characteristics were more likely to abuse their children.

This study and the growing desire to identify dangerous parents and their prevalence prompted a body of research reinforcing the theory that child abuse is possible to predict and therefore prevent.[67] The conclusions of Creighton's research, however, are best described as a hypothesis rather than a firm conclusion. The questions were pre-considered to show risk indicators, which restricted the type and number of indicators considered in the study. The resultant data showed higher than average prevalence amongst certain groups, which was then applied to the whole population to conclude that families with certain characteristics were more likely to abuse their children.

Although such studies yield useful and interesting data, applying their finding to the whole of the population is risky. Methodological issues with such an approach include:

- The methodology of the study took population averages of certain demographics from the Office of National Statistics and measured whether the abusing cohort scored higher than the average on these factors. The intention was to compare the abusing group with the overall population mean. However, without a control group there is no indication whether a random control group may yield a similar result in respect of above average results for some demographic factors. There is no indication of whether the measures on those characteristics in the abusing group are statistically significantly different from those of the whole population.

- The characteristics on which comparisons were made were pre-set by the researchers: they were searching for specific bits of information to confirm a theory. For example, if a methodology matches various characteristics of abusing families against a sample of the general population the results are only indicative of the characteristics tested. There may be other, untested characteristics that are more relevant or that reveal relevant results.

- The report looked at one characteristic at a time and consequently potential interaction between characteristics was not examined.

- Although the results conclude that in the majority of cases the theory is *not* confirmed, i.e. the characteristics the researchers are searching for do *not* occur in the majority of cases, this finding is ignored.

- The data categorising the parents in relation to the pre-selected characteristics is collected retrospectively and from a variety of methods including self-reporting. It may therefore be subject to inaccuracy.

- The operational parameters in relation to the scope of 'child abuse' were vague; the views of the authors of the study differed from the views of the participants (it was possible for a research subject to be categorised as 'abused' although they did not define themselves as such); few cases were reported as suspected child abuse at the time. Some researcher definitions are neither medical nor criminal. Syndromes such as FII and categories of emotional abuse are controversial.[68]

- No confidence limits are calculated.

Dr Marietta Higgs[69] and Professor Sir Roy Meadow[70] also developed theories which they applied to child abuse detection and prevention programmes. The common theme in this work is the speculative nature of the hypotheses, and the high false positive rate likely to be yielded by them. This was borne out by the high profile miscarriages of justice evident from application of their theories in the family courts and in the criminal justice system. These instances had disastrous consequences, one leading to a public inquiry,[71] the other to a Law Commission Review into the use of expert evidence in criminal trials.[72] Regardless of this, since the 1960s, when radiographers identified baby battering as a child abuse phenomenon,[73] other branches of the medical profession have understandably strived to predict and identify abuse.[74] An unfortunate consequence of this well-intentioned aim has been to contribute to the idea that child abuse is something that medical experts can and should reliably predict and identify. This raised the expectation that the medical profession and social workers are able to 'diagnose' and thus prevent child abuse. Pressure on experts to identify and take steps to predict and prevent child abuse increased, despite the problems that led to the Cleveland public inquiry[75] and the series of miscarriages of justice in relation to Sally Clark and similar cases.[76]

As a result, there is an emphasis in child protection and safeguarding discourse that child abuse can be predicted and prevented, entrenched by the use, methodology and findings of Serious Case Reviews. Partly as a result of this theory there are now firmly entrenched policies in England of early intervention. Such strategies begin at the primary and secondary levels of non-coercive intervention. However, this also means local authority social services that are used by families at these early stages have increased the opportunities for surveillance and interference, not only when such families are considered to have abused their children but also when it is predicted that they might do so in the future as a result of a risk being identified.

In some studies risk assessment is considered to be analogous to germ theory and disease control. If protecting children from abuse is viewed through the filter of analogy whereby child abuse can be likened to a disease,[77] then the child protection and safeguarding procedures set up to deal with child abuse arguably follow a procedural pattern similar to that of disease control.[78] For example, Gough explains that as child abuse is sometimes referred to as a disease in our society it can be eradicated by means of a programme based upon a model for the eradication of disease.[79] The descriptor 'eradicated' reveals a belief that it is possible to prevent all child abuse by greater understanding of where it is likely to occur, and by the provision of a system to intervene in such situations. This approach, however, assumes all that is needed is a logical system to be rigidly enforced upon parents.[80] This approach is controversial. Popper refers to the underpinning methodology of such approaches as 'pseudo-scientific'.[81]

An example of this approach in child protection literature is seen in Browne and Saqi's chapter in *Early Prediction and Prevention of Child Abuse*.[82] The book was produced following a conference organised by the Society for Reproductive and Infant Psychology intended to 'bring together what is known that would be helpful in predicting and preventing the abuse and neglect of young children.'[83] The conference and resulting publication were important in shaping risk prediction ideology. Browne and Saqi's chapter in this book states in the opening paragraph that it is easier to 'accommodate the parents than to discover what is really going on'.[84] From the outset this statement implies concealed guilt; taken in the context of Smith's schema it illustrates that social work assessment of a family may not be an impartial 'fact finding' exercise but a matching operation where parental behaviours are construed as evidence that 'something' is 'going on'. Browne and Saqi's subsequent findings, however, indicate that the prediction is wrong in over 97 per cent of cases.[85]

Using a sample population of 10,000 families Browne and Saqi predicted that 12.3 per cent of the families would abuse their children. Analysis of their data shows that of the 12.3 per cent (those families predicted to abuse their children), they were wrong in 97.3 per cent of their predictions;[86] 97.3 per cent of the 12.3 per cent did *not* abuse their children. No data is given to show the false negative rate (families *not* predicted to abuse their children who then did so).

In the paper Browne and Saqi do not link this significant false positive number back to his initial statement concerning discovering 'what is really going on'. Browne and Saqi do not distinguish between unsubstantiated cases and substantiated ones, considering that all referrals constitute actual cases of 'child abuse' or at least a 'child in need'.

In a more recent publication, Browne adopts the same position. He considers risk factors for 'child abuse' (which is not defined for this study) to include evidence of parental non-compliance with government ideals,[87] although he clearly states that 'it is important to note that not all families with these risk factors will go on to maltreat their child(ren)'.[88] Browne advocates tutelage for such families via counselling and informing parents of 'sensitive interactions' and 'appropriate routines'.[89] Social work assessment using this model can be argued to start from a premise that there is 'something to discover' and the parents require at least some level of tutelage.

This approach is an early attempt at a risk strategy to assess families at high and low risk of child abuse.[90] This strategy of risk assessment has since been routinely used despite the extremely high rate of incorrect prediction. Browne and Saqi suggest midwives and health visitors screen from the ante-natal period onwards using a checklist, which includes thirteen demographic points selected on the basis they can be 'routinely and easily obtained by the health visitors and nursing colleagues'.[91] This data is obtained without consent. The researchers test this prediction strategy on a sample group and attempt to predict who will abuse their children. They then compare their estimates with cases that proceed to a child protection case conference.[92] In contrast to the NSPCC's methodology, their approach is prospective, as opposed to retrospective. They conclude that their data shows an apparent above average prevalence of certain characteristics in families who had abused their children. They use this conclusion to suggest other families with those characteristics should be considered at high risk of abusing their children (see Table 2.2).

Although Browne and Saqi refer to 'large numbers' of false positive results, they do not explain how large the number is, stating only that 'the most optimistic estimates of screening effectiveness implies that a screening programme would yield large numbers of false positives'.[93] The authors do not comment further on this, identify it as a serious problem, suggest further research in this area or suggest what should be done about the families wrongly categorised if unwanted interventions take place.

Table 2.3 is an analysis of Browne and Saqi's data demonstrating the results of their risk assessment strategy. This illustrates the likely outcome of using risk prediction strategies to predict abusing parents.

Seven years later the use of risk indicators in attempting to predict child abuse remained problematic. Gibbons *et al.* conclude in regard to predictive systems that 'it is likely that any predictive system will produce large numbers of "false positives" in respect of children identified by the screening system who do not subsequently suffer abuse'.[94] They inform this conclusion with evidence from other research.[95] Parton also commented on the lack of ability for most referrals to be substantiated.[96] Although the use of predictive models for risk of child abuse is an inefficient method which labels as abusers a large number of non-abusing families, whilst missing families who may be abusing their children, this methodology is still routinely applied. Consequently there are likely to be a large number of false positive identifications using risk prediction.[97] If the resultant State processes are harmful to those families this consequence should be considered in evaluative studies with a view to finding

Table 2.2 Summary of Browne and Saqi's risk prediction outcomes

	Predicted to abuse	*Not predicted to abuse*	*Total*
	12.28%	87.72%	100%
Abuse found	33	7	40
No abuse found	1,195	8,765	9,960
Total	1,228	8,772	10,000

	predicted correctly
	predicted incorrectly

Source: Derived from Browne and Saqi (1988), Figure 1, p. 71.

Table 2.3 Applying Browne and Saqi's (1988) analysis to 2014 population data (England)

		Browne and Saqi's analysis scaled to 2014 population (England)	Comments/notes
Population	10,000	11,500,000	Children in England
Abuse rate (prevalence)	0.40%		using Browne and Saqi's rate
Number abused	40	46,000	cf. NSPCC estimate of 10% abuse, i.e. 1,150,000 children
Number not abused	9,960	11,454,000	

Apply Browne and Saqi's checklist			
82% sensitivity – Correct identification (number correctly predicted as abused)	33	37,720	cf. 2014 CPP register number of 48,300
82% sensitivity – Missed identifications (number incorrectly predicted NOT abused)	7	8,280	
88% specificity – false alarms (number incorrectly predicted as abused)	1,195	1,374,480	cf. 2014 number of referrals of 657,800
88% specificity – non-abusers identified (number predicted correctly NOT abused)	8,765	10,079,520	
Efficiency of detection process	2.7%		Extremely low ratio
Percentage of false positives	97.3%		Extremely high error rate
Population identified as likely abusers	1,228	1,412,200	cf. actual 2014 referrals of 657,800

Source: Derived from Browne and Saqi (1988), Figure 1, p. 71.

a resolution for such families. False negatives are also of concern: percentage-wise these constitute a very small number, but translate into quite a substantial actual number with dire consequences for the children concerned. The publication of the report of the inquiry into child abuse in Cleveland[98] did not prompt a review of this approach in respect of the consequences of either false positive or false negative categorisations. It cannot be considered a historic problem as risk prediction is embedded in modern child protection and safe-guarding practice. This is particularly concerning as it is possible that an over-loaded system attempting to filter out a large number of false positive referrals is contributing to the small number of false negative cases that are missed, with fatal consequences.

Of particular concern is the rising use of algorithmic risk prediction. This involves a computer program which enables the characteristics of families to be matched against characteristics the program identifies as 'risky'. The resultant score would be the basis of decisions about interventions. The accuracy and implications of such programs are not adequately researched or controlled, and their use is unregulated. The programs themselves are generated by private companies for profit.

Conclusion: issues of measuring success

This chapter has been concerned with a discussion of how the child protection and safeguarding system should be considered in evaluative terms, whether it is possible to accurately define and measure child abuse and how well solutions are working. The difficulty of attempting to measure success in relation to predicting and preventing child abuse includes not only the problems already identified earlier in this chapter but also the problem of defining the meaning of 'success' in this context. This issue is evident in research studies evaluating the success of child welfare interventions, particularly those where social conformity is conflated with welfare.[99]

Risk assessment is useful to inform further research questions. However, suggesting it as a viable solution in relation to predicting children who are likely to be abused has informed 'strengthening' of the existing system, without adequate consideration of the adverse consequences of categorising large sections of the population as 'risky'. One measure of this policy may be to calculate the system's efficiency, or perhaps a theoretically acceptable margin of error with appropriate remedies in place for those affected. There may be several answers to the question of an acceptable level, all subjectively valid. However, an acceptable margin of error is a sensitive question and may depend upon external factors, such as the feasibility of an appropriate remedy being available for cases involving false positives and false negatives. It is therefore difficult to draw firm conclusions in relation to these questions. Compounding the difficulties of an objective standard of success is the popularity of risk prediction despite its known high false positive rate. This in itself would suggest the system is unsuccessful if only in relation to its raw ability to predict child abuse, and prevent serious cases (false negatives) and families suffering unnecessary intervention (false positives).

The difficulties highlighted in this chapter are evident in the responses to the various strategies to detect child abuse. All have been criticised in relation to both over- and under-inclusiveness: it is very difficult to 'get the balance right'. Arguments about over- and under-inclusiveness may originate from different and possibly irreconcilable ideological positions in relation to child welfare and the justification for surveillance and interference. There is common ground, however, in the concern that the system is not infallible in relation to either position. For example Broadhurst *et al.* explain the implications of over-inclusion: 'The child protection "net" was perceived to be catching too many families, who were then subject to intrusive and inappropriate intervention, with local authorities providing little by way of effective family support.'[100] This reflects a post-refocussing view. Earlier research took the contrary view, observing it was considered that there is no accurate way to estimate the extent of child abuse, and concluded it was more prevalent than reported cases indicated. This represents the under-inclusive position: 'Most estimates are based on cases which have come to the attention of someone outside the immediate family, i.e. they are the cases that are reported, rather than all of those that actually occur.'[101] Hallett states:

> Some researchers claim that the cases that are reported (the incidence rate) represent a small proportion of the actual number of maltreated children in society (the prevalence rate), and suggest that a lot of child abuse and neglect is not detected.[102]

The NSPCC conclude:

> the known facts reveal only a fraction of the problem. This is because most cases of abuse go unreported, and [we] have conducted research that has concluded approximately 1 in 10 children suffer abuse during childhood.[103]

The above examples demonstrate how easy it is to identify conflicting views in literature delineating between those who identify problems because it is over-inclusive, those who identify problems because it is under-inclusive and those who believe the system is problematic on both counts. Although these critiques start from different ideological perspectives there is a consensus that the system does not work well. The inability to accurately define, measure or predict child abuse has not prevented these conflicting narratives raising concerns about over- and under-interventions from taking polemic stances. It has also not prevented policy from drifting towards over-reliance on concerns about under reporting, and under-reliance on concerns about over reporting.

Notes

1 This is not a recent issue. *Messages from Research*, for example, devoted a section to considering the problems of definition at the beginning of the book. Department of Health (1995) *Child Protection: Messages from Research*, HMSO, London, pp. 11–24.
2 World Health Organisation (1999) *Report of the Consultation on Child Abuse Prevention: Social Change and Mental Health, Violence and Injury Prevention*,

Geneva, pp. 29–31. Online at: http://apps.who.int/iris/handle/10665/65900 (Accessed 8 February 2016).

3 Ibid., pp. 13–17.

4 Ibid., pp. 13–14.

5 Female Genital Mutilation Act 2003 c.31. This was preceded by the Prohibition of Female Circumcision Act 1985 c.38.

6 Irfan, S. and Cowburn, M. (2004) 'Disciplining, Chastisement and Physical Child Abuse: Perceptions and Attitudes of the British Pakistani Community', *Journal of Muslim Minority Affairs* 24(1): 89–98. Also see: Mumby, J. dicta in: *Re K* [2005] EWHC 2956 (Fam), where he argues that reasonable parenting should be judged in accordance with the standards of the parents' ethnic and cultural community. These comments would have to be considered, however, in line with legislation and attitudes towards, for example, female circumcision. Also see: WHO (1999) 'Report of the Consultation on Child Abuse Prevention', *Social Change and Mental Health, Violence and Injury Prevention*, March, WHO, Geneva, pp. 29–31.

7 European countries which have banned corporal punishment in legislation are: Austria (1989), Bulgaria (2000), Croatia (1999), Cyprus (1994), Denmark (1997), Finland (1983), Germany (2000), Greece (2006), Hungary (2004), Iceland (2003), Latvia (1998), Netherlands (2007), Norway (1987), Portugal (2007), Romania (2004), Spain (2007), Sweden (1979) and Ukraine (2001). European countries that have committed themselves to banning it in the near future are: Czech Republic, Estonia, Ireland, Lithuania, Luxembourg, Slovakia and Slovenia. From: Council of Europe: Commissioner for Human Rights (2008) *Children and Corporal Punishment: The Right Not To Be Hit, Also a Children's Right*, CommDH/IssuePaper (2006)1REV Updated version January 2008. Online at: https://wcd.coe.int/ViewDoc.jsp?id=1237635andSite=CM (Accessed 10 February 2016).

8 Set out in: HM Government (2015) *Working Together to Safeguard Children*, TSO, London.

9 Gibbons, J., Conroy, S. and Bell, C. (1995) *Operating the Child Protection System: Studies in Child Protection*, HMSO, London, p. 20, Table 2iv.

10 Taken from: Department of Health, Department of Education and Skills, and Department for Children, Schools and Families *Annual Reports*: 1989, 2000, A/F 00/13 (2001), SFR 28/2003, SFR 41/2004, SFR 22/2009, SFR 43/2014.

11 c.100.

12 'Emotional abuse to be made a criminal offence' was announced in the Queen's speech before Christmas 2014: see Puffett, N. (2014) 'Emotional Abuse of Children to Become Criminal Offence', *Children & Young People Now*, 5 June. Online at: www. cypnow.co.uk/cyp/news/1144640/emotional-abuse-of-children-to-become -criminal-offence (Accessed 12 October 2016). It was made law before the May 2015 General Election. The provisions to amend the Children and Young Persons Act 1933 c.12 were added to the Serious Crimes Bill and debated in Parliament: see Hansard (2014) *House of Lords Debate*, 16 June, Col. 651, Baroness Smith of Basildon. S.66 Serious Crimes Act 2015 c.9 when it came into force amended the wording of s.1 Children and Young Persons Act 1933 to include 'whether the suffering or injury is of a physical or a psychological nature'. In addition the crime has been relabelled from a 'misdemeanour' to an 'offence' in the same section.

13 See for example: Department of Children Schools and Families (2009) *Referrals, Assessments and Children and Young People who are the Subject of a Child Protection Plan, England: Year Ending 31 March 2009*, SFR22/2009, 17 September, TSO, London.

14 c.31.
15 ONS (2008) *General Household Survey 2006: Overview Report*, p. 3. Online at: http://webarchive.nationalarchives.gov.uk/20160105160709/http://www. ons.gov.uk/ons/rel/ghs/general-household-survey/2006-report/index.html (Accessed 29 February 2016).
16 See for example discussion in: Department of Health (n. 1), p. 12.
17 Maria Colwell (1973), Jasmin Beckford (1984), Tyra Henry (1984), Heidi Koseda (1984), Kimberley Carlile (1986), Doreen Mason (1987). From: David Batty (2003) 'Catalogue of Cruelty', *Society Guardian*, 27 January. Online at: www.guardian.co.uk/society/2003/jan/27/childrensservices.childprotection/ print (Accessed 29 February 2016).
18 Children Act 1989 c.41.
19 This is evidenced by the preceding Law Commission Reports: Law Commission (1987) *Family Law: Review of Child Law – Care, Supervision and Interim Orders in Custody Proceedings (Consultation Paper)* [1987] EWLC C100. Online at: www.bailii.org/ew/other/EWLC/1987/c100.pdf (Accessed 13 January 2016); Law Commission (1987) *Family Law: Review of Child Law – Wards of Court (Consultation Paper)* [1987] EWLC C101. Online at: www.bailii.org/ ew/other/EWLC/1987/c101.pdf (Accessed 13 January 2016); Law Commission (1988) *Review of Child Law Guardianship (Report)* [1988] EWLC 172 (01 January 1988). Online at: www.bailii.org/ew/other/EWLC/1988/172.pdf (Accessed 13 January 2016); and the findings of Department of Health (1988) *Report of the Inquiry into Child Abuse in Cleveland in 1987*, HMSO, London; and Department of Health and Social Security (1974) *Report of the Committee of Inquiry into the Care and Supervision Provided in relation to Maria Colwell*, HMSO, London.
20 Home Office (1945) *Report by Sir Walter Monckton on the Circumstances which Led to the Boarding-Out of Dennis and Terence O'Neill at Bank Farm, Minsterley and the Steps Taken to Supervise their Welfare*, Cmd 6636, HMSO, London.
21 Susan Creighton was Senior Research Officer in the Public Policy Department of the NSPCC Headquarters. She managed the Register research from 1975.
22 Cawson, P., Wattam, C., Brooker, S. and Kelly, G. (2000) *Child Maltreatment in the United Kingdom: A Study of the Prevalence of Child Abuse and Neglect*, NSPCC, London.
23 Radford, L., Corral, S., Bradley, C., Fisher, H., Bassett, C., Howat, N. and Collishaw, S. (2011) *Child Abuse and Neglect in the UK Today*, NSPCC, London. Online at: www.nspcc.org.uk/Inform/research/findings/child_abuse_neglect _research_PDF_wdf84181.pdf (Accessed 25 November 2011).
24 Creighton, S. (1992) *Child Abuse Trends in England and Wales 1988–1990 and an Overview from 1973–1990*, NSPCC, London. The Child Abuse Register research was considered by Creighton p. 40 to be the 'largest continuous survey of child abuse conducted in this country'.
25 Creighton, S.J. (1988) 'The Incidence of Child Abuse and Neglect' in: Browne, K., Hanks, H., Stratton, P. and Hamilton, C. (eds) *Early Prediction and Prevention of Child Abuse*, Wiley, Chichester, pp. 1–43.
26 Cawson *et al.* (n. 22).
27 Radford *et al.* (n. 23).
28 Child Abuse Registers were originally called Non Accidental Injury Registers. They have existed since 1974 when they were set up following DHSS Circular LASSL (74) 13 (DHSS, 1974) as a response to the public inquiry findings in respect of the death of Maria Colwell in 1974. The same DHSS circular set up Area Review Committees (ARCs) which brought together senior policy makers from all 'agencies' involved with children as a way to integrate policies relating

to child abuse investigation and prevention. Part of this policy was to set up a central record of information in each area concerning reported cases of 'child abuse'. The NSPCC set up Special Units at the same time and in some areas the ARC delegated management, including that of the Register, to these NSPCC units. The non-consensually obtained data concerning each family that were entered onto the register was then used by the NSPCC for research, including attempts to consider the prevalence of 'abuse'.

29 Creighton (n. 24), p. 31.
30 Ibid., referring to Select Committee on Violence in the Family (1977) *Violence to Children*, First Report, Vol. 1, HMSO, London.
31 Creighton (n. 24), p. 31, referring to Oliver, J.E., Cox, J., Taylor, A. and Baldwin, J.A. (1974) *Severely Ill-Treated Children in North East Wiltshire*, Oxford Unit of Clinical Epidemiology, Oxford.
32 Creighton (n. 24), p. 31, referring to Gil, D.G. (1970) *Violence Against Children: Physical Child Abuse in the United States*, Harvard University Press, Massachusetts.
33 Creighton (n. 24), p. 31, referring to Kempe, C.H. (1973) 'Child Abuse (the Battered Child Syndrome)', position paper for the hearings of the Subcommittee on Children and Youth of the Committee on Labour and Public Welfare, United States Senate, 31 March, Denver, Colorado.
34 Creighton (n. 24), p. 33.
35 Ibid., p. 34.
36 Ibid., p. 33, referring to Strauss, M.A. (1979) 'Family Patterns and Child Abuse in a Nationally Representative American Sample', *Child Abuse and Neglect* 3(1): 213–25; and Strauss, M.A. and Gelles, R.J. (1986) 'Societal Change and Change in Family Violence from 1975 to 1985 as Revealed by Two National Surveys', *Journal of Marriage and the Family* 48: 465–79.
37 Creighton (n. 24), p. 34.
38 Ibid., p. 40.
39 In the Department of Health and Social Security (1986) *Child Abuse: Working Together – Draft Guidelines*, HMSO, London, the 'sexual abuse' of children is added as a separate category of abuse despite its vague operational definitions and the existing coverage of sexual offences under criminal legislation. Prior to this, sexual acts against children were treated as physical abuse and emotional abuse in addition to potentially amounting to sexual offences in the criminal law.
40 Ibid., p. 40.
41 Department of Health (n. 19); and Department of Health and Social Security (n. 19).
42 Cawson *et al.* (n. 22).
43 Ibid., p. 89.
44 Ibid.
45 Ibid., p. 90.
46 Publishers note: 'Received 20 May 2002; Received in revised form 30 April 2004; accepted 14 May 2004.'
47 May-Chahal, C. and Cawson, P. (2005) 'Measuring Child Maltreatment in the United Kingdom: A Study of the Prevalence of Child Abuse and Neglect', *Child Abuse and Neglect: The International Journal* 29(9): 943–1070.
48 For example, in the discussion section of the article, examples are provided illustrating the varying prevalence rates found by other studies. Ibid., 981. Also, see reference in ibid., 972 to the problem of 'no standardized definition of neglect although there is some agreement amongst community samples', which cites Dubowitz, H., Klockner, A., Starr, R.H. and Black, M. (1998) 'Community and Professional Definitions of Child Neglect', *Child Maltreatment* 3: 235–43.

Stone, however, notes there is much disagreement amongst professionals in relation to the same issue. Stone, B. (1998) *Child Neglect: Practitioners' Perspectives*, NSPCC Policy Practice and Research Series, London.

49 May-Chahal and Cawson (n. 47), 982.

50 Ibid., 971. A system called Computer Assisted Personal Interviewing (CAPI) was used.

51 Ibid., 969. Physical abuse, sexual abuse, emotional abuse and neglect.

52 Ibid., 982. Surprisingly this document is not referenced by the 2011 NSPCC follow-up study report, discussed later in this chapter.

53 Cawson *et al.* (n. 22).

54 'Study Reveals 1 in 10 Children in the UK Suffer Abuse – December 2008', The Lantern Project website. Online at: www.lanternproject.org.uk/categories/childabuseintheuk-thefacts/1 (Accessed 11 October 2010).

55 Rayner, J. (1999) 'Why this NSPCC Advert is Harmful to Children – The Way to Protect our Children is to Let Them Play (Again) . . . Not to Scare the Parents to Death', *The Observer*, Sunday, 8 August. Online at: www.guardian.co.uk/lifeandstyle/1999/aug/08/foodanddrink.childprotection (Accessed 14 February 2016).

56 For example, the media reports concerning the death of Peter Connolly in Haringey. 'Baby Peter's horrifying death was down to the incompetence of almost every member of staff who came into contact with him, official reports say'; Sellgren, K. (2010) 'Baby Peter Was Failed by All Agencies', 26 October, *BBC News Online*. Online at: www.bbc.co.uk/news/education-11621391 (Accessed 29 February 2016).

57 Radford *et al.* (n. 23), Section 1.5, p. 24, and Appendix C, pp. 158–79.

58 Ibid., p. 14. The overview to the Report was published in February 2011: NSPCC (2011) *Child Cruelty in the UK 2011: An NSPCC Study into Childhood Abuse and Neglect Over the Past 30 Years*. Online at: www.nspcc.org.uk/news-and-views/our-news/nspcc-news/11-02-15-report-launch/overview-report_wdf80875.pdf (Accessed 1 April 2011). The full report was published in September 2011.

59 Child protection registers have historically held the names of children deemed to be 'at risk of significant harm' and were held by social services departments. Registers have been replaced by a record of children who are the subject of 'child protection plans' that will be contained in electronic files held by children's social care departments.

60 Creighton, S. (n. 24).

61 Ibid., p. 4.

62 Ibid.

63 Ibid.

64 Ibid.

65 Using forms 35 and 37 reproduced in appendix III of Creighton's report, ibid., pp. 73–5.

66 For example, parents who suffered unemployment, separation or divorce, bereavement, were battered, had a disabled child or were physically or mentally ill were all considered high risk categories.

67 This approach was developed during the 1980s when commentators such as Gough theorised that eradicating child abuse is analogous to germ theory whereby once identified a germ can be targeted and eliminated. Gough, D. (1988) 'Approaches to Child Abuse Prevention' in: Browne, K., Hanks, H., Stratton, P. and Hamilton, C. (eds) *Early Prediction and Prevention of Child Abuse*, Wiley, Chichester, p. 107.

68 Munchausen syndrome by proxy has been renamed fabricated and induced illness (FII) following the miscarriages of justice involving the expert evidence

of Professor Sir Roy Meadow. However, the inclusion of such syndromes in the DSM-IV remains controversial. Such 'culture bound' syndromes are included in Appendix 1 of the American Psychiatric Association (1994), *Diagnostic and Statistical Manual of Mental Disorders*, 4th edn, DSM-IV, American Psychiatric Association, Washington, DC. The Association's website is online at: www.psychiatry.org/practice/dsm/ (Accessed 13 May 2016).

69 In relation to the Cleveland issues.

70 In relation to MSBP (FII) and SIDS death issues.

71 Dame Elizabeth Butler-Sloss (1988) *Report into the Inquiry into Child Abuse in Cleveland 1987*, July, Cm 412, HMSO, London.

72 Law Commission (2011) *Expert Evidence in Criminal Proceedings in England and Wales*, LC325, 21 March, HC 829, TSO, London. Online at: www.lawcom.gov.uk/wp-content/uploads/2015/03/lc325_Expert_Evidence_Report.pdf (Accessed 21 July 2015).

73 Scheibner, V. (2001) 'Shaken Baby Syndrome Diagnosis on Shaky Ground', *Journal of Australasian College of Nutritional and Environmental Medicine* 20(2) (August). Online at: www.whale.to/v/sbs35.html, (Accessed 27 February 2016); Parton, N. (1981) 'Child Abuse, Social Anxiety and Welfare', *British Journal of Social Work* 11(1): 391–414. Online at: www.bjsw.oxfordjournals.org/content/11/1/391.full.pdf (Accessed 27 February 2016); American Academy of Pediatrics (2009) 'Policy Statement: Diagnostic Imaging of Child Abuse', *Paediatrics* 123(5): 1430–5. Online at: http://pediatrics.aappublications.org/content/pediatrics/123/5/1430.full.pdf (Accessed 1 May 2016); American Academy of Pediatrics (2000) 'Policy Statement: Diagnostic Imaging of Child Abuse', *Pediatrics* 105(6): 1345–8. Online at: http://pediatrics.aappublications.org/content/pediatrics/105/6/1345.full.pdf (Accessed 1 May 2016).

74 For example, in the 1960s and 1970s: baby battering (see: Parton, N. (n. 73)). In the early 1980s: sexual abuse; in the late 1980s: see Department of Health (n. 19); Munchausen syndrome by proxy (MSBP) (see: *Meadow v General Medical Council* [2006] EWHC 146 (Admin) (17 February 2006) and *GMC v Meadow* [2006] EWCA Civ 1390).

75 Butler-Sloss (n. 71).

76 For example: *R v Clark 2000* WL 1421196; *R v Clark* [2003] EWCA Crim 1020 and *R v Cannings* [2004] EWCA Crim 1.

77 Gough (n. 67). 'Child abuse' is considered in a similar fashion to germ theory whereby identification of a germ leads to its eradication and therefore eliminates disease. Germ theory (also called the pathogenic theory of medicine) states that many diseases are caused by the presence and actions of specific micro-organisms within the body. This theory became widely accepted in the late nineteenth century. See for example: Online at: http://archive.is/germtheorycalendar.com (Accessed 1 May 2016).

78 Gough (n. 67), p. 107. For an example of a critique of this approach see: Gibbons *et al.* (n. 9), Chapter 6: 'Filtering Cases out of the Child Protection System', p. 52, which describes different approaches to risk assessment in child protection. Gibbons *et al.*'s general point is that these systems are not evidence-based and are ultimately based on subjective opinions sometimes themselves derived from assumption about 'risk indicators'.

79 Gough (n. 67), p. 107.

80 Lord Laming stated 'it is unrealistic to expect that it will ever be possible to eliminate the deliberate harm or death of a child – indeed no system can achieve this.' Quoted in: Conway, H. (2003) 'The Laming Inquiry: Victoria Climbié's Legacy', *Family Law* 33: 513.

81 Popper, K. (1963) *Conjectures and Refutations*, Routledge & Kegan Paul, London, esp. 'Science as Falsification', pp. 33–9. Online at: www.stephenjaygould. org/ctrl/popper_falsification.html (Accessed 8 January 2016).

82 Browne, K. and Saqi, S. (1988) 'Approaches to Screening for Child Abuse and Neglect' in: Browne, K., Hanks, H., Stratton, P. and Hamilton, C. (eds) *Early Prediction and Prevention of Child Abuse*, Wiley, Chichester, pp. 57–85.

83 Browne and Saqi (n. 82), 'Foreword'.

84 Browne and Saqi (n. 82), p. 57.

85 Ibid., pp. 70–1; calculating the number of non-abusing families who are wrongly predicted to be abusing as 'false alarms' (1,195) as a percentage of the total number of families predicted as 'high risk' of abuse (1,228).

86 Using the risk factors the Browne and Saqi (n. 82) researchers identified, they predicted that in a population of 10,000 families 12.3 per cent would be at risk of abusing their children, i.e. 1,228 families. However, the researchers reported that in their sample of 10,000 families only 40 cases of actual abuse were found (i.e. 0.4 per cent). Using their 82 per cent sensitivity checklist (from Fig. 1, p. 71) they found that 33 of the 40 abusers were found in the 12.3 per cent identified by risk analysis, whilst 7 were not identified by this method at all. This appears a good result at first sight, except that to identify the 33 real abusers they also wrongly identified 1,195 (i.e. 1,228 less 33) non-abusers as abusers. That equates to a detection efficiency of 2.7 per cent (i.e. 33/1,228) or an error of 97.3 per cent in their prediction and completely missing 17.5 per cent of cases of actual abuse (i.e. 7/40).

87 World Health Organisation Regional Office for Europe in collaboration with Browne, K., Hamilton-Glachritsis, C. and Vettor, S. (2007) *Preventing Child Maltreatment in Europe: A Public Health Approach*, Violence and Injury Prevention Programme, WHO Regional Office for Europe, Rome, Italy, p. 13. Online at: www.euro.who.int/__data/assets/pdf_file/0012/98778/E90618. pdf (Accessed 12 October 2016).

88 Ibid.

89 Ibid.

90 Browne and Saqi (n. 82), p. 57.

91 Ibid., p. 59.

92 This point is assumed to be an accurate indicator that child abuse has occurred. This is not a reliable assumption.

93 Browne and Saqi (n. 82), p. 70.

94 Gibbons *et al.* (n. 9).

95 Star, R.H. (1982) *Child Abuse Prediction: Police Implications*, Ballinger, Cambridge.

96 Parton, N., Thorpe, D. and Wattam, C. (1997) *Child Protection: Risk and the Moral Order*, Macmillan Press, Basingstoke, Hampshire, p. 214. 'Substantiated' refers to whether the events that gave rise to the referral can be shown to have happened.

97 See: Taylor–Russell diagram in: Sarewitz, D., Pielke, R. and Byerly, R. (eds) (2000) *Prediction: Science, Decision Making, and the Future of Nature*, Island Press, Washington, DC.

98 Butler-Sloss (n. 71).

99 See, for example, adoption studies which aimed to measure success but conflated success with social conformity: Bohman, M. and Sigvardson, S. (1990) 'Outcome in adoption: Lessons from longitudinal studies' in: Brodzinsky, D. and Schechter, M. (eds) *The Psychology of Adoption*, Oxford University Press, Oxford, pp. 93–101.

100 Broadhurst, K., White, S., Fish, S., Munro, E., Fletcher, K. and Lincoln, H. (2010) *Ten Pitfalls and How to Avoid Them: What Research Tells Us*, NSPCC, London, p. 3.

101 Browne *et al.* (n. 82), p. 33.

102 Hallett, C. (1988) 'Research in Child Abuse: Some Observations on the Knowledge Base', *Journal of Reproductive and Infant Psychology* 6(3): 119–24.
103 NSPCC (2002) *Child Abuse in Britain*, NSPCC Website. Online at: www.nspcc. org.uk, (Accessed 1 September 2011) (see earlier discussion about this prevalence number which derives from the *Cawson Report*; see n. 22).

3 Identifying families for policing

The modern surveillance role of the State: identifying children for referral

The practicalities of identifying the right families for referral into the social work system are legally and socially complex. The previous chapter explained the difficulties involved. These include the problems of reaching a consensus on exactly what is meant by child abuse, whether that is equivalent to the legal term 'significant harm', the problems of estimating the prevalence of child abuse, 'safeguarding' extending child protection measures and the accuracy issues surrounding risk prediction methods. Given these issues the question of how families are identified for referral for social work assessment merits examination.

All children and families are now intended to be subject to continual State surveillance. This chapter examines the enabling legal mechanisms, and the 'referral triggers'. This highlights the question of whether there are sufficient inbuilt controls, including whether the process contains protection for children and parents from excessive State interference. Particular attention is given to whether parents and/or children can effectively challenge and stop surveillance and its consequences if it is not needed, if it is causing harm or if it cannot evidence any significant benefit. The examination also raises the question of whether there is an appropriate balance between the requirement for the State to interfere into private life to fulfil its statutory duties, on the one hand, and remedies for families (either for the family unit or for individual family members), on the other. Questions such as how the current system of surveillance and referral is justified are addressed, including whether families can potentially be failed by the system through either over, or under scrutiny.

The significant increases in the number of referrals of children for social work assessment is driven by the modern role of the State, and of agencies working with children to focus on identifying children who should be targeted. Notably this includes the introduction of s.11 Children Act 2004 requiring professionals working with children to report any concerns under the broad concept of 'safeguarding'. This is achieved via mass surveillance of all families to identify children for referral to local authority children's social care departments. These developments have created an increasingly low threshold for referral, dramatically increasing the number of families referred for assessment by 311 per cent over the past twenty-two years, and the number of assessed children by 302 per cent.[1] It is of note however, that there is no corresponding proportionate rise in the amount of child abuse detected following referral: data showing referral and assessment trends since the Children Act 1989 shows the number of cases where referred children were found to be at risk of significant harm are an increasingly small percentage of referred cases, dropping over the twenty-two-year period from 24.1 per cent to 7.3 per cent of referred cases.[2]

The expansion of the level of intrusion and the adoption of targeted early intervention policies have eroded privacy and increased the risk of families becoming stuck in a cycle of continuing intervention once under the State's intensive scrutiny. This is counter to the aim of early intervention as a means of helping families back to autonomy. It is also counter to the aim of the Children Act 1989 to interfere into private family life only where necessary, thus preserving parental autonomy unless there is a real danger of significant harm to a child.

Introducing mass surveillance and recording of information about children: part of the e-Government agenda

The use of surveillance to police all parents in relation to their parental responsibilities aligns with the ideology of the e-Government agenda introduced across most areas of government. The White Paper *Modernising Government*[3] and *Privacy and Data Sharing: The Way Forward for Public Services*[4] set out the government's policies and plans in relation to increased surveillance and data collection and sharing in relation to citizens generally. In 2009 the House of Lords published a Report entitled *Surveillance: Citizens and the State*,[5] which aimed to bring together comments on this issue from a number of disciplines and organisations. This report clarifies exactly what is meant by the term 'surveillance' as it identifies two broad types of surveillance which is used in the UK, mass surveillance and targeted surveillance: 'Mass surveillance, also described as "passive" or "undirected" surveillance is not targeted on any particular individual, but gathers images and information for possible future use. CCTV and databases are examples of mass surveillance.'[6] Targeted surveillance is:

> Surveillance directed at particular individuals and can involve the use of specific powers by authorised public agencies. Targeted surveillance can be carried out overtly or covertly, and can involve human agents. Under the *Regulation of Investigatory Powers Act 2000* (RIPA), targeted covert surveillance is 'directed' if it is carried out for a specific investigation or operation.[7]

The House of Lords explain several meanings of 'surveillance':

> The term 'surveillance' is sometimes applied to the collection and processing of personal data. The combined term 'dataveillance' covers 'the systematic

use of personal data systems in the investigation or monitoring of the actions or communications of one or more persons.[8]

[The organisation] JUSTICE suggested that a common feature of surveillance was 'the use of personal data for the purpose of monitoring, policing or regulating individual conduct.' Dr David Murakami Wood, Lecturer at the School of Architecture, Planning and Landscape, University of Newcastle upon Tyne, and representative of the Surveillance Studies Network, said that the use of definitional extremes – which regard all (or at least all unwanted or unjustified) information gathering as surveillance – was unhelpful. He argued that 'information gathering with the intent to influence and control aspects of behaviour or activities of individuals or groups would be our working definition'.[9]

The e-Government agenda explains the commitment to a rise in the use of surveillance generally. In relation to families, databases exist and all agencies concerned with children are encouraged, and indeed required under s.11 Children Act 2004, to comply with 'safeguarding' requirements. In practice this means they are required to collect information in relation to all aspects of children's lives, including subjective impressions in order to risk profile and enable early intervention strategies to be applied to certain families. Such strategies aim to target children categorised as 'at risk', described as 'vulnerable'. Data from areas as diverse as children truanting from school and mandatory joint birth registration are collected and used to profile and risk assess children. Subjective interpretations of children's behaviour, interpreted as 'signs' of abuse are also triggers.

The driving force behind the notion that information sharing is fundamental to protecting children was the *Laming Report*.[10] Previous inquiries concluded that failure to share information had contributed to situations where children had been harmed;[11] the *Laming Report* not only restated this view but placed considerable focus on it; and it was heavily critical of the response to referral:[12]

The *Laming Report* is clear that the lack of protection [for Victoria] came, not because no one was willing to refer Victoria, but because of mismanagement, unprofessional performance and the failure to put basic good practice into operation.[13]

The report made recommendations on how methods of surveillance and interference might yet again be 'strengthened' despite Lord Laming's conclusion that 'It is unrealistic to expect that it will ever be possible to eliminate the deliberate harm or death of a child – indeed no system can achieve this.'[14] This acknowledged that eradicating child abuse is an unattainable goal. This is consistently proved to be the case, but has been marginalised in child protection narratives. The focus remains on the embedding of more stringent controls rather than re-evaluating whether the system can achieve its aim and, if not, what an acceptable measure of success is. These recommendations not only failed to grasp the need to consider more fundamental problems with the direction mass surveillance and targeted interference was taking but also underpinned the government's e-agenda in relation to child protection and safeguarding, evident in increased surveillance, databasing and reliance on privately commissioned IT systems to manage risk and child protection processes across government agencies.

It is perhaps not coincidental that public inquiry recommendations agreed with policies already foreseen in the e-Government agenda for increasing surveillance and databasing of citizens generally. Largely as a result of the *Laming Report*,[15] databasing and surveillance became inextricably linked with the idea that child fatalities could be avoided: it was an easy step to introduce the idea that placing *all* children and families under surveillance was desirable. In September 2003, eight months after the *Laming Report* was published, the government published the Green Paper *Every Child Matters*.[16] This detailed five 'priority outcomes' for children. These were 'Being healthy, staying safe, enjoying and achieving, making a positive contribution and achieving economic well-being'.[17] Having created objectives for every child, attempting to ensure those objectives were met (assuming it was possible) was to happen through programmes of 'early intervention', 'safeguarding', provision of 'services' and 'child protection' procedures. These reinforced notions of differing levels of entry into social work scrutiny although they had a common theme: that of detailed and thorough assessment of the child and family members, including wider family. The notion that it was achievable for the government to predict and prevent child abuse remained dominant. The *Laming Report* and the *Every Child Matters* initiative heralded a cessation of debate and a rolling out of the Labour Government's agenda in the lead into the implementation of the Children Act 2004.

Policing by surveillance of all families: intelligence gathering and its limits

The use of databases is now an important tool used by the State to detect child protection and safeguarding issues, primarily via the use of risk indicators. Consent is not required for intelligence gathering and all families are now subject to surveillance via a plethora of State databases. The success of the systems is heavily reliant on the accuracy of the data it collects and retains. Accuracy of data and the question of how 'truth' is established is therefore a key issue.

S.12 Children Act 2004 introduced legislation to enable extensive databasing by local authorities of all children, and by extension their families. This included the power to place details about all children on a central database (Contact-Point, which is no longer operational) to join together information from the *ad hoc* databasing that was already being undertaken by various State agencies. As a result, all children and their families were to be 'tracked and traced'. Children moving to a different local authority area or abroad are reported to local authorities by schools to ensure continuous surveillance of all children.[18] By the time a child reaches adulthood he or she will be likely to have been DNA profiled, fingerprinted, identified by a unique identifying number,[19] and have his or her sensitive data contained on numerous databases.[20] The relentless profiling is analogous to the type of data collected and stored in relation to citizens in the criminal justice system.[21]

The government's wider e-Government agenda has led to surveillance in many areas of private life as the technology has become available to do so. Collecting data 'just in case' it shows a failure to comply with the law has become widespread in the last decade, notably the use of CCTV cameras in public places, and the efforts by local authorities to police private life, for example by using the RIPA powers intended to counter terrorist activity in relation to the use of domestic bins and for families' school applications.[22]

Enabled under s.12 Children Act 2004, the Labour Government's flagship central database, ContactPoint, was implemented by the Children Act 2004 Information Database (England) Regulations 2007.[23] This multi-million pound database was stopped without warning soon after the Conservative/Liberal Democrat Government was voted into power in May 2010. There has been no statement on what has happened to the data it contained. Equally there has been no reported scandalous rise in child deaths at the hands of dangerous parents, which was the rationale for establishing ContactPoint. ContactPoint could thus be seen as both a 'kneejerk reaction' to child fatalities to pay lip service to the concerned public and a convenient way to further the e-Government agenda in addition to providing a means of policing parents.

Regardless of ContactPoint, which did not contain any data concerning children and families that was not available elsewhere, the other databases remain. In reality little has changed. The only difference is the lack of a central database which contains a list of all children and a collection of basic data. It is incorrect to assume there is any material difference to the databases: there is simply a difference to the method of organising and distributing this data. Since the demise of ContactPoint other, more direct, means of making personal information available without the consent of individuals (or checks about accuracy) are increasing. For example, recent developments such as Multi-Agency Risk Assessment Conferences (MARACs) and Multi-Agency Safeguarding Hubs (MASHs) provide a means of information sharing between agencies without the consent of the subjects of the data sharing. Recent case law suggests such data sharing may be unlawful in some circumstances.[24]

MARACs refer to a multi-agency conference where information is shared about cases considered to represent the highest risk of domestic abuse. MARACs work on the assumption that no single agency or individual can see the 'complete picture', but all may have insights and information to share. MARACs bypass data protection controls over information sharing. The person considered to be at risk does not have to be asked for their consent, and cannot attend the meeting. They are considered to have representation via an Independent Domestic Advice Adviser (IDVA). The alleged perpetrator is not informed of the MARAC referral. The meeting includes representatives from the police, health professionals, local authority social workers, housing practitioners, IDVAs and other specialists on an *ad hoc* basis from the statutory and voluntary sectors. Cases are referred to the relevant MARAC if they are aged 16+ and are considered at high risk of domestic violence from an adult (16+) partner, ex-partner or family member, regardless of gender or sexuality.

After sharing all relevant information, the representatives create an action plan. The main focus of the MARAC is on managing the perceived risk to the adult, but in doing this it will also consider other family members including any children involved. It will also consider measures to manage the behaviour of the alleged perpetrator. The MARAC is not an agency and does not have a case management function. This means that the responsibility to take appropriate actions following the MARAC rests with individual agencies. It is, in effect, an information sharing and recommendation-making body.

There are a number of serious concerns about the formation of this type of inter-disciplinary group. The meeting acts as a means of bypassing data protection controls in order to share information that may or may not be accurate without the knowledge of the accused, or the consent of the person considered to be at risk. Early indications are that referred women with children are finding themselves entered into the safeguarding system on the basis that they are failing to distance themselves from an allegedly abusive relationship. The meaning of domestic abuse is widening, including the criminal offence of coercive or controlling behaviour in an intimate or family relationship, where at the time of writing there is yet to be a conviction. It is therefore unclear how widely this offence will be interpreted.[25]

MASHs originated in Devon, piloting a first response to safeguarding and child protection referrals at all levels of concern. Chilvers explains that:

> A multi-agency safeguarding hub (MASH) is generally a co-located team of people, drawn from the relevant local agencies, and still in their employment. Children's services, the Police and the NHS all contribute staff members. The team works in a 'sealed intelligence hub', meaning that they can share information within the team, but there are agreed rules in place covering the release of information to staff in the rest of the organisations involved.[26]

Although the Data Protection Act 1998 does contain legitimate ways to bypass the consent for data to be shared (including sensitive data), the policy drive towards creating ways for this sharing to happen does not, of itself, legitimise sharing in all circumstances. The use of the MASH as a route through which all referrals travel seems to be an extension of the rationale of ContactPoint, providing a means of data protection controls to be bypassed on a case to case basis. The recent case of *AB and Anor, R. (on the application of) v The London Borough of Haringey*[27] opened the possibility of a successful challenge in respect of bypassing parental consent and data sharing within a MASH at an early stage of assessment.

The justification underpinning the databases is that all data concerning children may be relevant for the State to have in relation to fulfilling its statutory duty. This is reinforced by the complaint voiced in public inquiries and Serious Case Reviews, which can be expressed as 'if only we had known (shared information) then we could maybe have prevented this tragedy'.[28] It has thus become received wisdom that poor information sharing is a key barrier to effective child protection and safeguarding. The need for accuracy and making sense of the data has been somewhat overlooked. For example, the Department for Education's guidance document on information sharing in relation to the broad concept of safeguarding contains a 'myth busting' section which makes it clear that information sharing can take place in most situations if 'safety concerns' (which are not defined) are the justification.[29] The document describes 'safeguarding' as a 'service', including a service to parents. That it is truly a 'service' is questionable. This guidance, placed in the context of Anderson *et al.*'s two major reports into data sharing and child welfare, does not grasp the complexity of the issues of mass data collection on children and families, its accuracy and the implications for its use.[30]

Overall, there is a concerning lack of accountability and control in relation to data collection and sharing via the databases. This is exacerbated by the non-consensual nature of the collection and storing, and the lack of effective legal remedy in relation to the data if it is misleading or incorrect. The latter problem is discussed below.

Databases exist in relation to all children through their family's involvement with State agencies predominantly from the ante-natal, birth registration and health visiting period through to education, housing, health and criminal justice records. Information (including facts and opinions) is recorded and shared, often without the consent or knowledge of families.[31] As opinion and supposition is recorded, the boundaries between fact and opinion are blurred. For example, a psychiatrist may give his opinion that a parent is mentally ill in accordance with a diagnostic criteria laid out in DSM IV.[32] Many diagnoses are unable to be verified by objective evidence and rely heavily on the experts' observations and opinions. The opinion is relied upon, becoming in effect a rebuttable presumption, albeit originating from an opinion.[33]

Regardless of the enabling database legislation, all information held about data subjects in the UK is controlled by the Data Protection Act 1998[34] and is also subject to European Union control. The Data Protection Act 1998 sought to implement EC Directive 95/46/EC[35] and *inter alia* sets out the:

- data protection principles;
- general conditions for lawful processing of non-sensitive (ordinary) personal data;
- special conditions for lawful processing of sensitive data.[36]

All processing of personal data must:

- comply with the data protection principles; and
- be based on one of the relevant conditions.

Local authority decision making in child protection and safeguarding is embedded in the ideology of data collection and sharing, both as a risk stratification and preventative tool as well as a means of collecting evidence for possible litigation. The Data Protection Act 1998 theoretically contains inbuilt safeguards but it is questionable whether they are sufficient. The key issues are whether those safe-guards are adequate, particularly in relation to issues of consent and the statutory 'gateways' that enable consent to be bypassed as well as controls over the record-ing and storage of data.

The Data Protection Act 1998 includes additions to the principle in the Direc-tive[37] that personal data shall be processed fairly and lawfully, 'and, in particular, shall not be processed unless [one of the general or, for sensitive data, one of the special conditions] is met'.[38] On first examination, therefore, the Data Protection Act 1998 could be perceived as providing a protection in relation at least to families who face unsubstantiated allegations. However, the Act[39] also contains exclusions so as to render its effect as a protection limited: it is frequently the *data* that is protected, not the *data subject*.

Under Schedule II the conditions for lawful processing fall into two broad categories. The first and arguably the most important for the data subject is that consent must be obtained for the processing, but even when consent is not obtained Schedule II contains provisions referred to as a 'statutory gateway' by which the data can be processed and consent can be bypassed:[40]

- Consent is necessary: data must be processed on the basis of 'consent'.
- If consent is withheld or not sought a 'statutory gateway' must be used: data must be processed on the basis of statutory authority (through the 'statu-tory gateway'). The statutory gateways include *inter alia* where process is 'necessary for the administration of justice, for the exercise of any functions conferred on any person by or under any enactment, for the exercise of any functions of the Crown, a Minister of the Crown or a government depart-ment or for the exercise of any other functions of a public nature exercised in the public interest by any person'.

This means that the data subject's consent can be dispensed with as long as a 'statutory gateway' is identified. It is these methods of dispensing with consent that Anderson *et al.* identified as particularly likely to be unlawful because they breach European Convention law.[41] Since the Lisbon Treaty, the Charter is also part of the EU Acquis. It is binding on both the EU institutions and the member States. The UK sought reservations in this regard but in practice it is unlikely to make any difference as EU law has supremacy. Anderson *et al.* explain that they consider the Data Protection Act 1998 includes:

> interpretations to the principles which are not contained in the Directive and also links the principles and the conditions in ways that could inadver-tently lead to interpretations of the Act that are inconsistent with the Direc-tive – and thus, possibly, with the European Convention on Human Rights (ECHR) and the Human Rights Act 1998 (HRA).[42]

Their concern is that, when considered in the context of how it may be inter-preted in relation to the databases, the Data Protection Act 1998 does not

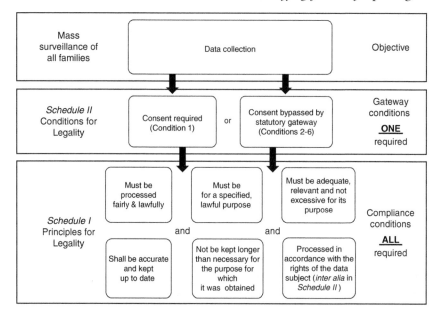

Figure 3.1 The legal requirements for data collection and storage.

provide adequate protection for the data subjects who may suffer harm as a result. Their argument centres on potential inconsistency with European Union law if the Data Protection Act 1998 is interpreted by the UK government to enable many of the databases they maintain. The Act[43] may therefore provide some limited protection if the consent/gateway problems identified by Anderson *et al.* are resolved (see Figure 3.1).

Schedule I sets out data protection principles which are intended to afford protection for data subjects regardless of which provision of Schedule II has been used in order to justify collecting the data. There are eight Schedule I principles[44] the first of which contains the requirement that personal data shall be processed fairly and lawfully. In particular, the first principle also contains the provision that data must not be processed at all unless one of the conditions in Schedule II regarding the need for consent or the use of a 'statutory gateway' has been met. The first principle also mentions sensitive personal data which must be processed in accordance with additional conditions contained in Schedule III.

The remainder of the eight principles deal with restrictions over how data will be processed. Principles two and three provide that there is a need for specified and lawful purposes for the data processing and for the data to be adequate, relevant and not excessive in relation to the identified purpose. Principle four provides that data must be accurate and kept up to date. Principles five and six concern the rights of the data subject not to have the data kept for longer than is necessary for the specified purpose, and that whilst it is kept the data will be processed in accordance with the data subject's rights under the Act. Principles seven and eight concern technical and organisational control over the data to prevent it from being processed by anyone unauthorised or in an unlawful manner, including control over accidental loss, destruction or damage to personal data and the restriction over transferring data outside the EU unless the receiving country ensures an adequate level of protection for the rights and freedoms of data subjects in relation to the processing of personal data.

The important question, therefore, in relation to data processing in child protection and safeguarding is whether the conditions contained in the Schedules provide any real balance or safeguards for the data subject who is concerned about the use of his or her data. This could arise in relation to either the surveillance via databases or data collected and processed if surveillance moves to an assessment.

The starting point is whether consent is necessary, or whether consent can be bypassed by the statutory gateway provisions. Consent is a recurring theme in relation to child protection and safeguarding practice, as by their nature assessments involve serious interference into private family life. The wider concept of safeguarding raises issues of consent particularly in respect of the mass surveillance that now takes place in relation to all children via all bodies and agencies covered by s.11 Children Act 2004. Data is collected and stored in relation to all families without consent. This occurs despite the requirement in the Data Protection Act 1998 concerning the necessity of consent for data processing to be lawful, unless the government contends it is justified in passing consent via a statutory gateway provision. Under the Data Protection Act 1998, if it is applied in accordance with the Directive, families are unable to give valid consent for data processing for a purpose that is too broadly specified. In any event, children are only able to give valid consent if they are of sufficient understanding and maturity to give valid consent. The state of being able to give valid, informed consent is described as being '*Gillick* competent'[45] which raises questions over how this is being interpreted by local authorities in relation to asking children to consent to their data being used.

Anderson *et al.* consider the concept of *Gillick* competence is being 'wrongly interpreted and improperly invoked as a basis for obtaining the "consent" of children, between the ages of 12 and 16, for the use and sharing of their data, without parental involvement'.[46] The decision in *Gillick* was clear that children's parents must be involved except in rare cases where the child insists that they not be. Therefore local authorities seeking the consent of children or young people without encouraging parental participation can amount, as Lord Fraser explained in *Gillick*, to a failure by the professional to discharge his or her professional responsibilities.[47] In addition, Lord Fraser was considering a specific, time-limited situation, in which consent was sought for a clearly defined purpose rather than for a purpose which is unable to be clearly defined.

Anderson *et al.* identify that the data sharing in relation to children and their families on the databases is often intended to allow access to a database or other record of information about a child.[48] This occurs over a long period of time, for a wide range of purposes which may not be at all apparent to the professional seeking the child's consent, let alone to the child at the time consent is sought.[49] Therefore, even if consent is sought at the outset, the data may then be used for unforeseen and other purposes. This is an issue not only in relation to consent, but also in relation to the purpose of the data collection, which must be specified. These issues fell outside the decision in *Gillick*.

Data that is sought by local authorities in relation to families includes data about wider family members and friends. Specifically this is part of the continuous assessment process laid out in *Working Together to Safeguard Children*[50] It is not possible for a person to consent to the processing of information about a third party. Processing personal information on parents, siblings, wider family and friends of a child without the consent of those other data subjects is unlawful. Although it is part of the assessment criteria, it is not clear how a local authority is expected to collect such data other than through interviewing the family. Consent is key here as without the family interview and access to the family home to observe the family members' interaction it is difficult to see how this data can lawfully be gathered from elsewhere.

Anderson *et al.* also identify that coercion is a feature of the relationship between local authorities and families. With regard to many of the databases consent may not be freely given but may be obtained, for example through fear of the consequences of refusal, because a child has been conditioned to acquiesce to the wishes of adults, because the child does not understand the implications of what he or she is consenting to or because the child may have been told that providing the information is in his or her own interests and that if they fail to consent they may not be able to obtain 'services' they might otherwise receive.[51]

Additionally, much of the personal data required in assessments is sensitive data. In relation to this type of data a series of more onerous special conditions apply, listed in Schedule III. The general conditions broadly correspond to what are termed 'criteria for making data processing legitimate' in the Directive.[52]

Although the principles and conditions are clearly set out, interpreting them in relation to the legality of mass surveillance with the intention of using the data for targeted interference is not as straightforward. Part II of Schedule I of the Act[53] contains provisions interpreting the principles. In relation to the reference to 'fairness' in the first provision:

> In determining for the purposes of the first principle whether personal data are processed fairly, regard is to be had to the method by which they are obtained, including in particular whether any person from whom they are obtained is deceived or misled as to the purpose or purposes for which they are processed.[54]

The second provision[55] links the question of fairness to the duty to inform data subjects of various matters (such as the purposes for which their data are to be used). Unless data subjects are informed of the purpose for which their data are to be used, personal data are not to be treated as processed fairly. Anderson *et al.* state:

> It should be stressed that these clarifications should not be read as suggesting that as long as there was no deception, and as long as the information duties

are fulfilled, the processing in question is 'fair'. In fact, 'fairness' can relate to any matter, including but not limited to these matters.[56]

On the question of 'lawfulness', guidance from the now obsolete Department for Constitutional Affairs states *inter alia:*

> Under the first Data Protection Principle, personal data are required to be processed 'fairly' and 'lawfully'. The requirement that the personal data be processed 'lawfully' means that those legal obligations both statutory and common law must be complied with. The *Data Protection Act* cannot render lawful any processing which would otherwise be unlawful. In the context of public sector data sharing this means that the public body must have the *vires* to carry out the processing (or the function to which the processing of the data is ancillary), that the processing is not in breach of the law of confidence, that the processing is not in breach of any other relevant domestic statute or common law principle, and that it is compliant with the Human Rights Act, the European Convention on Human Rights (Article 8 in particular) and any applicable principles of EU law. Accordingly, the Data Protection Act overlaps with other areas of law.[57]

Mass surveillance can be argued to be so wide as to be unable to be described as for a 'specified purpose' in relation to Schedule I of the Act[58] which provides that 'Personal data shall be obtained only for one or more specified and lawful purposes, and shall not be further processed in any manner incompatible with that purpose or those purposes.'[59] However, the Act does not specify how precise the 'specified purpose' is required to be, leaving it unclear where the parameters lie in relation to data collected by statutory agencies for the purposes of child protection and safeguarding processes. This problem is exacerbated by the fact that the parameters of child abuse are unable to be defined. Without clearly defined parameters this illustrates how easy it is to shift meaning of the terms 'at risk', and 'at risk of significant harm'[60] to 'at risk from failing to achieve the government's five targets for children' or 'at risk of social exclusion'.[61]

Considered in the context of data protection, defining the parameters is important. If the purpose of the data collection, processing and sharing is wider than that of 'protecting children' and encompasses 'safeguarding and promoting welfare' then the 'specified purpose' for which the data are processed is widened. If this is the case, Anderson *et al.* argue that the question then arises whether the wider purposes are still sufficiently specific in terms of the Data Protection Act 1998:

> One particularly pervasive example – the shift in meaning of the term 'at risk' from 'at risk of significant harm or neglect' to 'at risk from failing to achieve the government's five targets for children' and 'at risk of social exclusion' – could render data protection in respect of children meaningless. It may be tempting to extend the broad data sharing that may be justified in child

protection cases to the much larger class of child welfare cases, but it is not in accordance with law.[62]

In 2003 the Department for Constitutional Affairs acknowledged the importance of certainty in its legal advice:

> It is a matter of statutory construction as to whether a particular statutory gateway authorises disclosure for the particular purpose or purposes contemplated. In construing the statute account must be taken of the HRA and of the DPA.[63]

With regard to the question of 'compatibility', the 1998 Act[64] significantly tightens the law compared to its predecessor, the Data Protection Act 1984.[65] Under the Data Protection Act 1998 the Information Commissioner has the power to take enforcement action if he or she considers that 'incompatible processing' has occurred.[66]

Anderson *et al.* conclude that 'analysis has shown that the legislative and regulatory framework for the kinds of data collection and sharing described in this study . . . fails to legitimise the proposed data sharing and processing'.[67]

The 'statutory gateway' clauses in Schedule II are likely to be used by local authorities as an argument why consent has been obtained either under duress, or has been bypassed. Additionally, local authorities may obtain 'consent' from a child who may not understand the implications of what he or she is 'consenting' to.

These issues highlight the fact that the framework of the Data Protection Act 1998 may not provide adequate protection, particularly if an allegation of child abuse is made, even if expressed as a 'concern'. Once an allegation has been made it will be recorded, and this record will not be removed. The following scenario explains what can happen in the case of an allegation (concern) referred to a local authority which turns out to be unsubstantiated:

- Allegation is made to a local authority social services department stating there are 'concerns about child X'.
- The allegation will be recorded by the local authority and, unless treated as a notification, will be classed as a referral. A file is opened and the assessment process is started. It is likely the police will be notified of the allegation.
- The family receive an unplanned visit from a social worker, possibly with a police officer, who will state they are assessing the family and that the social worker requires access to the family home.
- The assessment takes place (although it is still unclear what happens if the family were to refuse, other than they are at risk of an s.43 order application or an EPO application). The assessment process may take several visits and extensive data collection via the various databases from any other agency the family is suspected to have had contact with. Other professionals such as the family GP and school will be told there are 'child protection or safeguarding concerns' but will not be told what they are. These other professionals will record that there are 'concerns' on their own notes.

- At the end of the assessment process the family will be told what will happen. If no further action is to be taken the local authority presume no further contact with the family will occur, or s.17 services may be offered. Under the 'signs of safety' framework which is being adopted by many local authorities it is very unlikely that they will fail to find something which requires some level of intervention.[68]

- In this situation the family is left with the record of the allegation but no process of removal. Suspicion is likely to remain; the intention of flagging up the 'concern' is to warn professionals to be vigilant in relation to the child concerned.

- The Data Protection Act provisions do not provide a remedy because the records will state that the allegation was made (a fact) and will argue that the contents of the assessment and comments about the family are a mix of fact and opinion, which does not give a family protection under the Data Protection Act provisions. At best, it may be recorded that no factual evidence was found to substantiate the allegation. The third party professional records may not even record this outcome.

The ability of a local authority to argue they can bypass consent via a statutory gateway coupled with the subjective nature of much of Schedule I makes it difficult to see what rights families have in relation to this scenario. With the exception of the requirement that data must be 'accurate and . . . up to date',[69] which may give limited protection in respect of certain factual inaccuracies, there seems to be no redress, and it does not help to address the complexity of 'fact', 'opinion' and professional interpretation that is fed through the assessment schema. Much of the data collected in relation to families can be argued to be 'opinion'. An opinion does not have to be factually accurate so there is no remedy in relation to, for example, a medical or psychiatric opinion, which amounts to a diagnosis.

For parents, the decision to have children carries with it an implied consent to loss of privacy. It is of note that the legal challenge of this position envisaged by Anderson *et al.* in 2006 has not occurred. This could be through lack of transparency in relation to the general public's understanding of the databases or their lack of appreciation of how their data could be used until they find themselves already in a more interventionist and frightening schema. There could be other reasons such as the difficulty and cost of litigation. Although an action challenging data breaching provisions of the Data Protection Act 1998 is initiated in the County Court, the cost of a challenge particularly if appealed could be prohibitive.

Conclusion: the challenge of balancing consent and coercion in the surveillance framework

With the exception of *AB and Anor, R (on the application of) v The London Borough of Haringey*[70] there is little relevant case law that directly challenges the databases and non-consensual information sharing. The most substantive review remains the report prepared by Anderson *et al.* in 2006.[71] Regardless of how data is stored and shared the principles are the same: families have little privacy or control over the continual monitoring of parents and children. This may be justifiable if it led to a significant reduction in child abuse, but this is not the case. The NSPCC's prevalence estimate, taken together with a data analysis of the ratio of referrals, assessments and detected abuse indicate that, although more children are referred each year, there is no proportionate increase in the amount of child abuse detected.[72]

Although the notion of databasing and sharing information about all children and families attracts periodic comment and criticism, partly as a response to media coverage, little in-depth reporting occurs. Anderson *et al.*'s 2006 report for the Information Commissioner criticised the databases, which were legislated for but had not at that time been implemented.[73] The report raised numerous serious legal, social and technological implications of databasing and information sharing but despite the findings there were no proposed changes to their legitimisation in the Children Act 2004. The agenda seemed set in stone regardless of Anderson *et al.*'s questions concerning the legality, desirability and potential adverse effects of the proposals.

These major concerns included the important considerations that many of the databases were either unlawful, or could be unlawful, and that there could be adverse consequences from such databases.[74] Obvious adverse consequences include the dangers for children and their parents of inadequate or inaccurate data being recorded. Anderson *et al.* raised a series of concerns in relation to consent, the shift from 'at risk' of harm to 'at risk of failing to meet government targets' and the recording of sensitive information, how it would be disseminated and the consequences of such a large amount of data recorded, held and stored on so many children and their families.[75] Opinion data and data that is based on vague impressions about 'signs' embedded in children's behaviour meant every child would be subjected to endless scrutiny and recording of their demeanour, attainment and behaviour. This amounts to profiling of every child and inferences drawn about parental behaviour on a grand scale.

When Anderson *et al.*'s *Children's Databases: Safety and Privacy, A Report for the Information Commissioner* was published in 2006, therefore, it was clear that there were serious differences of opinion about the desirability of extensive surveillance, but before the debate gathered momentum Peter Connolly died on 3 August 2007 aged seventeen months in the same London Borough where Victoria Climbié had died seven years earlier. He was 'known to social services' prior to his death. The criminal trials of his mother, her boyfriend and her lodger in 2008 attracted media attention sensationalising the apparent repetition of organisational failures within Haringay. This prompted the government to act in a defensive manner. Sharon Shoesmith, the Director of Children's Services for Haringay was sacked. She has since spoken publicly to voice her professional concerns about the government's response, and has won her unfair dismissal claim on appeal.[76] The Government's response exemplifies the problems of a culture of public responsibility towards children and defensive practice amongst those responsible for demonstrating they have discharged their duty.

In the wake of these events Lord Laming was asked to produce a further report (although not a public inquiry), entitled *The Protection of Children in England: A Progress Report.*[77] He published his report in 2009, reiterating his *Climbié Report*[78] findings in relation to surveillance and data sharing. By this time, the Children Act 2004 was fully operational and all children were placed onto ContactPoint.[79] The findings of Lord Laming's report appeared to validate this position. The public were led to believe that more children would be protected. Despite the odd ripple of concern in the media about surveillance, and Anderson *et al.*'s *Children's Databases – Safety and Privacy* report[80] this discourse remained dominant.

The up-to-date position is therefore that multi-agency databases containing data about children and families are now the cornerstone of modern State surveillance of families. They are designed to predict and detect not only child abuse but any welfare concern, risks, signs of abuse and potential youth offending. They enable early intervention strategies to be implemented in relation to children and their families following assessment via the information sharing databases introduced in s.12 Children Act 2004 and implemented following the Children Act 2004 Information Database (England) Regulations 2007.[81] Although ContactPoint contained data relating to all children and families it was populated from existing data already in the possession of the State.[82] Also, even though ContactPoint was dismantled in August 2010 by the Coalition Government the populating databases remain.[83] The basic position has not therefore changed. The drive has been towards collecting extensive information on children, much of it based on 'signs' in children's behaviour, purporting to indicate they may have been abused. This information is recorded, shared and acted upon, but has remained largely unquestioned either in relation to its reliable evidence base or as a rationale for interventions.

The intensive scrutiny of children involving collecting consensual and non-consensual data on children and their families is enabling increasing referrals, the gateway through which the State moves from surveillance to interference into private family life. Interference without parental consent takes place as a result of an allegation of suspected 'child abuse' which enables local authorities, under the provisions of s.47 Children Act 1989 to investigate families, making 'such enquiries as they consider necessary'.[84] In recent years, however, it is evident that the boundary between consensual and non-consensual assessment and intervention has become increasingly blurred. This is despite the evidence that the vast majority of referred families do not proceed beyond assessment. In the majority of referred cases, either the State takes no action at all or the State interferes to the extent that it completes an assessment, leaving the family to cope with the aftermath. There are consequently a large number of families who are affected by these stages but who are not involved in any further local authority action.

Whilst the legal and procedural framework surrounding the use of mass surveillance of families should be sufficiently robust to achieve its aim, it also needs to ensure that it provides sufficient safeguards for parents and children by restraining

State actions within clear limits. It is not clear that it strikes the right balance between 'protecting children' on the one hand whilst ensuring adequate protection for parents and children against unwanted surveillance and interference on the other. It is also unclear whether sufficient processes are in place setting appropriate thresholds and providing opportunities for parents and children to effectively challenge or stop the collecting of data, to check its accuracy or to prevent action being taken as a result of its collection. In relation to this important question of balance in child protection and safeguarding controls Harris-Short and Miles note that it 'is a difficult balance, but, perhaps nowhere more than here, is getting that balance right of such vital importance to the child.'[85] It is also of vital importance to the parents and to society.

Notes

1 Devine, L. and Parker, S. (2015) *Rethinking Child Protection Strategy: Learning from Trends*, Working Paper, Centre for Legal Research, Bristol Law School, UWE, Bristol, Online at: http://eprints.uwe.ac.uk/25258/ (Accessed 28 February 2016).
2 Ibid.
3 Cabinet Office (1999) *Modernising Government*, Cm 4310, TSO, London.
4 Cabinet Office Performance and Innovation Unit (2002) *Privacy and Data Sharing: The Way Forward for Public Services*, Cabinet Office, London.
5 House of Lords (2009), *2nd Report of Session 2008–09 Surveillance: Citizens and the State – Vol. I: Report*, Select Committee on the Constitution HL Paper 18–I, TSO, London. Online at: www.publications.parliament.uk/pa/ld200809/ldselect/ldconst/18/18.pdf (Accessed 1 February 2016).
6 Ibid., para. 24.
7 Ibid., para. 25.
8 Ibid., para. 26.
9 Ibid.
10 Lord Laming (2003) *The Victoria Climbié Inquiry Report*, HC 570, TSO, London (the Laming Report). Online at: www.publications.parliament.uk/pa/cm200203/cmselect/cmhealth/570/570.pdf (Accessed 1 February 2016).
11 For example, see the findings of the Dennis O'Neill inquiry where the lack of information sharing was considered a key failing in: Home Office (1945) *Report by Sir Walter Monckton on the Circumstances which Led to the Boarding-Out of Dennis and Terence O'Neill at Bank Farm, Minsterley and the Steps Taken to Supervise their Welfare*, Cmd 6636, HMSO, London.
12 Department of Health (2003) *The Victoria Climbié Inquiry: Report of an Inquiry by Lord Laming*, Cm 5730, TSO, London.
13 Conway, H. (2003) 'The Laming Inquiry: Victoria Climbié's Legacy', *Family Law* 33: 513.
14 Ibid., 516.
15 Laming (n. 10).
16 Chief Secretary to the Treasury (2003) *Every Child Matters: Green Paper Presented to Parliament by the Chief Secretary to the Treasury*, Cm 5860, TSO, London.
17 Ibid., p. 11.
18 State schools use a data sharing system called S2S for sharing data about pupils to the local authority and other schools. Pupil movements are uploaded via S2S and lost pupil data collected. Page 14 of the schools handbook states:

> The regulation is that pupils can be removed from the register if they have been continuously absent for a period of four weeks or more. The school should only do this after consulting its local Education Welfare Service, as the school and Local Authority are required to make reasonable enquiries to locate pupils before removing them from the register.

From: Department for Education and Skills (2005) *School to School (S2S) – The S2S Handbook for Schools*, Version 2.4 – June 2005. Online at: http://media.education. gov.uk/assets/files/pdf/t/the%20s2s%20handbook%20for%20schools%20v%20 2%20-%204.pdf (Accessed 5 March 2016).

19 The Guthrie Test (heel prick test) undertaken on babies at five days old to ascertain whether they have phenylketonuria (the inability to metabolise certain types of protein), sickle cell anaemia and cystic fibrosis routinely took blood. It is also used to profile the child's DNA and is stored without parental consent. See, for example: Evans, M. (2010) 'DNA Database Created from Babies' Blood Samples', 23 May, *Telegraph*, London. Online at: www.telegraph.co.uk/health/7756320/DNA-database-created-from-babies-blood-samples.html (Accessed 4 March 2016). Children in school are frequently fingerprinted so as to be able to access services such as the school library or school canteen, or in order to register. The justification for the use of biometric technology is that it makes services 'faster and more efficient'. The *Guardian* provides a useful synopsis of the concerns of parents about consent issues and the Data Protection Act 1998 and Article 8 Human Rights Act 1998 issues. See online article: Norton, E. (2010) 'Can I Refuse to Have my Child Fingerprinted at School?', *Guardian*, 16 July. Online at: www .guardian.co.uk/commentisfree/libertycentral/2010/jul/16/fingerprint ed-child-school (Accessed 4 March 2016). All children now have a 'unique identifying number' allocated to them which tracks their progress through schools. The UIN is used on the IS (information sharing) databases to identify and track children throughout their childhoods.

20 See: Anderson, R., Brown, I., Dowty, T., Inglesant, P., Heath, W. and Sasse, A. (2009) *The Database State*, The Joseph Rowntree Reform Trust, York, p. 2, concerning the legality of such databasing. Online at: www.jrrt.org.uk/publications /database-state-full-report (Accessed 1 January 2016).

21 A comprehensive review of the databases in the UK has been conducted by Anderson *et al.* (ibid.).

22 See for example the reference to the Labour Government's Home Office Consultation in 2009 into the use of RIPA (Regulation of Investigatory Powers Act 2000 c.23) in relation to both school applications and the regulation of domestic rubbish disposal. Dobson, N. (2009) 'Local Government, Surveillance Powers, Tenancy and Effective Consultation', June, *Law Society Gazette*, London and the Office of Surveillance Commissioners website generally for information about RIPA. Online at: http://surveillancecommissioners.independent.gov.uk/ (Accessed 20 May 2016).

23 Children Act 2004 Information Database (England) Regulations 2007/2182, updated by Children Act 2004 Information Database (England) (Amendment) Regulations 2010/1213.

24 *AB and Anor, R (on the application of) v The London Borough of Haringey* [2013] EWHC 416 (Admin) (13 March 2013).

25 S.76 Serious Crime Act 2015 c.9, under Part 5 Domestic Abuse.

26 Chilvers, A. (2012) 'Will MASH Make Our Children Safer?', *Journal of Family Health Care* 22(6): 10–13, 11.

27 EWHC 416 (Admin) (13 March 2013).

28 Laming (n. 10); Lord Laming (2009) *The Protection of Children in England: A Progress Report*, HC 330, March 2009, TSO, London. Online at: www.cscb. org.uk/downloads/policies_guidance/national/The%20Protection%20of%20 Children%20in%20England%20-%20%20a%20progress%20report%20by%20 Lord%20Laming,%202009.pdf (Accessed 1 January 2016).
29 HM Government (2015) *Information Sharing: Advice for Practitioners Providing Safeguarding Services to Children, Young People, Parents and Carers*, Dept for Education, London, pp. 13–14.
30 See: Anderson, R., Brown, I., Clayton, R., Dowty, T., Korff, D. and Munro, E. (2006) *Children's Databases: Safety and Privacy, A Report for the Information Commissioner*, Foundation for Information Policy Research, Bedfordshire. Online at: www.fipr.org/press/061122kids.html (Accessed 1 January 2016); Anderson *et al.* (2009) (n. 20).
31 See government advice to local authorities etc.: Department for Constitutional Affairs (2003) *Public Sector Data Sharing Guidance on the Law, November 2003*. Online at: http://webarchive.nationalarchives.gov.uk/+/http://www.justice. gov.uk/guidance/docs/data_sharing_legal_guidance.pdf (Accessed 5 May 2016).
32 American Psychiatric Association (1994) *Diagnostic and Statistical Manual of Mental Disorders*, 4th edn (DSM IV-TR), American Psychiatric Association, Washington, DC. The Association's website is at: www.psychiatry.org/practice /dsm/ (Accessed 13 May 2016).
33 The word 'diagnosis' is derived from Greek meaning 'to discern'. It concerns the identification of the nature and cause of anything, and a doctor's diagnosis is his opinion as to the nature and cause of an illness or injury, or a collection of behaviours that give rise to a 'syndrome'.
34 Data Protection Act 1998 c.29.
35 Directive 95/46/EC of the European Parliament and of the Council of 24 October 1995 on the protection of individuals with regard to the processing of personal data and on the free movement of such data.
36 For example, data on health, criminal convictions, religious belief, sexual orientation and sex life.
37 EC Directive 95/46/EC.
38 Data Protection Act 1998 c.29 Schedule 1, Part 1.
39 Ibid.
40 Ibid., Schedule II.
41 Anderson *et al.* (2006) (n. 30).
42 Ibid., p. 84.
43 Data Protection Act 1998 c.29.
44 Contained in Article 6 of the Framework Directive, and in the first eight paragraphs of Part I of Schedule 1 to the Data Protection Act 1998 c.29, in terms close to those used in the Directive.
45 Used as a guide to the competence for children to be able to consent, from: *Gillick v West Norfolk and Wisbech Area Health Authority* [1986] AC 112.
46 Anderson *et al.* (2006) (n. 30), para. 7.3(3), p. 119.
47 *Gillick v West Norfolk and Wisbech Area Health Authority* [1986] AC 112, 174.
48 Anderson *et al.* (2006) (n. 30), para. 7.3(3), p. 119.
49 It was announced at the end of March 2011 that the government intends to 'track' children until the age of 30 using existing data to identify whether any of the outgoing Labour Government's interventions have been 'successful'. 'Life Chance Indicators' are to be identified and tracked. See: *Daily Mail* (2011) 'Social Mobility Drive to Track Us to Age of 30', 31 March. Online at: www. dailymail.co.uk/news/article-1371742/Social-mobility-drive-track-education -work-achievement-age-30.html (Accessed 1 May 2016).

50 HM Government (2015) *Working Together to Safeguard Children*, TSO, London.
51 Anderson *et al.* (2006) (n. 30), para. 7.3(3) and para. 7.3(4), pp. 119–20.
52 EC Directive 95/46/EC.
53 Data Protection Act 1998 c.29.
54 Ibid., Schedule 1, Part II, para. 1(1).
55 Ibid., para. 2.
56 Anderson *et al.* (2006) (n. 30), para. 7.3(3), p. 85.
57 Department for Constitutional Affairs (n. 31), section 6.5. Online at: http://webarchive.nationalarchives.gov.uk/+/http://www.justice.gov.uk/guidance/docs/data_sharing_legal_guidance.pdf (Accessed 5 May 2016).
58 Data Protection Act 1998 c.29.
59 Ibid., Schedule 1(I) para. 2.
60 S.47(1)(b) Children Act 1989 c.41.
61 The agenda laid out in: Chief Secretary to the Treasury (n. 16).
62 Anderson *et al.* (2006) (n. 30), para. 7.3(1), p. 85.
63 Department for Constitutional Affairs (n. 31), para. 3.15. A 'statutory gateway' is used to describe statutory provision(s) requiring or authorising disclosures of data.
64 Data Protection Act 1998 c.29.
65 c.35.
66 Under Part V, s.40 Data Protection Act 1998 c.29.
67 Anderson *et al.* (2006) (n. 30), at Section 7.3.
68 Bunn, A. (2013) *Signs of Safety in England: An NSPCC Commissioned Report on the Signs of Safety Model in Child Protection*, NSPCC. Online at: www.nspcc.org.uk (Accessed 25 January 2016).
69 Data Protection Act 1998 Sch. 1(I) para. 4.
70 [2013] EWHC 416 (Admin) (13 March 2013).
71 Anderson *et al.* (2006) (n. 30).
72 Devine and Parker (n. 1).
73 Anderson *et al.* (2006) (n. 30).
74 For a summary example see: ibid., Section 7.3, which starkly points out that their analysis shows legislation 'fails to legitimise the proposed data processing and sharing'. These issues are considered in detail in Chapter 5.
75 Ibid., and see the report's findings generally.
76 *R (on the application of Shoesmith) v Ofsted* [2011] EWCA Civ 642.
77 Laming (n. 28).
78 Laming (n. 10).
79 Introduced under the Children Act 2004 Information Database (England) Regulations 2007, SI:2007/2182 Children and Young Persons, England, 24 July 2007.
80 Anderson *et al.* (2006) (n. 30).
81 See note 79 above.
82 ContactPoint was populated primarily from DWP child benefit data, which prompted a major security breach when the child benefit data was lost in 2007 precisely the same time it was being used to populate the database. See for example: BBC News (2007) 'Child Database System Postponed', 27 November, *BBC News Online*. Online at: http://news.bbc.co.uk/1/hi/education/7115546.stm (Accessed 1 May 2016). The link between the loss of the child benefit data and ContactPoint was officially acknowledged when a report by Deloittes into ContactPoint's security was ordered by Margaret Hodge following the loss of the child benefit data. See: Hoyle, D. (2010) 'ContactPoint. Because Every Child Matters?', infed.org, *The Encyclopaedia of Informal Education*. Online at: www.infed.org/socialwork/contactpoint.htm (Accessed 20 May 2016).

83 The full text of the Conservative and Liberal Democrat coalition agreement announces *inter alia* the abolition of ContactPoint. It does not address any other database issue in relation to children. See: BBC News (2010) 'Full Text: Conservative-Lib Dem deal', 12 May, *BBC News Online*. Online at: http://news.bbc.co.uk/1/hi/uk_politics/election_2010/8677933.stm (Accessed 20 May 2016).

84 S.47 states:

> 1) Where a local authority—
>
>> (a) are informed that a child who lives, or is found, in their area—
>>
>>> (i) is the subject of an emergency protection order; or
>>> (ii) is in police protection; or
>>
>> (b) have reasonable cause to suspect that a child who lives, or is found, in their area is suffering, or is likely to suffer, significant harm, the authority shall make, or cause to be made *such enquiries as they consider necessary* to enable them to decide whether they should take any action to safeguard or promote the child's welfare.

85 Harris-Short, S. and Miles, J. (2007) *Family Law Text, Cases and Materials*, Oxford University Press, Oxford, p. 900.

4 The policing of parents
Social work involvement

Social work response to referrals: State power and private rights

Social work assessments underpin the operation of child protection and safeguarding interventions, and also the operation of the Public Law Outline 2014 which sets out the process of public family law proceedings.[1] Assessments enable local authorities to gather as much information as possible about a family. They have a wider remit than simply an investigation of the substance of the referral which brought the family to the attention of social services. Assessment aims to establish whether the child is either in 'need of services', or 'is suffering or is likely to suffer significant harm'. Assessment also aims to risk assess, and predict what is likely to happen in the future.

Under the latest guidance, social workers carry out a continuous assessment, enabling them to treat the index intelligence (referral) as a gateway to obtaining as much information as possible about a family.[2] Despite the policy intention to recast assessment as a safeguarding-focussed needs assessment, the statutory framework remains unchanged; assessment must therefore also be described as a forensic evidence-gathering process. However, the framework of assessment is not analogous to the type of investigation carried out by the police. Whereas the police investigate an *allegation*, social services investigate the *child and the family members* in a much fuller sense. They are responding to a referral rather than specifically an allegation, and use assessment to see what can be inferred from the information and impressions they gather and record.[3]

Assessment policy and practice has changed and developed since its introduction into social work practice. Although by the 1950s child welfare legislation demanded that local authorities act on information about suspected child abuse if it was presented to them,[4] the precise nature of how local authorities investigated suspected child maltreatment and abuse was not clearly defined. Forty years from the implementation of the first statutory measures enabling the State to investigate suspected child abuse, the government produced statutory guidance. The latest version of the guidance, *Working Together to Safeguard Children*, produced by the Department for Education and published in 2015, is 109 pages long,[5] reduced from the 390 pages contained in the 2010 HM Government version.[6]

The *Framework for the Assessment of Children in Need and their Families*[7] is 109 pages. This reflects the post-Munro[8] move towards less procedural bureaucracy. Parton's discussion paper about the length and complexity of the statutory guidance provides a comprehensive overview of the different versions of the guidance, its rationale and development.[9] This statutory guidance sets out the steps that a local authority must take following referral of a child to them.

The threshold for a local authority to act follows referral of a suspected 'child in need' or a 'child at risk'. The categorisation may not be apparent at referral. Both are assessed via a continuous assessment.[10] The relevant provisions are set out in *Working Together to Safeguard Children*[11] and *Framework for the Assessment of Children in Need and their Families*[12] to which local authorities are legally bound to have regard when exercising their functions.[13] In relation to children who may be 'at risk', the provisions of the Local Authority Social Services Act 1970[14] and the Children Act 2004,[15] states that *anyone* believing a child may be suffering, or may be at risk of suffering, significant harm *should* always refer his concerns, specified in *Working Together to Safeguard Children* as meaning referring them to children's social care departments.[16] This is a different requirement from *must* which is covered in s.11 Children Act 2004. The actual means and process of referral is not restricted, can be done by anyone and may be as informal as by anonymous telephone call.

The refocussing debate of the mid-1990s and subsequent Labour policies of Early Intervention led to the adoption of this holistic assessment to look at all aspects of a child's life and situation. Social work response to referral thus moved from a child protection focus, criticised as being harmful and often inappropriate which filtered out the majority of cases,[17] to a more general safeguarding assessment to establish whether a child was in need. Prior to 2015 this was undertaken by an Initial Assessment, completed in seven days, from which it was intended that families would be referred on into the child protection framework if necessary where a Core Assessment would usually take place.[18] From 2015 this has changed to an integrated continuous assessment which aims to consider risk and need together.

Although the refocussing debate was a response to a 'screening out' process, altering practice to 'screening in', ultimately it laid the groundwork for the distinction between the two to be swept away. Even before this the distinction may have been blurred as, despite their apparent differences in approach, all assessments followed the same framework. In reality little has changed. The 2006 version of *Working Together to Safeguard Children* (the first version published by HM Government as opposed to a specific government department) defined '*safeguarding and promoting the welfare of children* [original emphasis]' for the first time. It was to be considered to be:

> defined for the purposes of this guidance as:
>
> - protecting children from maltreatment;
> - preventing impairment of children's health or development;

- ensuring that children are growing up in circumstances consistent with the provision of safe and effective care; and
- undertaking that role so as to enable those children to have optimum life chances and to enter adulthood successfully.[19]

This definition made it clear that it would be difficult to look at safeguarding issues without also looking at issues relating to child protection and vice versa. This policy decision represents a move away from the distinctions in the Children Act 1989 to keep ss.17 and 47 separate, emphasising the separation between the consensual nature of s.17 and the non-consensual nature of s.47.

As a consequence of the successive versions of the statutory guidance *Working Together to Safeguard Children*[20] the role of the State has developed in a direction that emphasises intervention at a level that is below that of the statutory s.47 provisions. The clear separations between consensual support and non-consensual interference into private family life have been eroded as a result of this changing approach to family assessment. This raises questions about where the boundaries lie and the operational feasibility: the assessment framework that is used was not designed or intended to investigate child abuse. Consequently it contains no inbuilt safeguards and controls to ensure there is a balance and separation between State powers and private rights.

Despite assessment being a process of law, families are not offered legal advice or representation before or during assessment as this is to a great extent considered incompatible with child welfare. This leaves families vulnerable with either no advice or limited advice which focusses on obeying social work instruction (described as 'working with' social workers)[21] or risking escalation through the stages of the Public Law Outline 2014 towards litigation.[22] The information gathered during assessment is used in any subsequent public family proceedings so there are potentially serious legal consequences to assessment, which may not be apparent at the time the assessment is started, particularly to a family who is simply seeking help and support services.

The framework of assessment

Figure 4.1, reproduced from *Working Together to Safeguard Children*,[23] represents the areas of investigation into private family life in order for a social work continuous assessment to be completed.

Given the intrusive, holistic nature of assessment, consent is a key issue. If consent is withheld, s.43 Children Act 1989 details the circumstances in which a person caring for a child (in most cases the parent) can be compelled by court order to enable assessment to take place without consent of the parent (or person responsible for the child). The threshold for application is 'reasonable cause to suspect that the child is suffering, or is likely to suffer, significant harm'. It is therefore applicable to assessment under s.47.[24] However, the type of assessment that may have been envisaged in 1989 has been expanded so it is unclear how s.43 is useful for completing a continuous assessment if consent is withheld.

Figure 4.1 Assessment framework.

The Munro Review of Child Protection: Final Report: A Child Centred System; *and changes to* Working Together to Safeguard Children

Recent changes to the statutory guidance were triggered by *The Munro Review of Child Protection, Final Report: A Child-Centred System*, published in May, 2011.[25] One of the first actions in relation to child welfare the Coalition Government took was to commission Professor Eileen Munro to review and produce this report on child protection. Her preliminary report, *The Munro Review of Child Protection, Interim Report: The Child's Journey*, which was published in January 2011, suggested *inter alia* that 'child protection' assessment was excessively bureaucratic.[26] *The Munro Review of Child Protection, Final Report: A Child-Centred System* is the most recent substantive government review of child protection and safeguarding processes. They indicate that the extent of government concern is in relation to procedural issues, but not the fundamental legal framework, which remains unchanged. It has become so entrenched in our society that child protection and safeguarding are essential services, delivered via the assessment framework that root and branch review of the drift towards increasing surveillance and the lowering threshold for referral seems unlikely.

Munro had previously expressed serious concerns about what she considered excessive and unlawful surveillance of families since 2006.[27] Despite this, the key findings of the new report were confined to looking at the functioning of the existing system, including the level of bureaucracy, without mentioning her previous areas of concern, such as the data protection and human-rights issues.[28] This inevitably led to the earlier concerns taking a back seat in favour of a scaling back of bureaucracy, including those which afforded a small level of certainty to parents in terms of the length of time they would be under investigation during the continuous assessment.

In the same week Munro's report was published the NSPCC claimed the scale of child abuse had increased from 10 per cent[29] of children to 25.4 per cent[30] with a corresponding pledge from the government to fund their activities with over £11.2 million more investment.[31] However, recent referral and assessment trend data analysis indicates that there is a significant difference between the NSPCC's prevalence numbers and the amount of detected significant harm, or risk of it, reported in the official statistics. This suggests either that the prevalence numbers should be revisited, or that the trend towards increasing referrals at a very low threshold level mask a large number of serious undetected cases.[32] Read in the context of the earlier discussion of the aim of Cawson *et al.*'s study[33] to measure child abuse prevalence, the data indicates government policy has made things worse by making the system less efficient and detecting a smaller proportion of child abuse year on year.

The *Munro Report* focusses on a systems theory analysis, emphasising scaling back the bureaucracy of child protection social work and early intervention processes:[34] 'The review began by using "systems" theory to examine how the current conditions had evolved.'[35] Systems theory, akin to cybernetics,[36] derived from an attempt to find a unified theory that would explain all systems in all fields of science.[37] It was developed in the 'hard sciences' but has been used by sociologists to examine human phenomena, and is used here as a basis on which Munro suggests child protection and safeguarding systems should be reformed, run and measured. Recommendation 9 of the Report states that 'The government should require LSCBs to use systems methodology when undertaking Serious Case Reviews (SCRs).'[38] This recommendation is the only one that was not accepted by government.

Munro considers from her initial report[39] that the current system of surveillance and interference has been shaped by four factors:

> The review's first report in October 2010 described the child protection system in recent times as one that has been shaped by four key driving forces:
>
> - the importance of the safety and welfare of children and young people and the understandable strong reaction when a child is killed or seriously harmed;
> - a commonly held belief that the complexity and associated uncertainty of child protection work can be eradicated;
> - a readiness, in high profile public inquiries into the death of a child, to focus on professional error without looking deeply enough into its causes; and
> - the undue importance given to performance indicators and targets which provide only part of the picture of practice, and which have skewed attention to process over the quality and effectiveness of help given.[40]

There is no consideration in her report, however, of potential harm caused by the surveillance and assessment system in shaping policy and practice. The system is considered the lesser of two evils,[41] but there is no evidence of adequate consideration of potential and actual harm caused by policies surrounding social work practice, nor is there evidence of consideration of the question of balance between rights, responsibilities and remedies:

> These forces have come together to create a defensive system that puts so much emphasis on procedures and recording that insufficient attention is given to developing and supporting the expertise to work effectively with children, young people and families.[42]

The Report does not acknowledge that the 'defensive system' has also led to insufficient attention to other issues of importance such as potential over-interference through fear of adverse social work consequence. The meaning of 'work effectively with . . .' is not clearly defined and the important issue of the overwhelming number of false positives are only mentioned in passing:

> Mistakes in assessing risk can be either of under-estimating (false negative) or over-estimating (false positive) the danger to the child. With hindsight, it can be deemed that the child was left in an unsafe home or was removed without sufficient cause. The former kind of mistake is more easily seen so there is more pressure in general to avoid false negatives than false positives.[43]

The overall tenet of the review is to leave the system of surveillance and assessments intact, and it refers to the importance of *Working Together to Safeguard Children*.[44] Paragraphs 3.11 and 3.13 state:

> As the local authority has a statutory duty to safeguard and promote the welfare of children, guidance on undertaking assessments of children in need should remain on a statutory footing . . . However, the review has observed that as *Working Together* has grown, so it has become more prescriptive and less useful. As was highlighted in the first report, it is now 55 times longer than it was in 1974.[45]

The Report promotes a drive towards a positive image for social work via the media:

> The College of Social Work, through its Policy and Communications Unit, is developing a range of tools and services that can help support social workers, their employers and the media to work together to promote a more balanced public image of social work. It will offer support for local authorities to help them prioritise this work, so that public sector employers of social workers can lead by example.[46]

In 2016 the College of Social Work was closed.

In paragraph 7.72 Munro suggests that 'Social workers may wish to consider making approaches to families or young people over 18 for their consent to share appropriate, positive and interesting stories with the media, working with communications and press colleagues for advice.'[47] Presumably this is intended to counter the negative impact on social work image that might occur as a result of publicity surrounding mistakes from either over- or under-interference. The negative aspect of social work, however, has attracted judicial support in relation to needing publicity in order to effect change. Mr Justice Ryder, for example, remarked in *Oldham MBC v GW & Ors*:[48] 'it would be complacent of us to assume that miscarriages of justice do not occur in the family justice system'. He went on to quote Munby, who in *Re B (A Child) (Disclosure)* warned that:

> We must be vigilant to guard against the risks and we must have the humility to recognise and to acknowledge the public debate, and the jealous vigilance of an informed media, have an important role to play in exposing past miscarriages of justice and in preventing possible future miscarriages of justice . . . We cannot afford to proceed on the blinkered assumption that there have been no miscarriages of justice in the Family Justice system . . . *open and public debate in the media is essential* [author's emphasis].[49]

Sir James Munby LJ is concerned with media and public debate. Multidisciplinary academic, professional and practitioner debates also have an important role to play in this sensitive area.

The Public Law Outline 2014

The Public Law Outline: Guide to Case Management in Public Law Proceedings came into force with effect from 6 April 2010.[50] A pilot scheme of a revised Public Law Outline was phased in between 1 July 2013 and 7 October 2013, and ran until 21 April 2014. The revised version was introduced on 22 April 2014. This followed on from previous statutory guidance for local authorities effective from 2008, which resulted from the *Review of the Child Care Proceedings System in England and Wales*, undertaken by the now obsolete Department for Constitutional Affairs to examine the child care proceedings system in England and Wales with two aims: to improve the system for children and families subject to proceedings; and to ensure that all resources in the system are used in the most timely, effective way.[51]

The Public Law Outline is primarily concerned with the forensic process of public child care proceedings. It sets out the stages and timescales for applications in public family law proceedings (see Figure 4.2). Although the majority of it deals with stages of social work involvement once litigation has commenced (usually under s.31 Children Act 1989), the stages make it very clear that all social

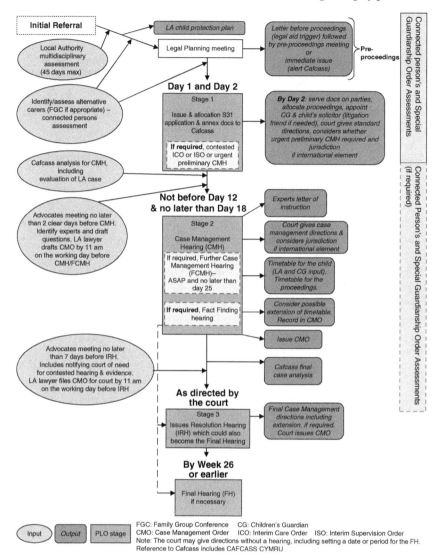

Figure 4.2 Public Law Outline 2014 (26 weeks).

work involvement at an early stage is a forensic process which can, and will, be used as part of the local authority's case to remove a child if they consider there are grounds for an application.

The Public Law Outline's objective is to set out streamlined case management procedures, with the aim of making the best decisions for the child within the timetable set by the court, and avoiding the need for unnecessary evidence or hearings. Under the revised s.32(1)(a) of the Children Act 1989 introduced by s.14 of the Children and Families Act 2014,[52] care and supervision proceedings must be completed by:

> disposing of the application—
>
> (i)   without delay, and
> (ii) in any event within twenty-six weeks beginning with the day on which the application was issued[53]

This places an increased emphasis on pre-proceedings work and the quality of social work assessments.

Sir James Munby LJ, President of the Family Division, has set out his interpretation of the revised Public Law Outline in *The Process of Reform: The Revised PLO and the Local Authority*. In the article it is made clear that social workers should be brought to the forefront of court proceedings in public law cases:

> One of the problems is that in recent years too many social workers have come to feel undervalued, disempowered and de-skilled. In part at least this is an unhappy consequence of the way in which care proceedings have come to be dealt with by the courts. If the revised PLO is properly implemented one of its outcomes will, I hope, be to re-position social workers as trusted professionals playing the central role in care proceedings which too often of late has been overshadowed by our unnecessary use of and reliance upon other experts.
>
> Social workers are experts. In just the same way, I might add, CAFCASS officers are experts. In every care case we have at least two experts – a social worker and a guardian – yet we have grown up with a culture of believing that they are not really experts and we therefore need experts with a capital E. The plain fact is that much of the time we do not.
>
> Social workers may not be experts for the purposes of Part 25 of the Family Procedure Rules 2010, but that does not mean that they are not experts in every other sense of the word. They are, and we must recognise them and treat them as such.[54]

The role of the local authority social worker is thus fourfold: as assessor in order to assess for provision of family help and support under s.17, as forensic investigator, as decision maker (with others) in terms of whether to proceed to litigation and as expert in those proceedings. If successful it is also the local authority that removes the child from their family and makes all decisions concerning the child subsequent to that decision. They are not independent, nor can they be described as impartial (one requirement of an expert) as they represent the applicant in s.31 proceedings.

The process of assessment

Following the 2015 *Working Together to Safeguard Children* and the Public Law Outline 2014, the nature of social work involvement has expanded and become increasingly confused. On the one hand the social work role is to intervene early, to build relationships and become a trusted partner with parents. On the other, this same involvement is part of a forensic process in which the role and power of the social worker extends far beyond that of, for example, the police in the criminal justice system. This places all concerned in a difficult and confused position from the outset, with a power imbalance weighted against parents and also against children if they do not agree with social work involvement and decisions.

Once a referral is made the local authority decides whether to assess. If so, the assessment process begins. Consent issues are particularly relevant because, despite the view of the serious case review panel in Khyra Ishaq's case,[55] the only non-consensual assessment that could be undertaken in respect of a family was following a decision to undertake a child protection inquiry under s.47 Children Act 1989 where the local authority has a duty to investigate reasonably suspected significant harm. Despite the desire in the 1989 Act to separate the stigma of non-consensual assessment from the provision of services, following the Children Act 2004 there is a lack of clarity over whether consent is required in relation to agreement to assessments that stop short of being a s.47 inquiry, particularly following the Department for Education's introduction of the continuous assessment.[56] The important issues are:

- whether parental permission should be sought prior to referral and assessment;
- whether consent should be sought before information is shared;
- whether social workers act without consent if consent is not forthcoming;
- whether consent is 'informed consent'; and
- whether consent is assumed and parents and children do not know they can refuse.

An issue of concern is what social services do if a family refuses to consent to an assessment at all, or refuses to talk to social workers during the conduct of an assessment, or wish to withdraw their consent part way through. If consent is not forthcoming for an assessment, a local authority must either simply not proceed, or consider what action it can lawfully take.

The serious case review findings in Khyra Ishaq's case concluded consent was not necessary for an Initial Assessment to take place.[57] The basis for this claim is not clear but it does flag up that there is an anomaly between the requirement on local authorities in *Working Together to Safeguard Children* to undertake an assessment in certain circumstances and the lack of specific statutory provision to bypass consent, other than the restricted circumstances set out in s.43 Children Act 1989. This suggests there are grounds for legal challenge over the *vires* of the *Working Together to Safeguard Children* requirement.

If assessment is not consensual there needs to be a mechanism for local authority social services to *inter alia* force entry to the family home, gain access to sensitive data on wider family members that may only be able to be obtained verbally from parents or the wider family members themselves, details of family income, sensitive medical details and details of parents' childhood experiences.[58] Even if this information is obtained upon interview, it is not clear how the 'truth' of the statements is ascertained in relation to, for example, data concerning wider family members and parents' childhood experiences. Even if an assessment of the nature detailed in *Working Together to Safeguard Children* could be forced, it is questionable whether statements made under protest by a family to comply with the assessment process should be relied upon in any subsequent litigation.

Continuous assessment of a family is intended to ascertain whether a family falls into a coercive 'child abuse' category, a non-coercive 'in need of services' category or neither. This is the means by which the mass surveillance of all families progress into increasingly coercive measures; it is entirely possible that a family that does not comply with an assessment for 'need' could be escalated into a s.47 inquiry where more coercive measures can be used to bypass consent. Whether any assessment should really be considered non-coercive, therefore, is a moot point. The use of coercive measures to obtain parental compliance, and compliance from children if they are not co-operative cannot be ruled out: the threat of litigation or imminent removal of a child via statutory measures in order that an assessment can be completed may secure acquiescence. The ethos of the Public Law Outline 2014 is to monitor compliance with social work requirements; what is lacking from the process is the plight of a family that disagrees with social work mandates, or that argues social work decision making is based on a flawed judgement or incorrect assessment of evidence. The process becomes a slippery slope where the backstop is the courtroom and the social worker is both the expert and the representative of the applicant. This is a dual role. In the modern climate of reduction in legal aid and the sharp rise of litigants in person this is a dangerously skewed framework which does not follow the same rationale as, for example, pre-action protocols in other areas of litigation and the ethos of the civil and criminal procedure rules in relation to the use of experts in litigation.[59]

Consensual assessment

Part III of the Children Act 1989 introduced measures that were intended to be supportive for children and their families. These measures were not intended to be coercive. As they are intended to work at a non-coercive level it is unclear what would happen if there is tension between a local authority who wants to provide services and a family who does not want them. The Public Law Outline 2014 implies escalation is at least a real possibility despite the fact that nominally all referrals are initially treated as non-coercive.[60] Ss.17 and 47 Children Act 1989[61] requirements in respect of 'children in need' and 'child protection' investigations are intended to be satisfied via a continuous assessment as opposed to the former model of separating out assessments, thus blurring the boundaries between the two sections. One now cannot take place without the other.

S.17(1) confers a general duty on local authorities to 'safeguard and promote the welfare of children in need'. The state of being 'in need' was defined in s.17(10):

For the purposes of this Part a child shall be taken to be in need if–

(a) he is unlikely to achieve or maintain, or to have the opportunity of achieving or maintaining, a reasonable standard of health or development without the provision for him of services by a local authority under this Part;

(b) his health or development is likely to be significantly impaired, or further impaired without the provision for him of such services; or

(c) he is disabled.

Although this may suggest that, budget considerations aside, children who are 'in need' will receive 'services' specific to their 'needs', the legal position is not as straightforward. Local authorities decide who is 'in need'.[62] As long as local authorities follow acceptable procedures it is not something that can readily be challenged by families.[63] Also, the services are not required to be specific and tailored towards the needs of an individual child. A child, therefore, even if he or she has needs, has no right to have those needs met as long as the local authority is 'providing a range and level of services appropriate to those children's needs'.[64] It is unclear whether families consenting to an assessment are aware that they may not receive services as a result, or that they may find themselves escalated to more coercive measures as a result of allowing the local authority access to their private lives. This knowledge might impact upon their willingness to consent to the assessment in the first place.

The problem with lack of provision of services once need had been established was sufficiently severe to be recognised in 1995 in the Department of Health's *Messages from Research*.[65] This report highlighted that 'children in need' were sometimes wrongly and deliberately recorded as at risk of 'significant harm' in order to obtain 'services' that they are not able to obtain via the s.17 route. In some respects, therefore, s.17 is less helpful than it first appears and may, in fact, be a coercive gateway.[66] Once assessment begins it may be found that there are risk factors that families cannot mitigate, leaving them vulnerable to unwanted interventions that they cannot take action to prevent. The same consent issue is relevant here. Parents who consent to an assessment to obtain services may not consent should they know of the risk of being categorised as potential 'child abusers' in order to obtain the services they presumably want. Knowing what they are consenting to, and being able to stop the process if they become uncomfortable with the assessment, is not given adequate consideration under the current framework. It seems that, once the process has started, families are left vulnerable to being escalated into the more coercive mechanisms if they withhold consent from a local authority or may consent to a process they do not want or need.

Coercive assessment

The Children Act 1989 vests responsibility with the State to make inquiries in cases of reasonably suspected significant harm in order to enable the local authorities to discharge their statutory duty to decide whether to take action.[67] It has been noted that 'the emphasis [in the Children Act is] placed on providing extensive State support for the family'.[68] However, despite provisions described as providing 'support' for the family, the Children Act 1989 Part V also confers paternalistic powers upon local authorities once the local authority decides to start an investigation. This is why such measures are contained in a separate section of the Children Act 1989 and are intended to be invoked only when necessary. The objective is to ascertain whether or not a child is at risk of 'significant harm' if action is not taken by the local authority.[69] Parental consent is not required, but it is not clear what would happen if a *Gillick* competent child objected. S.43(8) of the 1989 Act concerning non-consensual Child Assessment Orders makes it clear that if the child is of sufficient understanding he or she can refuse to submit to an assessment. This implies that if such an order is sought a child may refuse, but this is only helpful to a child who is aware he or she can refuse.

In order to understand the meaning that has been attributed to the phrases used in s.47,[70] other sections of the 1989 Act and case law jurisprudence are of relevance. The judiciary have been afforded the opportunity to interpret what was intended by Parliament in cases that have travelled further through the system than the assessment stages. These cases can help explain what is meant by terms such as 'significant' and 'harm'. There is a lack of litigation over local authority social services assessment, but in limited circumstances it is possible to mount a successful legal challenge.[71] Despite the lack of litigation it would be wrong to assume this is because this stage is unproblematic.

S.31(9)[72] defines 'harm', and 'significant' is defined in s.31(10).[73] There is no further guidance in the legislation, leaving the issue open to judicial interpretation. The meaning of 'significant' can be interpreted widely particularly given the rise of the category of cases involving alleged emotional abuse. The case law considering the meaning of 'significant' is particularly relevant to the early investigation stages because this forms part of the threshold for investigative interference.[74]

In *Humberside CC v B*[75] Booth J held that 'significant harm' should be denoted as: 'being harm that the court should consider was either considerable or noteworthy or important . . . harm which the court should take into account in considering a child's future'.[76] Whilst these descriptive terms may be helpful they do nothing to assist with achieving certainty. There could, perhaps, be a more clearly defined approach to this whereby each concept, word and procedure is defined precisely although this approach would no doubt be criticised as unduly restrictive.

The question of whether a child can be considered to be 'suffering' or 'likely to suffer' has also been subject to judicial interpretation. In relation to the question of when the child had to be 'suffering significant harm' the Lords decided that it referred to 'suffering' at the time when the local authority first interfered rather than the time of the application to the court.[77] *Re G*[78] for example concerned a related issue where evidence of 'suffering' was obtained *after* the local authority intervened. In these circumstances the Appeal Court drew a distinction between evidence up to the point of interference, and unrelated evidence obtained afterwards. It was held that evidence obtained afterwards was not able to be used to 'retrospectively valid[ate] a concern which was not in fact justified at the time'.[79] This does not, however, stop the local authority from starting again and undertaking a new assessment of a family.

Substantiation

One problematic area occurs where an assessment concludes that the allegations are unsubstantiated, raising a question of what should happen in such cases. This issue is particularly important as it is the outcome in the majority of cases.[80] In respect of referrals that amount to an allegation unable to be disproved by the parents there remains a residual fear that an outcome of 'unsubstantiated' is simply a failure to obtain sufficient evidence to justify further interference. The onus should not be on parents, but it is difficult to see what else they can try to do other than strive to 'clear their names'.

Even where an allegation is considered by the local authority to be substantiated, the statutory duty conferred upon local authorities under s.47[81] does not confer a duty upon the local authority to act on their findings although it would be reasonable to presume they would do so. The duty set out in s.47(b)[82] is to 'make enquiries', but the decision to 'take any action' is a decision for the local authority, rather than a duty: 'the authority shall make, or cause to be made, such enquiries as they consider necessary to enable them to decide whether they should take any action to safeguard or promote the child's welfare.'[83] As a matter of policy, it may be undesirable to place local authorities in a position where they could be held to be in breach of a statutory duty to 'take any action' if, for example, budget constraints would make it difficult to do so. As the type of 'action' is unspecified it is difficult to see how the local authority could be in breach of a statutory duty regardless of what action it takes or fails to take if the wording of the Children Act 1989 is interpreted literally. However, case law has found in favour of children in relation to claims of under-interference resulting in a failure to protect them, establishing a common law duty of care. It is the local authority who has *locus standi* to bring an action in respect of care proceedings.[84] S.47 therefore acts as an information gathering gateway, an essential precursor to litigation. This has not, however, prevented public inquiries and Serious Case Reviews from taking place when a child has been seriously harmed or killed following assessment and local authority failure to act. This case law in relation to under-interference has created a defensive culture and sensitivity to risk.[85] The political and media pressures on local authorities in relation to criticism of under-interference are a compelling reason for a local authority to be cautious about any failure to take action. A 'blame culture' towards both local authority social services departments and individual social workers and managers working within them has developed as a result of the public inquiries and Serious Case Reviews. It is therefore certainly implied that there is an expectation a local authority should not put themselves at risk of adverse consequences as a result of under-interference. The consequence of this may be to cause a tendency for over-interference.

The limits of Working Together to Safeguard Children

In order to carry out its statutory duty to investigate under s.47(b), local authorities draft their own documents to set out their expectation of social workers in the conduct of their enquiries. *Working Together to Safeguard Children*[86] drafted and published by the Department of Health, HM Government and most recently the Department for Education, forms the core procedural set of rules from which each local authority works having drafted their own, internal set of procedures. As it is statutory guidance it can reasonably be assumed that local authorities' individual procedures will be based on those set out in *Working Together to Safeguard Children*.[87] This is, however, an assumption: local authorities draft and set their own, so there may be regional variations. The stages start with an assessment which can lead to possible further investigation and potential litigation to remove children from their families.[88]

S.47(b)[89] enables local authorities to make 'such enquiries as they [the local authority] consider necessary'. This enabling section should in theory also be adequate in relation to an appropriate level of statutory protection for a family about whom a local authority decides to 'make enquiries'. The legal position is that the powers could not be considered to be unlimited. However, public perception, particularly where there have been reports of social work excess, or where social work practice appears to have been unlawful, has fed concerns that State control appears to be excessive, erratic and potentially lacking in clear boundaries.[90] Paradoxically, where practice has the potential to be found unlawful this demonstrates that some boundaries can be retrospectively enforced via remedies.[91]

Updated versions of *Working Together to Safeguard Children*[92] have become longer and more comprehensive although the Department for Education's 2015 version considerably scales the length back.[93] This potentially erodes the balance between the duty upon a local authority to make inquiries and the right of a family not to suffer excessive interference into their private family life. Local authorities make their own decisions over how far they implement the duty to 'make enquiries', and according to statute they simply need to 'consider it necessary' in order for it to be justified. This can be compared and contrasted with the powers of the police, noting that families under investigation by social workers do not have the protection of PACE[94] or a similar framework of due process and protection. This is because social work involvement is seen as primarily a welfare role, in the interests of the child. As such, social work is seen as building a relationship with a family in order to help the child, not a forensic process. This is, however, at odds with the legal framework and with policy, creating conflict, confusion and difficulties for social work practitioners and families.

There is a long history of the tensions between the need for the police to investigate crime against which must be balanced the right of citizens to be free from unwarranted State interference. The lack of debate outside welfarist discourse in relation to child protection and safeguarding has not been conducive to ensuring robust controls are in place to try to ensure reasonableness and proportionality in local authority investigations. The job of a social worker is not to fight or investigate crime but a social worker is caught in the welfare/policing dichotomy of being support worker and forensic investigator. Social work practice aiming to build trust and relationships with families is based on the principles of s.17, but this approach is not able to reconcile the complex and different nature of a forensic, evidence-gathering process under s.47.

Anderson *et al.* identify this issue as a point of concern in relation to s.2 Local Government Act 2000[95] which despite the limits set out in s.3 has led to local authorities unsuccessfully applying these provisions to *inter alia* school applications and household recycling habits. Anderson *et al.* observe that:

> No-one would try to claim that Section 2 Local Government Act 2000, which allows local authorities to do 'anything which they consider is likely

to promote or improve [the economic, social or environmental] well-being of their area', allows those authorities to arrest people without other legal authority, or to close down a local newspaper, or indeed to break down someone's front door. Yet this is one of the main provisions on which the authorities seek to base the sharing of sensitive data on children.[96]

The wording of the statute and case law on abuses of s.2 does raise the possibility that families would have to bring actions to control excesses.[97] The 2013 judgment in *AB and Anor, R (on the application of) v The London Borough of Haringey* illustrates this.[98]

If the enabling statute confers extensive powers on local authorities, and *Working Together to Safeguard Children*[99] is used as a basis for increasingly intrusive local procedures, it is difficult to see how assessments are adequately controlled to ensure an appropriate balance between State powers and private rights. The absence of any Code of Practice over the way assessments and inquiries are carried out leaves families potentially vulnerable to increasing levels of coercion in relation to welfare decisions in order to head off escalation. Whilst it is possible for a challenge to be made to *Working Together to Safeguard Children* and the manner in which it is applied during assessment, there is little protection for families against State powers in this circumstance.

Statutory measures to compel compliance with assessment

In addition to the statutory powers examined above, there are also statutory provisions that can be invoked by a local authority to compel compliance. These are not processes of assessment in themselves, but they are steps that a local authority can take to either enforce assessment or to remove a child from his or her family in order that assessment can take place. These powers are undeniably draconian, and may therefore operate as a very persuasive measure in relation to parents, who may consent to an assessment for fear of the consequences of refusal. They all occur in Part V of the Children Act 1989. S.43 is directly relevant to an application to compel assessment, whereas Ss.44, 45 and 46 are more concerned with the sudden removal of a child under an Emergency Protection Order (EPO). These measures occur at the tertiary level of interference and are more likely to escalate to a quaternary outcome of total severance than de-escalation back towards the secondary or even primary stages of intervention.

S.43 CHILDREN ACT 1989 ORDERS

The only statutory mechanism that exists specifically to compel parents to comply with assessments generally is found in s.43 which relates to Child Assessment Orders.[100] The purpose of s.43 is to compel a child to be produced for assessment in circumstances where the applicant has reasonable cause to suspect the child is suffering, or is likely to suffer, significant harm, that an assessment is necessary in order to determine whether or not this is the case and that without an Order an assessment is unlikely to take place.[101] This is in contrast to the wording of s.11

Children Act 2004 which also emphasises the concept of 'safeguarding and promoting welfare', but is not concerned with 'significant harm': s.11 is concerned with 'safeguarding and promoting the welfare of children' not investigating child abuse. In any event, s.43 orders are intended to be used in relation to child abuse inquiries and a *Gillick* competent child can refuse to comply.

It is generally assumed in *Working Together to Safeguard Children*[102] that families do consent to assessment, to the extent that consent is not mentioned as an issue of importance at all. S.43 Orders are designed for ordering production of the child for examination in the event of non-compliance and last for seven days. For example, if a child was suspected of having sustained physical injury as a result of child abuse an order could be made compelling the parents to produce the child for physical examination. Under s.43(8) a child can refuse to consent so the orders are limited although *South Glamorgan County Council v W & B* suggests that the court can exercise its inherent jurisdiction to overrule a child's lack of consent.[103]

As s.43 orders were created in the Children Act 1989 they were not designed to deal with non-compliance with modern assessment. Therefore, although the court can order 'production for assessment' of the child, the order cannot compel the parents to produce themselves for assessment, nor can it compel the type of dialogue and inspection essential for modern assessments to be effectively completed.

S.43 orders are therefore suitable in circumstances where a point of fact needs to be established and the child needs to be produced for that purpose, for example a physical examination by a doctor.[104] They have limited use in modern safeguarding contexts as it is difficult to envisage how they are adequate to force compliance with the type of enquiries made in such assessments. It is possible, therefore, that refusal to consent to an assessment may cause the local authority to escalate matters through the stages of the Public Law Outline 2014. If families are told their refusal will cause this to happen it is doubtful that assessments can really be considered to be consensual.

The confusion, therefore, over what requires consent and what does not require consent is not clarified by identifying the different ideology behind s.17 (which is concerned with 'partnerships') and s.47(which is not), nor by the statutory provision designed to compel assessment set out in s.43. This confusion has enabled this blurred boundary in relation to the 'hybrid' continuous assessment which is not on the face of it a child abuse inquiry but seems to cover ss.17 and 47 together. There is, however, no adequate statutory measure to compel compliance. It seems more likely that under the framework of the Public Law Outline 2014, refusal to consent may trigger escalation to non-consensual stages beyond assessment which are increasingly difficult to halt.

EMERGENCY PROTECTION ORDERS

Another avenue open to a local authority to override resistance to assessment would be to apply for an Emergency Protection Order. These orders are clearly designed to swiftly remove a child from his or her family if *inter alia* an assessment is taking place and access to the child is 'unreasonably refused'.[105] The orders are enabled under s.44 Children Act 1989 and were introduced to replace Place of Safety Orders.[106] They are used either with, or without notice (*ex parte*) and, if successful, a child will be removed from his or her family immediately.

A low standard of proof, 'reasonable cause to believe' is required. It is the applicant (the local authority or the NSPCC) who have to have 'cause to believe'. Similarly, in respect of s.47 inquiries being frustrated by lack of access to a child, it is the local authority or the NSPCC who have to have 'reasonable cause to believe' that 'access to the child is required as a matter of urgency'.

In terms of protection for parents, and also for children, McFarlane J has made it clear that the judicial reasons for granting an EPO must be explained, and that this must be more than a simple reliance upon the testimony of a social worker:

> The need for justices to state their reasons and the basis for those reasons is well established in the rules . . . A failure to give reasons is a serious deficiency and should only occur in quite exceptional cases. In *S v Oxfordshire County Council* [1993] 1 FLR 452, Connell J said: 'It would be unjust to this child to allow a decision to stand which so affected his future without at least understanding the main bases upon which the decision was reached.' That was not an EPO case, but the principles of justice and fairness must equally apply in an emergency case given the draconian effect of the order that is being made . . . The emergency nature of the application, whilst requiring prompt determination, does not absolve the court of its duty to give a reasoned explanation for its decision.[107]

Although this confirmed other authority to the same effect[108] it is difficult to see how the granting of EPOs can be based upon anything other than the court's trust and good faith that the information given to them is reliable. There may also be an understandable reluctance to fail to act when a professional is stressing the urgent nature of perceived danger to a child.

Once applied for, the chance of an EPO being granted is extremely high: 'Judicial Statistics indicate that approximately 90% of EPOs are granted.'[109] In respect of the other 10 per cent Masson *et al.* note that these are generally applications that do not proceed only because parents have acquiesced to whatever measures the local authority have demanded. This supports the idea that the threat of, or actual granting of, an EPO is a way of forcing consent to assessment.

There is no right of appeal against an EPO so parents are in a very difficult position should one be granted. There is a limited safeguard in the judicial guidance on the care that must be taken in light of the Human Rights Act 1998 which has influenced judicial thinking about the justification for Emergency Protection Orders leading to the judicial guidance in *X Council v B (Emergency Protection Orders)*[110] and *Re X: Emergency Protection Orders*.[111] In *X Council v B*, Sir James Munby LJ listed 14 key points which:

> should be copied and made available to the justices hearing an EPO on each and every occasion such an application is made . . . It is the duty of the

applicant for an EPO to ensure that the *X Council v B* guidance is brought to the court's attention.[112]

The guidance emphasises the care that should be taken when applying for an EPO:

> An EPO, summarily removing a child from his parents, is a terrible and drastic remedy. The European Court of Human Rights has rightly stressed . . . that such an order is a 'draconian' and 'extremely harsh' measure, requiring 'exceptional justification' and 'extraordinarily compelling reasons' . . .[113]

Even with this guidance, given that the 'EPO is a drastic order, often made in the absence of the parents and with little effective scrutiny by the courts',[114] they raise several concerning issues, the most important of which is the power imbalance and lack of ability for parents and children to challenge a local authority once a decision has been made to apply for an EPO or where one has been granted. In view of its draconian nature it is a very powerful coercive threat. Although an EPO is a pre-emptive action which can be argued to exist to protect against potential or actual harm whilst assessment is carried out, there is the potential for error, over-reaction and the threat of its use as a coercive tool to enforce compliance with an assessment. These issues must be balanced against any harm the use of EPOs is considered to have prevented. This is a particularly difficult balancing act as it would be very difficult to quantify how much harm has been prevented as these harmful acts, by definition, have not occurred.

S.46 relates to police powers of protection and provides that:

> Where a constable has reasonable cause to believe that a child would otherwise be likely to suffer significant harm, he may–
>
> (a) remove the child to suitable accommodation and keep him there;
>
> or
>
> (b) take such steps as are reasonable to ensure that the child's removal from any hospital or other place in which he is being accommodated is prevented.[115]

This provision allows the police to remove a child and place the child into police protection for up to 72 hours where a police officer has 'reasonable cause to believe' that the child would otherwise 'suffer significant harm'. Masson *et al.* note that 'this power is widely used both at the request of social services and where the police come across a child "at risk" independently.'[116] One major difference, however, between the police's powers under s.46 and those of the local authority or the NSPCC under s.44 is that the police do not acquire parental responsibility for the child[117] whereas the local authority and the NSPCC do.

Masson *et al.* discovered that, far from being a last resort, police protection is 'widely used as a first step by local authorities'.[118] This statutory power therefore has the potential to be used to bypass consent in relation to assessment, and it also raises the same issue in relation to whether the threat of police protection is, or is capable of, being used to gain acquiescence to assessment or bypass a refusal. Considering the extremely distressing and abrupt nature for the family, including the child, of police protection and the lack of necessity for an application to the court before such action is taken, this is of concern.[119] The findings of the *Inquiry into Child Abuse in Cleveland*[120] made it clear that a removal of a child from his or her family in this manner has an extremely shocking and distressing effect upon a family and long-term consequences for them. From such a disempowered position parents accused of child abuse and children who are the subjects of such allegations are not in an equal position in relation to subsequent proceedings. They are likely to be extremely traumatised. On the other hand, the local authority would argue they have acted to prevent harm to a child. This tension between competing interests merits careful examination.

These powers should be used judiciously and only in unavoidable circumstances. However, the fact remains that the threat of their existence may have an impact on a family when it is faced with a local authority's demand for an assessment.

Conclusion: issues of safeguards and controls over State powers of assessment

The legal framework enabling the policing of parents via referral and assessment does not provide sufficient inbuilt safeguards for families who for whatever reason do not, or cannot, comply with social work demands. State powers are evident but private rights are less prominent. A non-compliant parent or family simply risks escalation through an increasingly coercive process. This is evident in the framework set out in the Public Law Outline 2014, which *inter alia* requires compliance to prevent escalation. Non-compliant families who disagree with social work decisions and assessments, and those who would like to comply but cannot for reasons beyond their control, are in a vulnerable position with little standing between them and litigation other than a social work decision to take 'no further action'. The pressure is on social workers to err on the side of caution so a family may be in a very difficult position indeed. The wording of the enabling statutes does not limit or regulate the power of local authorities, who are using *Working Together to Safeguard Children*[121] to guide them in relation to the conduct of a continuous assessment. Under this framework there is an unacceptable potential for the parents' consent to be bypassed at a very low level of concern, or simply at the level of a request for help and support.

In addition to questions surrounding the parents' consent, the child's consent or refusal is not relevant other than perhaps for a s.43 order unless the refusal is successfully challenged in court by the local authority. Whilst the interests of the parent and of the child may conflict, throughout this chapter mention is also made of the 'family' as well as 'parents' and 'children' in circumstances where local authority social services interaction with a family may potentially be unwanted by both parents and child. This is particularly relevant in relation to older children. In trying to achieve its aim of protecting and safeguarding children the policy interpretation of the legal framework is overly paternalistic in a manner that can cause stress, distress and uncertainty to children as well as their parents, creating consequences that could have a negative impact on any or all members of the family.

Through its constant development and evolving policy towards increased surveillance and early, rationed intervention, the statutory guidance has led to a position which is insufficient in relation to providing inbuilt safeguards for families not abusing their children who do not want or need interventions. Coercion can be used by local authorities to gain consent through acquiescence when families either do not know they have a choice, or are put in fear of the consequences of refusal. These issues are particularly relevant because the overwhelming majority of assessments do not yield evidence of 'significant harm' and therefore the use of coercive measures on such families seems excessive. The extent to which assessments cause long-term distress and damage and erode trust in State agencies must be considered in this context. Of equal importance is the consequence for a family. If the best outcome they can hope for is that an allegation is 'unsubstantiated', or that they are eligible for services because they are 'high risk', it hardly seems satisfactory for them. If this were made clear to families at the outset the question of consent may become increasingly contentious. This stance may be argued to be justified if it was demonstrably reducing significant harm to children, but the data is showing that, although an increasing number of referrals are made year on year, the proportionate detection of significant harm is dropping.[122]

Notes

1 Public Law Outline 2014, PD12A. See: Ministry of Justice (2008) *The Public Law Outline Guide to Case Management in Public Law Proceedings*, TSO, London. Online at: www.familylaw.co.uk/system/uploads/attachments/0000/2168/public _law_outline.pdf (Accessed 25 January 2016).
2 See Department of Health (2002) *Initial Assessment Record v.0*, TSO, London.
3 HM Government (2015) *Working Together to Safeguard Children*, DFE-00130-2015, TSO, London, lays out the framework for these assessments and makes it clear that the assessment is not an investigation of an allegation, but a 'holistic' assessment of the entire family, wider family and their 'needs'. Figure Assessment Framework on p. 22 of *Working Together* lays out the framework for these comprehensive assessments. Online at: www.gov.uk/government/uploads/system /uploads/attachment_data/file/419595/Working_Together_to_Safeguard _Children.pdf (Accessed 1 May 2016).
4 Children Act 1948 c.43.
5 HM Government (2015) (n. 3).
6 HM Government (2010) *Working Together to Safeguard Children: A Guide to Inter-Agency Working to Safeguard and Promote the Welfare of Children*, TSO, London.
7 HM Government (2000) *Framework for the Assessment of Children in Need and their Families*, TSO, London.

8 Munro, E. (2011a) *The Munro Review of Child Protection, Interim Report: The Child's Journey*, DFE-00010-2011, Department for Education, London. Online at: www.gov.uk/government/uploads/system/uploads/attachment_data/file/206993/DFE-00010-2011.pdf (Accessed 27 February 2016); Munro, E. (2011b) *The Munro Review of Child Protection: Final Report, A Child Centred System*, Cmd 8062, May 2011, Department for Education, TSO, London. Online at www.official-documents.gov.uk/document/cm80/8062/8062.pdf (Accessed 4 May 2016).

9 Parton, N. (2011) *The Increasing Length and Complexity of Central Government Guidance about Child Abuse in England: 1974–2010*, Discussion Paper, University of Huddersfield, Huddersfield. Online at: http://eprints.hud.ac.uk/9906/3/The_Increasing_Complexity_of_Working_Together_to_Safeguard_Children_in_EnglandJune101RevisedOct10.pdf (Accessed 5 May 2016).

10 HM Government (2015) (n. 3), paras 517–18, p. 24.

11 Ibid.

12 HM Government (2000) (n. 7), appendix A, p. 89.

13 HM Government (2010) (n. 6), Part 1, p. 25.

14 c.42, s.7(1): 'Local authorities shall, in the exercise of their social services functions, including the exercise of any discretion conferred by any relevant enactment, act under the general guidance of the Secretary of State.'

15 c.31, ss.10(8), 10(10), 11(4), 12(12), 12B(4), 16(2), 18(7), 19(2) and 25(8).

16 HM Government (2015) (n. 3).

17 Gibbons, J., Conroy, S. and Bell, C. (1995) *Operating the Child Protection System Studies in Child Protection*, HMSO, London.

18 Devine, L. (2015) 'Considering Social Work Assessment of Families', *Journal of Social Welfare & Family Law* 37(1): 70–83. Online at: http://dx.doi.org/10.1080/09649069.2015.998005 (Accessed 28 February 2016).

19 HM Government (2006) *Working Together to Safeguard Children*, TSO, London, para. 1.18.

20 HM Government (2015) (n. 3).

21 Lindley, B. and Richards, M. (2002) *Protocol on Advice and Advocacy for Parents (Child Protection)*, Centre for Family Research, University of Cambridge, Cambridge. Online at: www.frg.org.uk/images/PDFS/advocacy-protocol.pdf (Accessed 25 January 2016).

22 Ministry of Justice (n. 1).

23 HM Government (2015) (n. 3), Figure 1, p. 22.

24 Children Act 1989 c.41.

25 Munro (2011b) (n. 8).

26 Munro (2011a) (n. 8).

27 Anderson, R., Brown, I., Clayton, R., Dowty, T., Korff, D. and Munro, E. (2006) *Children's Databases – Safety and Privacy: A Report for the Information Commissioner*, Foundation for Information Policy Research, Bedfordshire. Online at: www.fipr.org/press/061122kids.html (Accessed 1 January 2016).

28 Ibid.

29 Cawson, P., Wattam, C., Brooker, S. and Kelly, G. (2000) *Child Maltreatment in the United Kingdom: A Study of the Prevalence of Child Abuse and Neglect*, NSPCC, London.

30 NSPCC (2011) *Prevalence and Incidence of Child Abuse and Neglect*, NSPCC website. Online at: www.nspcc.org.uk/inform/research/statistics/prevalence_and_incidence_of_child_abuse_and_neglect_wda48740.html (Accessed 1 April 2011); NSPCC (2011) *Child Cruelty in the UK 2011: An NSPCC study into Childhood Abuse and Neglect Over the Past 30 Years*. Online at: www.nspcc.org.uk/news-and-views/our-news/nspcc-news/11-02-15-report-launch/overview-report_wdf80875.pdf (Accessed 1 April 2011).

31 Department for Education (2011) 'Press Notice: Government Confirms Future Funding for Children's Charity and Helpline', 15 February. Online at: www.education.gov.uk/inthenews/pressnotices/a0074369/government-confirms-future-funding-for-childrens-charity-and-helpline (Accessed 10 March 2011).

32 Devine, L. and Parker, S. (2015) 'Rethinking Child Protection Strategy: Learning from Trends', Working Paper, Centre for Legal Research, Bristol Law School, UWE, Bristol, Online at: http://eprints.uwe.ac.uk/25258/ (Accessed 28 February 2016).

33 Cawson *et al.* (n. 29).

34 Munro, E. (2011b) (n. 8), Executive Summary, para. 2, p. 6.

35 Ibid., p. 6.

36 Bailey, K.D. (1994) *Sociology and the New Systems Theory: Toward a Theoretical Synthesis*, SUNY Press, Albany, NY.

37 Von Bertalanffy, L. (1976) *General System Theory: Foundations, Development, Applications*, rev. edn, George Braziller, New York.

38 Munro (2011b) (n. 8), Executive Summary, p. 12.

39 Munro (2011a) (n. 8).

40 Munro (2011b) (n. 8), Executive Summary, p. 6.

41 When compared with the actual and potential harm to some children if the State does not have these processes.

42 Munro (2011b) (n. 8), Executive Summary, para. 3, p. 6.

43 Ibid., para. 1.11, p. 17.

44 HM Government (2010) (n. 6).

45 Munro (2011b) (n. 8), Executive Summary, paras 3.11 and 3.13, p. 42.

46 Ibid., para. 7.57, p. 122.

47 Ibid., para. 7.72, p. 127.

48 Ryder, J. in: *Oldham MBC v GW & Ors* [2007] EWHC 136 (Fam), para. 75.

49 Munby, J. in: *Re B (A Child) (Disclosure)* [2004] 2FLR 142, para. 101.

50 Ministry of Justice (2008) *The Public Law Outline: Guide to Case Management in Public Law Proceedings*, TSO, London. Online at: www.familylaw.co.uk/system/uploads/attachments/0000/2168/public_law_outline.pdf (Accessed 25 January 2016).

51 Department for Constitutional Affairs (2006) *Review of the Child Care Proceedings System in England and Wales*, May 2006, TSO, London. Online at: http://webarchive.nationalarchives.gov.uk/+/www.dca.gov.uk/publications/reports_reviews/childcare_ps.pdf (Accessed 25 January 2016).

52 This section was prospective as of 27 February 2016.

53 Children and Families Act 2014 c.6, s.14.

54 Munby LJ, Sir James (2013) 'View from the President's Chambers – The Process of Reform: The Revised PLO and the Local Authority', *Family Law* 43(5): 680.

55 Radford, J. (2010) *Serious Case Review Under Chapter VIII 'Working Together to Safeguard Children' In respect of the Death of a Child Case Number 14*, 26 April 2010, Birmingham Safeguarding Children Board, specifically p. 167. Online at: http://northumberlandlscb.proceduresonline.com/pdfs/kyhra_ishaq_scr.pdf (Accessed 1 May 2016).

56 This is apparent from its failure for inclusion in relevant procedures and texts. For example, standard social work textbooks and guidance does not consider consent in detail. See for example: Brayne, H. and Carr, H. (2010) *Law for Social Workers* (11th edn), Oxford University Press, Oxford, Chapter 10, pp. 294–307, and the source document HM Government (2010) (n. 6), paras 5.32–5.47, pp. 143–9, although para. 5.35 states that the consent of parents should be sought before discussing a referral about them with other agencies. However, this is a different

issue to giving consent for the assessment itself. Given the circumstances in which a local authority has the power to escalate the level of inquiry to operate under s.47 and take legal action by applying for a s.43 order if consent is not forthcoming, and that failure of parents to co-operate could be seen as weakening their chances of success in such proceedings, one may wonder how often such consent is real consent. This is a strong ground for producing a Code of Practice governing such actions (discussed in Chapter 6). It could be argued that in cases of Initial Assessment the relevant guidance would be *Assessing Children in Need and Their Families* or *the Common Assessment Framework*, not *Working Together to Safeguard Children*, which illustrates the dichotomy in relation to consent: assessments that are intended to be non-coercive cannot be such if they can proceed without consent if consent is not forthcoming. The Khyra Ishaq serious case review findings assumed that Initial Assessments are non-consensual and were generally critical that social workers did not continue with an assessment without parental consent, but did not explain why this should be if it operates under s.17. The findings also did not explain why social work response to the referral was not elevated to start a s.47 investigation given the circumstances. See generally: Radford (n. 55), specifically p. 167.

57 Radford, J. (n. 55), p. 167.
58 HM Government (2010) (n. 6), paras 5.32–5.47, pp. 143–9, sets out a long list of assessment criteria. This is analogous to the situation in a police inquiry where a suspect refuses to answer questions. In a criminal investigation a suspect can only be cautioned as to the consequences of his or her failure to answer questions and cannot be forced to speak.
59 The Criminal Procedure Rules, Part 33, Civil Procedure Rules, Part 19 and the Family Procedure Rules, Part 25 contain the rules relating to the use of experts in the courtroom.
60 Children Act 1989 c.41.
61 Ibid., ss.17 and 47.
62 These decisions are subject to judicial review. Judicial review does not provide a remedy for a contested decision but does enable the process followed to reach the decision to be questioned. See: *Re J (Specific Issue Order: Leave to Apply)* [1995] 1 FLR 669.
63 For example: *R (on the application of A) v Croydon LBC*; *R (on the application of M) v Lambeth LBC* [2008] EWCA Civ 1445; *X (Minors) v Bedfordshire CC*; *M (A Minor) v Newham LBC*; *E (A Minor) v Dorset CC (Appeal)*; *Christmas v Hampshire CC (Duty of Care)*; *Keating v Bromley LBC (No. 2)* [1995] 2 AC 633.
64 Per Lord Millett in: *R (on the application of G) v Barnet London Borough Council*; *R (on the application of W) v Lambeth London Borough Council*; *R (on the application of A) v Lambeth London Borough Council* [2003] UKHL 57; [2004] 2 AC 208 at 109.
65 Department of Health (1995) *Child Protection: Messages from Research*, HMSO, London.
66 See Masson on the use of voluntary care, which gives a comparable example of a non-coercive provision that is used as a coercive gateway. Masson is critical of the 'coercive' use of Part III given power disparities, particularly where the local authority uses Part III because they are not confident that they would be able to satisfy s.31 for a care order. Masson, J.M. (2005a) 'Emergency Intervention to Protect Children: Using and Avoiding Legal Controls', *Child & Family Law Quarterly* 17(1): 75–96, and Masson, J.M. (2005b) 'Emergency Intervention: The Use of EPOs', *Family Court Journal* 3(1): 13–24.
67 This duty was enacted in s.47 Children Act 1989 c.41.
68 Fox-Harding, L. (1991) 'The Children Act 1989 in Context: Four Perspectives in Child Care Law and Policy', *Journal of Social Welfare and Family Law* 13(3): 285.

69 It is noted that s.37(1) Children Act 1989 c.41 also confers a duty upon local authorities to 'investigate a child's circumstance' by court order if 'in any family proceedings in which a question arises with respect to the welfare of any child' there is a question of whether 'it may be appropriate for a care or supervision order to be made'.

70 Children Act 1989 c.41.

71 *AB & Anor, R (on the application of) v The London Borough of Haringey* [2013] EWHC 416 (Admin) (13 March 2013).

72 S.31(9) Children Act 1989 states that 'harm' means ill treatment or the impairment of health or development; 'development' means physical, intellectual, emotional, social or behavioural development; 'health' means physical or mental health; and 'ill treatment' includes sexual abuse and forms of ill-treatment which are not physical.

73 S.31(10) Children Act 1989 states that 'significant' is decided on an assessment of the child's health or development, which should be compared with that of 'a similar child'.

74 Under s.47 Children Act 1989 c.41.

75 *Humberside CC v B* [1993] 1 FLR.

76 Ibid., 263.

77 *Re M (A Minor) (Care Orders: Threshold Conditions)* [1994] 2 AC 424, at 433–4.

78 *Re G (Care Proceedings: Threshold Conditions)* [2001] EWCA Civ 968, [2001] FLR 1111.

79 Ibid., para. 15.

80 Some 92 per cent of allegations are unsubstantiated if the 'cut off point' identified by Gibbons *et al.* (n. 17) *Operating the Child Protection* is used.

81 Children Act 1989 c.41.

82 Ibid.

83 Ibid., s.47 (as originally drafted).

84 Also the NSPCC and anyone else if authorised by the Secretary of State. This latter provision has never been utilised.

85 For example: Lord Laming (2003) *The Victoria Climbié Inquiry Report*, HC 570, 24 June. Online at: www.publications.parliament.uk/pa/cm200203/cmselect /cmhealth/570/570.pdf (Accessed 1 January 2016); The 'Baby P' inquiry: Lord Laming (2009) *The Protection of Children in England: A Progress Report*, HC 330, March, The Stationary Office, London. Online at: www.cscb.org. uk/downloads/policies_guidance/national/The%20Protection%20of%20Chil dren%20in%20England%20-%20%20a%20progress%20report%20by%20Lord%20 Laming,%202009.pdf (Accessed 1 January 2016); and the review into Khyra Ishaq's death: Radford (n. 55).

86 HM Government (2015) (n. 3). The point is that, over time, successive versions have been published by different government departments, or by HMG itself.

87 Ibid.

88 Ibid. Provides guidance for assessment, whereas litigation moves back to direct statutory authorisation via s.31 Children Act 1989 c.41.

89 Children Act 1989 c.41.

90 For example, publicity from groups such as Parents Against Injustice (PAIN) and associated research from its case files, particularly: Prosser, J. (1995) 'A Case Study of a UK Family Wrongly Accused of Child Abuse', *Issues in Child Abuse Accusations*, Vol. 7, pp. 1–12, 10, published online by IPT. Online at: www. ipt-forensics.com/journal/volume7/j7_3_2.htm (Accessed 14 May 2016). And Prosser, J. and Lewis, I. (1992) 'Child Abuse Investigations: The Families' Perspective', Parents Against Injustice (PAIN), 3 Riverside Business Park, Stansted, Essex CM24 8PL, where observations are made about the methodology of

investigations in relation to several families where practice has been reported as unlawful or excessive.

91   Remedies are discussed in Chapter 6, and refer to the mechanisms by which surveillance and assessment can be challenged where it is potentially excessive or unlawful.

92   HM Government (2015) (n. 3).

93   For example, *Working Together to Safeguard Children* 2010 has 393 pages, whilst the 1999 version had 128 pages. For a review of the development of the guidance see: Parton, N. (2011) 'The Increasing Length and Complexity of Central Government Guidance about Child Abuse in England: 1974–2010', Discussion Paper, University of Huddersfield, Huddersfield (unpublished). Online at: http://eprints.hud.ac.uk/9906/3/The_Increasing_Complexity_of_Working_Together_to_Safeguard_Children_in_EnglandJune101RevisedOct10.pdf (Accessed 5 May 2016).

94   The Police are regulated by Police and Criminal Evidence Act 1994 c.60 (PACE).

95   c.22.

96   Anderson *et al.* (n. 27), p. 105.

97   Local Government Act 2000 c.22. Similarly abuses of the Regulation of Investigatory Powers Act 2000 c.23 by local government undermine Anderson's assumptions about local government behaviour. See: Oates, J. (2008) 'Local Council Uses Snooping Laws to Spy on Three-year-old: Spying Laws Used to Check School Applications', *The Register*, 11 April. Online at: www.theregister. co.uk/2008/04/11/poole_council_ripa/ (Accessed 18 April 2016).

98   [2013] EWHC 416 (Admin) (13 March 2013).

99   HM Government (2015) (n. 3).

100   Children Act 1989 c.41.

101   Ibid., ss.43 (1)(a)(b) and (c).

102   HM Government (2015) (n. 3).

103   *South Glamorgan County Council v W & B* [1993] 1 FLR 514, decided in relation to an Interim Care Order application.

104   Child Assessment Orders last for a maximum of seven days, but are not appropriate when an EPO is a more suitable course of action. Under s.43(1)(3) a court may treat the application as an application for an EPO under s.44. Under s.43(8) a child can refuse to be assessed if they have sufficient understanding to make an informed decision. The threshold for granting the Order is comparatively low: under s.43(1)(a) it is 'reasonable cause to suspect' that a child may be suffering or likely to suffer significant harm that is required rather than belief. Information generally available to families about the nature and purpose of s.43 Order is limited. For example, the Children's Legal Centre state the purpose of the Order is to 'allow social services to talk to the child and decide whether any further action is needed'. They advise compliance because 'a refusal to co-operate . . . may indicate there is something to hide'. They consider it is more likely that social services will move directly to an EPO under s.44 rather than use s.43. See: Children's Legal Centre online at: www.childrenslegalcentre.com/OneStopCMS /Core/CrawlerResourceServer.aspx?resource (Accessed 20 September 2011), p. 4.

105   See s.44(b)(ii) and (c)(ii) and (iii) Children Act 1989 c.41.

106   In, for example: Parton, N. and Martin, N. (1989) 'Public Inquiries, Legalism and Child Care in England and Wales', *International Journal of Law and the Family* 3: 21–39. Online at: http://lawfam.oxfordjournals.org/content/3/1/21.full.pdf (Accessed 18 April 2016).

107   Per Mr Justice McFarlane in: *Re X: Emergency Protection Orders* [2006] EWHC 510 (Fam) paras 52–3.

108   *T v W (Contact: Reasons for Refusing Leave)* [1996] 2 FLR 473; *Stray v Stray* [1999] 2 FLR 610 and *S v Oxfordshire County Council* [1993] 1 FLR 452, all of

which concern the requirement for reasons to be given in relation to decisions concerning children.

109 Masson, J.M., Winn Oakley, M. and Pick, K. (2004) *Emergency Protection Orders: Court Orders for Child Protection Crisis, Executive Summary*, School of Law, Warwick University, funded by the NSPCC and the Nuffield Foundation. Online at: www.nspcc.org.uk/Inform/publications/downloads/EPOsummary_wdf48088 .pdf (Accessed 11 March 2011). In 2010, there were 1,350 EPO applications and 1,030 granted, from Table 2.4 of: Ministry of Justice (2011) *Judicial and Court Statistics 2010*, published 30 June 2011, revised July 2011, p. 51. Online at: www.justice.gov.uk/downloads/publications/statistics-and-data/courts-and -sentencing/judicial-court-stats.pdf (Accessed 19 May 2016).
110 *X Council v B (Emergency Protection Orders)* (2005) 1 FLR 341.
111 *Re X: Emergency Protection Orders* (2006) EWHC 510 (Fam).
112 *X Council v B (Emergency Protection Orders)* (2005) 1 FLR 341, paras 15 and 16.
113 Ibid., paras 1 and 2.
114 Harris-Short, S. and Miles, J. (2007) *Family Law: Text, Cases and Materials*, Oxford University Press, Oxford, p. 971.
115 Children Act 1989 c.41, s.46.
116 Masson *et al.* (n. 109), p. 2.
117 S.46(9), although they have to do what is reasonable to safeguard and promote the child's welfare.
118 Masson *et al.* (n. 109).
119 As this is a police power, not an application that must be made by the local authority. Masson, J.M. (2005a) (n. 66).
120 Dame Elizabeth Butler-Sloss (1988) *Report into the Inquiry into Child Abuse in Cleveland 1987*, July, Cmd 412, HMSO, London.
121 HM Government (2015) (n. 3).
122 Devine and Parker (n. 32).

5 Paradigms, policy and policing

State practices of referral and assessment are underpinned by a variety of theories derived primarily from child welfare and psychology. Child protection and safeguarding is designed from a welfare perspective which prioritises interventions and children's rights over privacy and wider justice concerns. However, the relationship between the State and its citizens can be considered from other perspectives, including justice, civil liberties and power relations. Considering the processes from other perspectives could focus on the experience of the child and also on the experience on the child's family, and other subjects of the system. This includes the child's parents, other children, the wider family and anyone else suspected of significantly harming a child. The position of parents is particularly difficult as they may have both been accused of causing significant harm to their child, one parent may have been accused but the other may not have been, neither parent may have been accused but a third party may have been, and one or both of the parents may have been accused of not protecting their child from harm from another source. Alternatively, there may have been no allegation at all but the family finds itself referred and assessed in order to receive services. This very complex matrix of possibilities has to be fed through an assessment process. The dual role of the investigators to assess need whilst considering risk makes the role of the social worker extremely complex.

Existing studies into State processes have identified phenomena in relation to how social workers make their decisions. Dingwall *et al.* identified the 'rule of optimism' in relation to social work investigation, which noted that social workers operated more comfortably within the welfare framework than the policing framework, erring on the side of finding that a family needed support as opposed to policing.[1] This could be considered a type of confirmation bias, which refers to the seeking or interpreting of evidence in ways that fit existing beliefs, expectations or a hypothesis.[2] Evidence that does not fit the expected or wanted result is filtered out, and confirmatory evidence is prioritised. It is well recognised that confirmation bias could be a problem in, for example, police investigations where a view is formed that a suspect is guilty.[3] However, it could equally be a problem in social work where social workers are either inclined to apply the rule of optimism and assume that all evidence points to the need for support, or to take a risk adverse approach where evidence to support an allegation of abuse is prioritised over other explanations. If the latter is the case, it suggests that a major change has occurred in social work attitudes in working with families since Dingwall *et al.*'s study.

Smith's work into schema seeks to explain how processes of investigation can make it increasingly difficult for a subject of investigation to remove themselves from it.[4] In modern social work, this exemplifies the dilemma of families who are subject to a referral: the new continuous assessment model is so focussed on the starting point being the identification of 'signs', whereby hidden meaning is inferred from children's behaviour, that it is extremely difficult to see how a family can easily remove itself from being an object of State interest. If the 'sign' does not produce sufficient evidence for abuse to be concluded to have occurred, it may very likely be concluded it is an indicator of need. It is therefore very difficult for a family to remove itself from the system altogether. From a starting point where signs are *de facto* evidence of 'something' all behaviours could be construed as pointing towards the 'something'. In terms of finding a way of understanding how this thinking may be inherently embedded within social work assessment, Smith's schema provides a useful model.

Smith's schema: exploring the 'fractured lens'

The original concept of schemata is linked to reconstructive memory.[5] Schemata refers to the processes by which information is filtered through the 'lens' of the observer to provide evidence to support a proposition, and to reject evidence that does not support it. Smith's investigation of schema explains how evidence is not objective: it is understood and classified according to the prior schema that is in operation. Thus, the 'lens' can become fractured.

Bartlett conducted a number of experiments to demonstrate how this operates.[6] By presenting participants with information that was unfamiliar to their cultural backgrounds and expectations and then monitoring how they recalled these different items of information, Bartlett was able to establish that individuals' existing schemata and stereotypes influence not only how they interpret 'schema-foreign' new information but also how they recall the information over time. His findings demonstrated that participants transformed details of stories in such a way that it reflected their cultural norms and expectations. In other words, the 'lived actuality' described in the story was processed and understood in line with their schemata. Bartlett's work demonstrates that long-term memories are constantly being adjusted as our schemata evolve with experience.

Much of what we remember is an adjusted and rationalised narrative that allows us to think of our past as a continuous and coherent string of events. This 'fractured lens' of understanding operates even though it is probable that large sections of our memory are irretrievable to our conscious memory at any given time. This phenomena is also a type of confirmation bias.[7] New information that falls within an individual's schema is easily remembered and incorporated into their worldview. However, when new information is perceived that does not fit a schema, other phenomena may be observed. The new information can be ignored or forgotten, or assimilated into the schemata.

Logically, new information would be assimilated, but this does not tend to happen because heuristics[8] are unconsciously applied: most everyday situations do not require much effort to understand because a heuristic, or 'automatic processing', is all that is needed. Through the use of heuristics, people can quickly organise new perceptions into schemata and act effectively without effort. Habitual use of heuristics provides a 'shortcut' to thought, and action, so as to prevent detailed questioning of events that objectively viewed could fail to fit the schema.

Smith's example examines what happens when a group of observers are led to believe a subject is mentally ill.[9] Once this is accepted, the observers construe all the behaviours of the subject as evidence of mental illness. The desire to fit events into this framework dominates thinking. The heuristic, or 'shortcut', of being able to categorise all the behaviours of the subject in this way mean the observers do not have to put mental effort into alternative explanations or examine exactly what behaviours are indicative of mental illness, and why.

Use of a heuristic saves time and makes new information easy to process, but it can influence and hamper the uptake of new information. This can lead to either a rejection of valid information or a revision of new information to fit the existing schema. Discourse that does not fit the dominant view can be reclassified in this process, which is why it takes time for new ideas to be understood and accepted; the mental structures of beliefs that use heuristics help save time and effort in thinking, but do not lead to challenge of the dominant belief. Schema can refer to processes or 'schemes' that are used in which 'lived actuality' is translated by the observers to lead to the outcomes the schema intends. These processes are implicit, not explicit, and can be observed in the assessment process of social services.[10]

Smith's approach in 'K is Mentally Ill: The Anatomy of a Factual Account'[11] provides explanation of how this operates. She is informed both by Foucault and by feminist theory, both discourses are principally concerned with power imbalances.[12] She considers:

> The conception of discourse used here originates with Foucault in whose work it defines an assemblage of 'statements' arising in an ongoing 'conversation', mediated by texts, among speakers and hearers separated from one another in time and space. The notion of discourse displaces the analysis from the text as originating in writer or thinker, to the discourse itself as an ongoing inter-textual process.[13]

She intends her concept of discourse to be placed 'in the context of Foucault's archaeology'[14] and explains the movement of the individual subject into a system as 'having the same force as structuralism in displacing the subject or reducing her to a mere bearing of systemic processes external to her'.[15] Her point being that once an individual has been classified as 'Other', all narrative and action generated by the Other is in danger of being construed as evidence to support a theory. This process occurs via a filtering though the heuristic. Evidence is extracted from the discourse of the Other to reinforce 'Otherness'. For example, a reason cited within child protection and safeguarding decisions for keeping a family under surveillance and subject to interference is the denial of the parents that abuse has occurred, or that need exists. This is seen as 'refusal to take responsibility' or a sign of 'denial' (in the psychiatric sense of denial of reality). The 'truth' is assumed to be derived from the referral itself and the decision to assess. For this reason the exercise of State power needs to be very carefully balanced against private rights. Smith explains:

> The various agencies of social control have institutionalised procedures for assembling, processing, and testing information about the behaviour of individuals so that it can be matched against the paradigms which provide the working criteria of class-membership.[16]

She identifies various stages through which a subject must pass, and constructs them into a methodology that can be used more widely to examine how discourse operates in the schema of State agencies.[17] When applied to targeted interference into private family life through the type of assessment carried out by social services, the process by which a family becomes the 'subjects' and finds their discourse restated through the 'fractured lens' of the schema is evident. This reinforces the need for appropriate safeguards and controls to ensure State powers are balanced appropriately with private rights.

Smith's schema (see Figure 5.1) shows how an account of events (the circumstances surrounding a referral) is entered into an organisational process, where

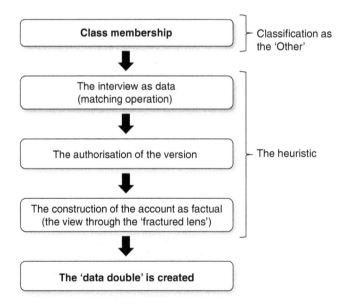

Figure 5.1 Smith's schema.

the data is articulated within the parameters of professional discourse. This discourse passes through the key stages of analysis.[18]

In Figure 5.2 the assessment stages are reproduced beside Smith's schema to tie the stages of each process together.

The stages of the assessment procedures in 'child protection' and 'safeguarding' schema

Stage 1 – Class membership: moving from surveillance to targeted interference – the referral

The first stage of Smith's schema mirrors the initiation of the assessment procedure following a referral, which may arise via a child being observed as failing to fulfil the prediction models of development, through the need for services, neglect, parental insufficiency or injury, or to have suffered 'child abuse'.[19] There were 657,800 such referrals in 2013/14.[20]

Class membership transfers families from a population comprising all families to a smaller class of referred families. This moves the family into the assessment process. Smith identifies the threshold for class membership as 'a definite rule must have been broken or a norm deviated from'.[21] A referral, put simply, is a suspicion that an individual, in this case a parent, has broken a societal rule, or 'norm', concerning the welfare of children. This could occur deliberately, through an inability to adequate provide for the needs of their child or failure to ensure an environment with an acceptably low level of risk. In such situations the family and its members

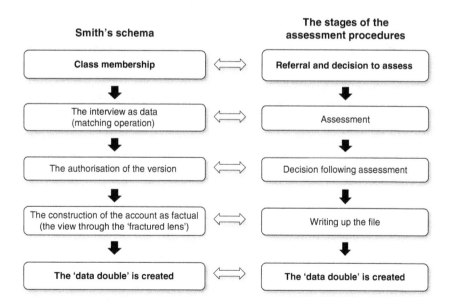

Figure 5.2 Mapping the assessment procedures.

become subjects of the system. However, the assessment process goes further than Smith's criteria of a 'definite rule' that has been broken: it requires assessment on 'reasonable suspicion' of significant harm, not on 'fact'. The parameters of the 'definite rule' is thus unclear: terms such as 'child abuse', 'safeguarding', 'concern', 'risk' and 'need' are not clearly defined. The plight of the subject within the schema who should not be there is not addressed, other than an assumption they reach a 'dead-end' in the process and progress no further. In modern safeguarding this may mean the outcome is recorded in terms of a need for early intervention. Recording a 'wrong' decision to refer is very unlikely to occur.

When receiving a referral, a local authority must translate the incoming data via a written account leading them to decide whether they 'have reasonable cause to suspect that a child who lives, or is found, in their area is suffering, or is likely to suffer, significant harm'.[22] Or is in need because:

(a) he is unlikely to achieve or maintain, or to have the opportunity of achieving or maintaining, a reasonable standard of health or development without the provision for him of services by a local authority . . .
(b) his health or development is likely to be significantly impaired, or further impaired, without the provision for him of such services; or
(c) he is disabled.[23]

At this stage 26 per cent[24] of referrals are not deemed suitable for any investigation but are kept as recorded data.

The subjects of those referrals, therefore, cannot be said to form part of the class membership. The remaining 74 per cent of referrals are considered to pass the threshold; they pass to the assessment stage of the procedures where a continuous assessment should be undertaken. There is an anomaly between procedure and practice at this stage: in theory all referrals should progress through the assessment process so that the family can be categorised as either not requiring any further action or requiring a level of interference either via 'services', further assessment or litigation.[25] This does not happen in practice as many families referred into the system on the basis that they are considered to possess the characteristics of 'class membership' do not progress further.

Following the referral a choice is made by social workers whether to investigate it or merely to note the call, record it onto relevant databases, notify any other agency who will have contact with the family[26] and take no further action. If no further action is taken, the parents may have no knowledge of this referral, although *Working Together to Safeguard Children* has generally encouraged consent to be sought prior to it being made:

professionals should seek . . . to discuss any concerns with the child and family and, where possible, seek their agreement to making referrals to local authority children's social care, *this should only be done where such discussion and agreement-seeking will not place a child at increased risk of suffering significant harm.*[27]

'Increased risk' assumes there is always some degree of risk. Where a referral will be made anyway there is a coercive element to 'agreement'.

Regardless of whether consent is sought or not, the referral and its circumstances will be recorded, stored and circulated to a large number of individuals and organisations with whom a family will have contact in relation to their children. At the early, decision-making stage where a 'no further action' decision will occur, the process of making this decision incudes information sharing in order to enable the local authority to reach its conclusion. This suggests information will be recorded by other agencies about the existence of the referral in order to justify disclosing information about a family. The existence of Multi-Agency Safeguarding Hubs (MASHs) is of concern in this context as discussions about whether to proceed can be made after information sharing has already occurred. This turns the referral itself into an information sharing gateway.

As part of the decision about whether to investigate further a social worker may contact all agencies with whom the family have contact to inform them of their decision. It is partly via this mechanism that circulation of a referral takes place, as for example a school, a GP, a health visitor, a hospital treating a child, a child minder and the parents' employers[28] may all be contacted to help in this decision-making process and to alert them to its existence. An entry may be made on List 99, now referred to as the 'Barred List' in relevant cases.[29] The 'vetting and barring' service also affects this category of family.[30] The Criminal Records Bureau (CRB) and the Independent Safeguarding Authority (ISA) have merged to become the Disclosure and Barring Service (DBS). CRB checks are now called DBS checks.[31]

Until 2013, after a decision to take no further action, paragraph 5.156 of *Working Together to Safeguard Children* stated in relation to record keeping that:

> Where a child has been the subject of a section 47 enquiry which did not result in the substantiation of referral concerns, his or her record should be retained in accordance with agency retention policies. These policies should ensure that records are stored safely and can be retrieved promptly and efficiently.[32]

The 2013 version of *Working Together* does not include this. It can be assumed that records are not destroyed irrespective of the outcome.

In addition to the local authority's records other organisations who may have been contacted in order to inform the decision-making process will keep their own records. It may therefore be the case that a family is unaware of a referral, whereas every organisation with whom they come into contact in respect of their child does know. The Information Sharing Proposals critiqued by Anderson *et al.*[33] concerned the drive towards profiling 'high risk' families for the purpose of predicting and preventing abuse that has not yet happened. Anderson *et al.* were concerned about the invasion of privacy, unlawfulness and potential consequences for families. They did not consider data collection and sharing was without adverse consequence.[34]

It would be naïve to imagine that agencies aware of a referral about a family would not be hyper-vigilant in their future dealings with them. A referral has at least this effect, as all agencies are primed to be risk adverse in relation to referring children. If a family is oblivious to what is happening then it could be argued they have not been directly harmed by it. However, equating knowledge with harm is not necessarily a reliable measure of harm, although it is one measure of it. The blurring of allegations and notifications of children thought to be in need into the catch-all phrase 'referrals' leaves any family facing uncertainty remaining about them if it is not explicitly clear that there is no allegation of child abuse or any parental insufficiency. If an allegation is able to be substantiated this may be reasonable. If not, it leaves families vulnerable. If all the interactions a family has with government agencies are primed to believe the parents may be abusing their child, or unable to adequately address their child's needs, parental contact with these agencies may be fraught, or cease altogether. Differences in the way agencies interact with them could cause harm, distress and alienation. The notification of a 'child in need' may also be perceived as stigmatising.

There are 174,000 referrals from the 2013/14 data which do not progress at all.[35] The family is not informed by the local authority that the referral has taken place, and therefore has no opportunity to address it. These referrals must be presumed to be the weakest in substance as social services do not proceed as far as an assessment.[36] This stage is therefore the stage where a family is entered into the system and is subject to an increased level of surveillance either with or without their knowledge via the recording of the referral. The bureaucratic procedures begin at this stage and professional discourse is produced which interprets the 'lived actuality' described by Smith within the framework of a theorised discourse.

The 'definite rule' phrase highlights the problem with the child protection and safeguarding system; there is a presumption that for a referral to be made there must be some need, risk or actual abuse: '. . . definite rule must have been broken, or a norm deviated from'.[37] The inherent point Smith makes here is that, in order for a referral to be made in the first place, there will be an assumption that a 'definite rule must have been broken, or a norm deviated from' (as opposed to a mistaken or unfounded referral, whether deliberate or accidental).

Gibbons *et al.* identify a problem with the threshold criteria for substantiation of child abuse and child protection conferences. They note that procedures are vague in respect of the threshold criteria and state that 'there were differences between the practices of different authorities'.[38] In their study they try to create a composite measure of the need for protection. The stigma created by a previous referral can be observed here as they state, *inter alia*, that a risk factor in a case of an allegation of child abuse is 'at least one previous investigation for abuse or neglect'. They indicate that where this is the case such families are more likely to be retained in the system. In other words, once cast as the 'Other' parents are unable to free themselves from stigma even where 'no further action' is the outcome of the first referral.[39]

Smith describes the use by government agencies of assumed 'knowledge', which explains why a previous referral would be used as evidence of future risk. There is an assumption that families will only be entered into the system in genuine cases, rather than by mistake or by accident. The schema provides an explanation of the type of bureaucratic discourse that operates in relation to the 'fractured lens' of State agencies. This discourse replaces a common sense approach that a referral may occur for a variety of reasons, ranging from reports of genuine abuse to referrals that are mistaken or inappropriate.[40]

In summary it is questionable as to whether it is acceptable to circulate allegations that suggest a parent would harm a child (a morally repugnant act in people's minds) but to give the parent no knowledge of what has been alleged or any process through which they are able to exonerate themselves. In relation to children 'in need' it is far from clear that this is not also stigmatising.

Stage 2 – The interview as data: the assessment procedures

The second stage concerns the enquiries that will be made in the course of assessment. Prior to 2015 these enquiries started with the Initial Assessment, which could lead to the longer Core Assessment. Assessments known as continuous assessments now incorporate both. S.47 Children Act 1989 states that 'the authority shall make, or cause to be made, such enquiries as they consider necessary'.[41] There is a statutory duty on health and education services to co-operate in the assessment procedures, which takes precedence over the privacy of the family and its members. The sharing of information after a referral is made is fundamental to the operation of the procedures.

Assessment relies upon dialogue with the subjects through interview. Smith identifies that the interview:

> is not being viewed as an account from which we are trying to infer back to what actually happened. The effect of questions is not merely to generate information. The difference between questions in different forms is not merely that some yield more and others less information. The form of the question tells the respondent what sort of work [he or] she is being asked to do. It asks her [or him] to operate on [his or] her knowledge, experience, *etc.* in a particular way.[42]

Smith concludes the interview is not an objective process, and can be restated as a 'matching operation, to find from [the interviewer's] own experience an instance . . . which can be properly matched against criteria of class-membership assumed to be known at large'.[43] The assessment by the local authority will be undertaken by a social worker, who will bring to the interview his or her professional understanding of child abuse, risk and need. The interview starts from the concern that there are problems that need to be addressed. His or her role is to look for instances of sub-standard parenting as well as specific examples of behaviour that can be matched against the referral.[44] This explains the disparity between the social worker's schema of 'matching' and the complaints of parents that they are 'guilty until proven innocent'.

In the year ending 31 March 2014, 483,800 families were subjected to Initial Assessment; of those 170,600 also underwent a Core Assessment.[45] All these families have become subjects of surveillance, interference and tutelage through discussions and decisions made about them. At this point of progress through the system, production of records concerning the transfer of the 'lived actuality' to professional discourse and data operates through the opening of a case file and the collection of data from other 'agencies' concerning the family.

This stage relates to the second stage described by Smith where the interview as data is used. Smith describes a matching operation against the criteria of class membership assumed to be known to be at large.[46] The size and prevalence of the class membership is informed by the NSPCC's prevalence estimates. The local authority social services department will interview the family concerned, marking the start of the matching operation. This is fundamental to all stages of the assessment procedures. The social worker will try to ascertain whether it is possible to find 'from [his or her] own experience an instance . . . which can be properly matched against criteria of class-membership assumed to be known at large'.[47] The family is potentially subjected to the disciplinary gaze of the criminal justice system whether or not police action is taken as the:

> [p]olice are notified as soon as possible where a criminal offence has been committed, or is suspected of having been committed, against a child . . . the police retain the opportunity to be informed and consulted, to ensure all relevant information can be taken into account before a final decision (to prosecute) is made.[48]

In practice, the member agencies of the Local Safeguarding Children Board[49] (LSCB) will all be 'informed and consulted' but this does not mean that action will be taken by each member body. Social services take the lead in the assessment procedures and the information relayed back to the police will inform a decision over whether further police involvement is necessary. The assessment procedures include information sharing with other member agencies of the LSCB who will process and keep the data generated by this process. In practice, unless there is clear and serious indication of criminal activity, social services will conduct the investigation as they are the body with the statutory requirement to do so.[50]

The family, now professionally constructed as a 'case', is subjected to a system of professional discussion and analysis during the assessment from which they are excluded.[51] Subjected to a high level of forensic surveillance via visits from social workers and associated data collection, families can only be realistically subjects of the assessment, not active partners 'working with' social workers as suggested by HM Government.[52] When considered in the context of Smith's schema, *Working Together to Safeguard Children*[53] can be seen to operate from an initial premise that child abuse, or the risk of it, is being concealed.

Smith describes this stage in terms of how a particular version of events is authorised through the investigation. Smith recognises that the use of the schema highlights how alternative versions are likely to be missed as they do not form part of the schemata but notes '[I] take it as axiomatic that, for any set of actual events, there is always more than one version that can be treated as what has happened.'[54] She highlights the dichotomy between logically recognising that first-hand events (lived actuality) must be capable of more than one interpretation, and theoretically recognising that professionals using schema view events through a 'fractured lens' where one discourse (or interpretation) dominates.

Stage 3 – Authorisation of the version: writing up the file

Smith's schema is concerned with 'construction of the fact', concerning what she describes as instructions in texts that tell the reader how it should be read. It is the construction of the 'professional' account that determines the outcome. Thus, the lived actuality is reduced and categorised:

> It is the use of proper procedure for categorizing events that transforms them into facts. A fact is something that is already categorized, already worked up to conform to the model of what the fact should be like. To describe something as a fact, or to treat something as a fact implies that the events themselves – what happened – entitle or authorize the teller of the tale to treat that categorization as ineluctable.[55]

Assessment is concluded with 'writing up' (the construction of an account) from which a decision is made. The subsequent decision about what to do with a child is informed by the writing up but regardless of which outcome is decided the assessment procedures are concluded by this act. However, this process has been shown to be unclear. There is no research specifically on this point relating to the English system; however, in relation to the similar US model, Robin concluded that 'in none of the eight sample authorities was it policy routinely to record the outcome of investigations'.[56] This in itself is concerning, but Smith makes a different and more conceptual point. Her concern derives from understanding that once data is recorded it is assumed to be factual, something that can be relied upon. This is an important issue in relation to how social work accounts of the assessment process are written up and read as the wider debate over whether there is or is not 'anything outside the text' that has been ignored in relation to the assessment procedures. Dominant 'risk assessment' discourse has reduced the writing up to an exercise of categorising parents. There are a number of powerful factors that can be observed in this stage of the process.

If an assessment is approached from a biased start, data may then be interpreted in a biased way, and may be used to fit the 'truth' that is assumed to be known. In this stage of the schema, Smith describes a process of entrenchment of views. She explains that, once a version is authorised, the construction of the account as providing objective, factual 'truth', which cannot be challenged, occurs.

This part of the schema separates the 'lived actuality' of the real events from the narrative that arises from them. The plurality of viewpoints in the telling of any given set of facts is important. There is no one account of how things happen, and to describe an event as a 'fact' confers upon it an assumption that it has already been objectively assessed as such. Smith explains:

> If something is to be constructed to be a fact, then it must be shown that proper procedures have been used to establish it as objectively known. It must be seen to appear in the same way to anyone.[57]

Smith clarifies this, detailing that:

> The account provides the reader/hearer with an itemised and specific account of . . . character and behaviour. The reader/hearer is thus apparently given an opportunity to judge for [him- or] herself on the basis of a collection of samples of the behaviour . . . from which [an individual] constructed the fact [in question].[58]

In order to do this, 'facts' must be constructed:

> The construction of a fact involves displaying that it is the same for anyone and that their recognition of it as a fact is based on direct observation, is constrained by the nature of the event itself, and is not constrained by a hearsay construction.[59]

This is an objective standard. Once a version of events has been accepted as 'fact' it will be recorded and repeated as such. Returning to the point of entry into the schema *before* subjective interpretations were applied becomes increasingly complex and difficult the further through the schema the actors move. This helps to explain why parents being assessed by social services complain of encountering increasing resistance to their version when they logically expected that the observable evidence that their children are not being abused or have unmet needs during their time under observation would suffice.[60]

The more complex point inherent within this part of the schema is the (often unconscious) use of encoded data within texts. Smith argues that hidden 'instructions' can be found within texts that lead the reader of the text to come to the conclusion pre-ordained by the author of the text. Such instructions, she states, mean that:

> The reader/hearer thus knows at the outset how this collection of characterological and behavioural description is to be interpreted. If the collection is viewed as a problem, then we have been told what the solution is. The problem presented by the account is not to find an answer to the question . . . but to find that this collection of items is a proper puzzle to the solution.[61]

Once the 'instructions' within the text are complied with by the reader of the text the version decided upon becomes 'authorised' (concluded as being fact). From this, decisions are made.

The important points to note about the procedures are the lack of clarity over consent requirements at any of the stages, the absence of any clear way out of the system for a family and the absence of restriction to specific investigation of the substance of the referral. Once the referral is in the system, the family progresses through various investigative stages that are assumed to occur without any need for a specific stage where informed consent is sought. The assessments are then used to inform progression further through the system. There is a danger that this becomes a self-reinforcing process with a pre-determined outcome.

Child protection and safeguarding policies of referral, assessment and early intervention are reliant on risk assessment. The consequence of a 'wrong assessment', where serious abuse is missed, is the start of a different set of bureaucratic procedures involving external scrutiny via public inquiries and Serious Case Reviews. These are intended to provide a mechanism for learning if incorrect assessments of risk are made.[62] These mechanisms only operate where abuse is present and missed; there is no mechanism for review where no abuse is present but is assumed to exist. The difference in consequence for the social worker therefore between entering a false negative as opposed to a false positive, however, is striking.[63] There is an impetus not to miss a false negative so as to avoid adverse consequence, both to individual social workers and managers and the local authority in question.[64] It is difficult to see where the motivation is to avoid a risk adverse approach.

As there is no specific reason to avoid a false positive finding it is not difficult to envisage the organisational and personal importance of ensuring there are a minimum of false negatives. A necessary part of this may be recording false positives as high risk 'just in case' to avoid adverse consequence. This is an unsatisfactory position not least because of the risk of harming families by the exercise of unnecessary State power. This also explains the unacceptably high number of families who formerly fell into the category of 'unsubstantiated' following a child abuse investigation and would now more likely be categorised as requiring early intervention.

Stage 4 – Construction of the account as factual: decision following assessment – the view through the 'fractured lens'

The fourth stage of Smith's schema mirrors the stage of assessment which is concerned with the decision of the local authority at the end of the assessment procedures. The options are whether to proceed to a child protection conference and beyond, take no further action or treat the family as containing a child in need.[65] It is generally the case that if evidence of child abuse is found, a case should proceed to a conference.

The data shows anomalies in outcomes. There are cases where an investigation has revealed evidence of child abuse but a conference does not then occur, and from Gibbons *et al.*'s research it can be inferred that this may occur in 15 per cent of cases.[66] She does not explain why. The latest[67] numbers indicate that 65,200 families (9.9 per cent) who are subject to a referral proceed to a conference, following which 59,800 (9.1 per cent) lead to some form of registration for a Child Protection Plan (CPP) or care proceedings.[68]

A small proportion of these may include situations where a child is deemed to be no longer at risk of continuing harm regardless of whether child abuse could be said to have occurred but the remainder are unaccounted for and will contain a number of cases where children are deemed to be 'in need'. Where a child has been shown to have suffered significant harm but the risk of a recurrence is considered minimal a conference may not be considered necessary. Also, where an investigation has revealed no evidence to substantiate that any 'abuse' has occurred and there is no risk or need, no further action may be possible once the discourse becomes more legal in nature and hard evidence is required.

There is an inherent assumption within the procedures that only families with 'problems' would be referred at the outset. It is assumed that children who are referred, if not actually abused, are at least children who can be defined as being 'in need' that require services to prevent neglect turning into abuse.[69] There is no mention of families who are not in need of services and whose children are not at risk of significant harm. This gives parents an uphill battle if it is already assumed they fall into one of these categories and there is no safeguard to prevent them being categorised as high risk simply because a referral has been made.

The data double

The data double refers to the process where the file is written up with conclusions, and a data identity is created over which the subject has no control. In a broad context the use of data to create an identity has become a largely accepted part of modern life, going far beyond George Orwell's vision in his novel *Nineteen Eighty-Four*, published in June 1949. The embedding surveillance and creation of the data double has been described as:

> a convergence of what were once discrete surveillance systems to the point that we can now speak of an emerging 'surveillant assemblage'. This assemblage operates by abstracting human bodies from their territorial settings and separating them into a series of discrete flows. These flows are then reassembled into distinct 'data doubles' which can be scrutinized and targeted for intervention. In the process, we are witnessing a rhizomatic leveling of the hierarchy of surveillance, such that groups which were previously exempt from routine surveillance are now increasingly being monitored.[70]

In the context of social work assessment, the creation of the data double occurs following the abstraction of facts, opinion and conjecture during the assessment. The information is put together and written up to create an 'identity' or 'profile' of the family and its members. Haggerty and Ericson explain 'The result is a decorporealized body, a "data double" of pure virtuality.'[71]

Decisions about what should happen following the assessment are made on the basis of the data double. The problem for families and particularly for those accused of significantly harming a child is that the data may or may not be accurate. The inability to change data or even to have access to it in order to challenge it is a significant hurdle for the data subjects, who are nevertheless affected by its existence. In terms of describing the data double, the intention may be for the data to be an accurate portrayal but in reality it may not be:

> And while such doubles ostensibly refer back to particular individuals, they transcend a purely representational idiom. Rather than being accurate or inaccurate portrayals of real individuals, they are a form of pragmatics: differentiated according to how useful they are in allowing institutions to make discriminations among populations. Hence, while the surveillant assemblage is directed toward a particular cyborg flesh/technology amalgamation, it is productive of a new type of individual, one comprised of pure information.[72]

The primary problem this creates for social work and legal decision making attempting to advance a welfare agenda is the potential inaccuracy of the data double.

Conclusion: implications for assessment

Examination of the assessment process using Smith's schema has provided a means by which the impact of assessment can be understood in the context of a discourse that is not welfare dominated. What is evident from this examination is that recognition of more than one version of events in respect of assessment is important for a balanced system. A balanced view taking into account alternative versions of events should be evident throughout the process rather than any assumption that if the parent is 'in the system' there must *de facto* be a problem. Smith explains this in her assertion that investigations should not start from a view that there is a single valid version of events. The same event can be construed in different ways. She states:

> I take it as axiomatic that, for any set of actual events, there is always more than one version that can be treated as what has happened . . . this is because social events or facts . . . involve a complex assembly of events occurring in different settings, at different times, sometimes before collections of persons.
>
>   Further, the moment of actual observation is at that point where the consciousness of the individual is, and any process of assembly from the past can no longer draw on the total universe of resources which were at successive 'moments' present to the observer. For these reasons, an endemic problem must always be how a given version is authorized as that version which can be treated by others as what has happened.[73]

It is also evident that within the assessment schema, social work interpretation plays an important role. Dingwall *et al.* consider the way in which parents' accounts of events are interpreted and understood by social workers.[74] They observe that judgements are made by social workers of parents' moral characters and truthfulness.[75] The account of the parents may be taken seriously or discounted, depending upon the perception by the social workers of the truthfulness and character of the person making the statement. For example, in one case they looked at, a family connection by marriage was observed to be sufficient for inferences about character to be drawn.[76] What is clear is that once cast as 'the Other' it is incredibly difficult for a parent to extricate themselves from this role and be considered blameless.

Having carried out an assessment, social workers make a decision based upon their opinion that the family contains a child 'in need',[77] a child 'at risk of significant harm',[78] a child with 'safeguarding' issues[79] or a child who does not require interference. This involves a process of 'authorisation of the version' in which the local authority has to make a judgement about what they think is happening. If there are conflicting accounts they have to authorise one version over others, creating the dominant discourse that will be applied from this point onwards and will decide the fate of the family in relation to the family and future social work interaction.[80] This places the role of assessment as central to all future interactions and decisions concerning a family: it will be the data double that professionals will engage with as the 'truthful version' from this point onwards. The implications are considered in Chapter 6.

Notes

1 Dingwall, R., Eekelaar, J. and Murray, T. (1984) *The Protection of Children: State Intervention and Family Life*, Blackwell, Oxford.
2 Nickerson, R. (1998) 'Confirmation Bias: A Ubiquitous Phenomenon in Many Guises', *Review of General Psychology* 2(2): 175–220.
3 Ask, K. and Granhag, P. (2005) 'Motivational Sources of Confirmation Bias in Criminal Investigations: The Need for Cognitive Closure', *Journal of Investigative Psychology and Offender Profiling* 2: 43–63.
4 Smith, D. (1990) *Facts, Texts and Femininity: Exploring the Relations of Ruling*, Routledge, London, published previously as Smith, D. (1978) 'K is Mentally Ill: The Anatomy of a Factual Account', *Sociology* 12(1): 23–53, as discussed below.
5 Bartlett identified the concept of schema (Bartlett, F. (1932) *Remembering: An Experimental and Social Study*, Cambridge University Press, Cambridge) from studies of memory he conducted in which subjects recalled fictional details of stories (false memories). He suggested that memory takes the form of schema which provide a mental framework for understanding and remembering information. Mandler and Rumelhart developed the schema concept (Mandler, J. (1984) *Stories, Scripts, and Scenes: Aspects of Schema Theory*, Erlbaum, Hillsdale, NJ; Rumelhart, D. (1980) 'Schemata: The Building Blocks of Cognition' in: Spiro, R., Bruce, B. and Brewer, W. (eds) *Theoretical Issues in Reading and Comprehension*, Erlbaum, Hillsdale, NJ). Schemata have also received significant empirical support from studies in psycholinguistics. For example, the experiments of Bransford and Franks (Bransford, J. and Franks, J. (1971) 'The Abstraction of Linguistic Ideas', *Cognitive Psychology* 2: 331–50) involved showing people pictures and asking them questions about what the story depicted; people would remember different details depending upon the nature of the picture. Schemata are also considered to be important components of cultural differences in cognition (Quinn, N. and Holland, D. (1987) *Cultural Models of Language and*

Thought, Cambridge University Press, New York). Research comparing novice and expert performance suggests that the nature of expertise is largely due to the possession of schemas that guide perception and problem-solving (Chi, M., Glaser, R. and Farr, M. (1988) *The Nature of Expertise*, Erlbaum, Hillsdale, NJ).

6 Bartlett (n. 5); Brewer, W.F. and Treyens, J.C. (1981) 'Role of Schemata in Memory for Places', *Cognitive Psychology* 13: 207–30.

7 Confirmation bias is explained for example in: Gilovich, T., Griffin, D. and Kahneman, D. (eds) (2002) *Heuristics and Biases: The Psychology of Intuitive Judgment*, Cambridge University Press, Cambridge; Harmon-Jones, E. and Mills, J. (1999) *Cognitive Dissonance: Progress on a Pivotal Theory in Social Psychology*, American Psychological Association, Washington, DC; Jones, E.E. and Harris, V.A. (1967) 'The Attribution of Attitudes', *Journal of Experimental Social Psychology* 3: 1–24. For explanation of the fractured lens see: D'Cruz, H. (2001) 'The Fractured Lens: Methodology in Perspective' in: Horsfall, D., Byrne-Armstrong, H. and Higgs, J. (eds) *Researching Critical Moments*, Butterworths, Oxford. D'Cruz explains the 'fractured lens' in the context of Foucault, Bordieu and Potter, feminist sociology, identity politics and critical discourse analysis, which she uses to investigate meanings and identities in reports of social workers reporting on 'child abuse'.

8 See for example: Kiss, O. (2006) 'Heuristic, Methodology or Logic of Discovery? Lakatos on Patterns of Thinking', *Perspectives on Science* 14(3): 302–17; Jaszczolt, J. (2006) 'Defaults in Semantics and Pragmatics', *The Stanford Encyclopedia of Philosophy*, Stanford University, Stanford, CA; Minsky, M. (1985) *The Society of Minds*, Simon and Schuster, London. And for an interesting discussion of confirmation bias, schemata and heuristics in relation to its application to the computer sciences see: Tae, K. and Lee, S. (2006) 'On Cognitive Role of Negative Schema' in: Gavrilova, M. (ed.) *Computational Science and its Applications*, ICCSA Part II, International Conference 2006, Glasgow.

9 Smith (1990) (n. 4).

10 See for example the following articles which have used 'K is Mentally Ill: The Anatomy of a Factual Account' to examine aspects of social work: most recently, Kendell, E. (2011) 'Reasoning Processes in Child Protection Decision Making: Negotiating Moral Minefields and Risky Relationships', *British Journal of Social Work* (March), 1–20. Online at: http://bjsw.oxfordjournals.org/content /early/2011/03/09/bjsw.bcr012.abstract (Accessed 4 May 2016); concerning social work assessments of mothers: Urek, M. (2005) 'Making a Case in Social Work: The Construction of an Unsuitable Mother', *Qualitative Social Work* 4(4): 451–67; psychiatrists' assessments in relation to insanity: Roca-Cuberes, C. (2008) 'Membership Categorization and Professional Insanity Abscription', *Discourse Studies* 10(4): 543–70; and concerning 'needs assessment' forms in mental health settings: McLean, C. (1998) 'Organising Madness: Reflections on the Forms of the Form', *Organisation* 5(4): 519–41.

11 Smith (1978) (n. 4).

12 An examination of feminist theory is not attempted in any detail, but for a general explanation of the complex strands of feminism see for example: Holub, R. (undated) *Feminist Theory*, University of California, Berkeley. Online at: http:// learning.berkeley.edu/holub/articles/Femthe2.pdf (Accessed 4 May 2016); Mitchell, J. and Oakley, A. (eds) (1986) *Reflections on Twenty Years of Feminism*, Pantheon Books, New York; and Mitchell, J. and Oakley, A. (eds) (1986) *What is Feminism?*, Pantheon Books, New York, which includes a discussion of 'child abuse'.

13 Smith (1990) (n. 4), p. 161.

14 Ibid.

15   Ibid.
16   Ibid., p. 12.
17   This methodology is drawn from Kitsuse, J. (1962) 'Societal Reaction to Deviant Behaviour', *Social Problems* 9(3): 247–56.
18   Smith (1990) (n. 4), pp. 12–51.
19   A 'referral' can be made as a result of observed evidence, suspicion, by mistake or by a deliberately false assertion.
20   Department for Education (2014) SFR24/2014, *Characteristics of Children in Need: 2013–14*, 29 October, p. 1. Online at: www.gov.uk/government/uploads /system/uploads/attachment_data/file/367877/SFR43_2014_Main_Text.pdf (Accessed 20 May 2016).
21   Smith (1990) (n. 4), p. 15.
22   S.47(1)(b) Children Act 1989 c.41.
23   S.17(10) Children Act 1989 c.41.
24   Calculated as: (number of referrals {minus} number of Initial Assessments {minus} number of continuous assessments) {divided by} number of referrals, using 2014 data from Department for Education (n. 20). NB continuous assessments were phased in during 2013/14 in some local authorities. Prior to 2013/14 a referral deemed to be above the threshold for assessment would have had an Initial Assessment, followed by a Core Assessment if serious enough. Post 2013/14, referrals above the assessment threshold were subject to a continuous assessment, which replaced the two-stage assessment process.
25   See the discussion in Chapter 2 concerning the public health model of primary, secondary, tertiary and quaternary levels of interference.
26   HM Government (2010) *Working Together to Safeguard Children*, April, TSO, London, paras 5.156–5.160; Anderson, R., Brown, I., Clayton, R., Dowty, T., Korff, D. and Munro, E. (2006) *Children's Databases: Safety and Privacy, A Report for the Information Commissioner*, Foundation for Information Policy Research, Bedfordshire. Online at: www.fipr.org/press/061122kids.html (Accessed 1 January 2016).
27   HM Government (2010) (n. 26), p. 140 (original emphasis).
28   This list is not exhaustive and is compiled from scrutiny of *Working Together to Safeguard Children*. The emphasis in 'child protection' and 'safeguarding' is on record keeping and communication between agencies and this occurs at every stage of the process, including the decision to investigate stage.
29   Originally this was administered under s.142 Education Act 2002 c.32. This Act was repealed by s.20 of the Safeguarding Vulnerable Groups Act 2006, c.47. Now implemented by the Independent Safeguarding Authority (ISA). The information held on the list is passed by the Secretary of State to ISA. Under s.21 ISA hold an up-to-date 'barred' list which they must produce on request to the Secretary of State for Health.
30   The Vetting and Barring Scheme was established from the Safeguarding Vulnerable Groups Act 2006, c.47. This legislation follows the Soham murders of Holly Wells and Jessica Chapman. The vetting and barring scheme was operated by the criminal records bureau and a new body created by the legislation: the Independent Safeguarding Authority (ISA).
31   Disclosure and Barring Service Checks.
32   HM Government (2010) (n. 26), p. 184.
33   Anderson *et al.* (n. 26).
34   Ibid.
35   Continuous assessments were trialled in 2013/14 in some LAs, whilst Initial Assessments and Core Assessments were used in the remaining LAs. The procedures imply all families undergoing Core Assessments would have had an Initial

Assessment first, so the 174,000 estimate is the number of cases referred which had neither an Initial Assessment nor a continuous assessment in the period. See: Devine, L. and Parker, S. (2015) *Rethinking Child Protection Strategy: Learning from Trends*, Working Paper, Centre for Legal Research, Bristol Law School, UWE, Bristol. Online at: http://eprints.uwe.ac.uk/25258/ (Accessed 28 February 2016).

36 Department for Education (2010) *Statistical Release OSR24/2010: Referrals, Assessments and Children who were the Subject of a Child Protection Plan (Children in Need Census – Provisional) Year ending 31 March 2010*, TSO, London. Online at: www.education.gov.uk/rsgateway/DB/STR/d000959/OSR24 –2010.pdf (Accessed 1 May 2016).

37 Smith (1990) (n. 4), p. 15.

38 Gibbons, J., Conroy, S. and Bell, C. (1995) *Operating the Child Protection System: Studies in Child Protection*, HMSO, London, p. 55.

39 Ibid., p. 5.

40 Smith (1990) (n. 4), pp. 12–51.

41 S.47(b) Children Act 1989 c.41.

42 Smith (1990) (n. 4), p. 16.

43 Ibid.

44 This is the gist of s.47 Children Act 1989 and the *Working Together to Safeguard Children* procedures for assessment. The point of the assessment process is to look for 'child abuse', whether it matches the specific allegation which has triggered the assessment process or a more general observation during the assessment process.

45 See: Devine and Parker (n. 35).

46 Smith (1990) (n. 4), p. 16.

47 Ibid.

48 Department of Health (1999) *Working Together to Safeguard Children*, TSO, London, p. 24.

49 Local Safeguarding Children Board member agencies are health authorities, health trusts, the police and children and young peoples' services departments.

50 Under the provisions of s.47 Children Act 1989 and procedural framework in: HM Government (2015) *Working Together to Safeguard Children*, HMSO, London.

51 This is because they are subjects of the system, not part of the decision-making team. They will be informed of decisions made about them, not involved in making the decisions themselves.

52 See discussion in this chapter concerning construction of the subject as 'the Other'.

53 HM Government (2015) (n. 50).

54 Smith (1990) (n. 4), p. 24.

55 Ibid., p. 27.

56 Robin, M. (1991) *Assessing Child Maltreatment Reports*, Haworth Press, New York, pp. 47–8.

57 Smith (1990) (n. 4), p. 27.

58 Ibid., p. 30.

59 Ibid., p. 28.

60 Ibid., p. 30. For a recent case example see: *AD and OD v United Kingdom* (App No 28680/06) [2010] ECHR 340.

61 Smith (1990) (n. 4).

62 Formerly, public inquiries were frequently called if a false negative was entered that resulted in a fatality. More recently 'Serious Case Reviews' are conducted. There is no adverse consequence for local authorities or the government in respect of a false positive outcome.

63 Throughout the book reference to 'false negative' and 'false positive' is made to describe situations that can be categorised according to the Taylor–Russell typology. See: Taylor–Russell diagram in: Sarewitz, D., Pielke, R. and Byerly, R. (eds) (2000) *Prediction: Science, Decision Making, and the Future of Nature*, Island Press, Washington, DC. Online at: http://books.google.co.uk/books?id =O0nxEU-dcAUCandpg=PA45anddq=%22Taylor+Russell+diagram%22andhl=e nandsa=Xandei=mu0_T5fcO4Sd8gPNtMWmCAandredir_esc=y#v=onepagean dq=%22Taylor%20Russell%20diagram%22andf=false (Accessed 13 May 2016). In this instance the term 'false positive' is used to denote cases that have been through assessment but have failed to identify risk which is later shown to be present, particularly in cases of child fatalities.
64 Most notably the dismissal of Sharon Shoesmith from her role as Director of Children's Services for Haringay following the death of Peter Connolly in 2007.
65 Under s.17 Children Act 1989 c.41.
66 Department of Health (1995) *Child Protection*, pp. 68–70, based on research by Gibbons *et al.* (1995) *Operating the Child Protection*.
67 Available numbers to 31 March 2014. Devine and Parker (2015).
68 Calculated from the 2008/9 figures, a proportion of referrals, i.e. 43,700/ 547,000 x 100 = 8.0 per cent and 37,900/547,000 x 100 = 6.9 per cent.
69 Department of Health (1995) (n. 66), p. 25.
70 Haggerty, K. and Ericson, R. (2000) 'The surveillant assemblage', *British Journal of Sociology* 51(4): 605–22, December, p. 606.
71 Ibid., p. 611.
72 Ibid., p. 614.
73 Smith (1990) (n. 4), p. 24.
74 Dingwall *et al.* (n. 1), pp. 167–79.
75 See for example ibid., pp. 152–65, section entitled 'A Battering Walsh'.
76 Ibid., pp. 211, 164.
77 S.17 Children Act 1989 c.41.
78 S.47 Children Act 1989 c.41.
79 S.11 Children Act 2004 c.31.
80 This is where the genealogy (origin) of the dominant discourse that will then be applied to decisions concerning the family can be observed. This is the point where the greatest risk occurs in relation to faulty decision making to create either a false positive or a false negative, although the consequences for families and social workers for each are not equal (see discussion in Chapters 4 and 5). The use of confirmation bias through schema and its heuristic may increase the danger of a false positive and diminish the objectivity and accuracy of subjective decision making during the assessment process. See for example: Kendell (n. 10).

6 The balance of State power and private rights

Considering the protections for children and parents

Having considered the means by which children are referred for assessment and how the assessments operate, this chapter assesses the balance between the support and protection intended to be given to children via referral and assessment against the potential harm caused by the processes. This issue is contentious as the discourse from welfare narratives prioritises the State's duty to protect children arguing this is more important than any potential harm caused by its attempts to do so. Legal narratives, however, must address these issues to ensure the law adequately strikes the right balance between the competing rights, responsibilities and interests of the parties involved. This includes consideration of the difficult question of how best to balance the competing and potentially irreconcilable differences between the respective rights of children and the rights, duties and responsibilities of the State, parents and others affected by the State's processes. If there are insufficient inbuilt controls and remedies there is an imbalance between State powers and private rights.

Attempting to erase the problems created by parental ownership of children by replacing it with parental responsibility may have created different problems if the methods of policing this responsibility are too intrusive, unsuccessful or cause harm. Longitudinal data, collected since the inception of the Children Act 1989 shows that the vast majority of families referred beyond the surveillance stage to the assessment stage do not proceed further as no evidence of abuse is found.[1] In the majority of referred cases the State either takes no action at all or completes an assessment, after which it may offer services or offer nothing. A very small minority of cases are sufficiently concerning to merit progression to the next stage of the process, a child protection conference and formation of a Child Protection Plan.[2] The important question in these scenarios is whether referral and assessment are adequate to protect children from parental harm, and also to protect parents from State harm.

Moving from 'ownership' to 'responsibility': disowned children and the burden of policing parental responsibility

Modern child welfare policy and practice derives from the belief that the State should have a role in protecting children from significant harm.[3] By incorporating the legal concept of parental responsibility, the Children Act 1989 sought to remove any notion that children are owned by their parents. The rationale was that ownership of children can leave them unprotected from parental maltreatment and from being treated as mere possessions. The current legislative position therefore does not vest ownership of children with either parents or the local authority but instead confers *responsibilities* on parents and *duties* upon the local authority. Alongside the responsibilities and duties lies the right of parents and the State in certain situations to make decisions concerning a child, including where they will live and with whom. Parents assume this responsibility unless or until the State considers it should intervene to fulfil its statutory duty and take over such decisions.

Children have thus moved from a status analogous to privatised possessions of their parents, particularly fathers, to a position where parents either automatically acquire or can apply to acquire parental responsibility for them.[4] Having acquired this responsibility, parents must discharge their responsibilities to the satisfaction of the State in order to avoid it intervening in order to discharge its duties. Parents must therefore be policed in the discharge of their responsibilities to the standard considered acceptable by the State. This standard can change over time. If parents fall below this threshold, or if a third party is trained to look for and report certain signs in children's behaviour or if the family falls into a risky category, they will be subject to referral. Although it was not the intention of the legislation, this could be construed as leaving children in a position analogous to nationalised State possessions.[5] The concept of parental responsibility[6] as opposed to rights has arguably left parents free from State interference only as long as they comply with State ideals, set out in *Every Child Matters*,[7] expanded with the Children Act 2004's expansion of safeguarding and the growth of policies of rationed early intervention, triggered by referral based on signs and risk indicators.[8]

However unpalatable the notion of ownership of children may be, children are *de facto* unable to care for themselves so finding an appropriate legal framework to support their wellbeing is important. Although the removal of the concept of ownership may protect children from excesses of harmful parental behaviours it could also be argued that the same framework may create the lack of a sense of adequate safety within families or the freedom from over-intrusive State policies envisaged in the Children Act 1989. If parents do not feel some sense of autonomy they may become insecure and uncertain in their parenting, and children may not feel secure within the family unit. There is a difference between intervening in a robust and timely manner to protect children from significant harm, as opposed to imposing potentially damaging coercive intervention at a very low level. This is why achieving the right balance is critical.

Alongside the negative aspects to the sense of children belonging to their parents it could be argued that the concept of ownership fosters a sense of belonging and security. It is where that concept is abused that problems begin. Children feeling safe, secure and knowing they belong to a family historically underpins family welfare policy and much psychological literature in relation to attachment and security. It is known that uncertainty for a family subject to State assessment is not conducive to children's or parent's feelings of safety, security and empowerment. In cases of significant harm, the rationale of intervention is to remove parental notions of autonomy, but what of parents who are requesting support, or find themselves referred into the system at a very low level based on signs their children are apparently exhibiting?

In a psychological and a practical sense, a lack of a sense of ownership is seen as analogous to a failure to take responsibility. 'Taking ownership' is used to mean 'taking responsibility' and being conscious of others' needs.[9] Social work assessment could be seen as undermining the ability of parents to demonstrate their responsibility for their children and is certainly an erosion of their autonomy at a very low threshold. These issues must be considered alongside the policy drive to intervene early. The ethos of consensual State support for families where it is needed is laudable, but the methods of delivery in the English system is inadequately considered and seems to have developed piecemeal through successive government policies as opposed to a considered move forwards. If law and welfare discourses are combined to find a more appropriate way to support families and to investigate suspected significant harm a new way to implement these aims must be found.

Under the present policy and statutory guidance, the State's statutory duties create the need to police parental responsibilities towards children to ensure compliance. The uncontrolled expansion of this has created the welfare/policing dichotomy in social work practice.[10] Children can be caught between these potentially competing responsibilities and duties. Where there are irreconcilable differences between the State and parents' views children can be argued to fall into the resultant 'gap' where the State and parents disagree on how they discharge their potentially competing obligations. In this position children are faced with potentially traumatic and stressful assessments with the associated family distress and uncertainty. The child in the middle of such a conflict faces uncertainty and is mostly powerless to stop action being taken by the State. This historical rupture[11] merits further examination as the aim of the Children Act 1989 was to create a framework where the State would not excessively interfere into private family life,[12] and only if significant harm or the risk of it was reasonably suspected.

Parents and children are permitted by the State to have a family life, but this permission can be withdrawn if a parent is deemed to have abrogated their parental responsibility towards a child. It is therefore important for parents to be aware of parenting practices the State deems acceptable: parents are in a frightening and uncertain position if they disagree with a local authority in relation to child welfare issues particularly if they do not understand what is expected. Disagreements are made particularly difficult as a result of the lack of certainty over the definition of child abuse and its relationship to the legal threshold of 'significant harm'.[13] Once abuse is able to be equated with non-compliance, together with an increasingly bureaucratic set of ideals in relation to child rearing it is easy for large numbers of parents to be investigated for holding differing views on parenting, rather than for significant harm. Cultural and religious differences, values and practice are not acknowledged in the legislative framework so it may be difficult for families to know what a local authority expects at a low threshold of referral.

If removing a child into the care of the State ensured a better standard of care, the outlook for a child at this point could be considered to be improved. In reality, if a child is removed from their family their welfare is far from certain: the State does not have a record of discharging its acquired parental responsibility towards children well, raising questions over which is the 'lesser of two evils' for a child in distress. Children in State care ('looked after children') notoriously can suffer impaired life chances and outcomes.[14] Morgan observes the State makes 'a lousy parent'.[15] It is therefore questionable whether in at least some cases one type of maltreatment is substituted for another. This unsatisfactory situation even applies to those cases where life threatening or other very serious forms of maltreatment of a child by his parents can be substantiated, as for some children the harm they faced in State care proved serious, or fatal.[16] Child fatalities, regimes such as 'pindown' and physical and sexual abuse scandals have all occurred when children are already in the care of the State.[17] Considered together, these are serious issues that question the State's suitability and ability to police parents in the manner now required of it. Ironically if a parent exhibited a similar track record to that of the State it would not be left in charge of children if the same risk criteria were applied.

What is the legal and policy framework of 'child protection' and 'safeguarding' trying to achieve?

Since the Children Act 2004 it is more difficult to clarify what the legal and policy framework is trying to achieve. Not only is there a mixture of surveillance and intervention which mixes consensual and non-consensual practices, but safeguarding, which under the Children Act 1989 was mentioned in s.17 in relation to 'children in need' and in s.47 in relation to children at risk of 'significant harm', was expanded under s.11 Children Act 2004 to apply to all children, not just those falling into these categories. This increased duty on the State has resulted in a system more inefficient than before due to its rapid expansion. As a result, surveillance, referral, assessment and intervention has become a costly and increasingly privatised growth industry.[18] It is of note that the Children Act 1989 pre-dates the Human Rights Act 1998, whereas the Children Act 2004 was implemented post. Despite the broad aim of the Human Rights Act 1998 to protect *inter alia* individual freedoms and privacy, the more recent legislation is more intrusive than the position prior.

The type of harm that the consolidating Children Act 1989 envisaged and aimed to prevent was influenced by public inquiry findings into child deaths as a result of parental or State harm. S.11 of the Children Act 2004 requires State agencies generally to ensure that their 'functions are discharged having regard to the need to safeguard and promote the welfare of children'.[19] This needs to be read in conjunction with the additional provision in s.12 of the Children Act 2004 to enable the State to collect and retain data about all families. S.11 of the Children Act 2004 seems to cross the Rubicon from selective non-consensual interference in respect of suspected 'significant harm' and consensual interference in respect of children 'in need' to potential assessment of any family to 'safeguard and promote welfare', facilitated by mass surveillance of all families via data collection and retention in databases.[20]

Whilst there is nothing inherently wrong with the notion of all children's welfare being considered by the State, this goes much further, creating a duty to intervene at a very low and unclearly ascertained level. There is a danger that because this expansion targets all children it could become a compliance mechanism enabling local authorities to socially engineer suspected parental non-compliance with government ideals of child rearing via a social policing framework. This goes much further than the provisions of the Children Act 1989. The current policy framework presents a Panopticon ideology of continual surveillance, mediating family behaviour and increasingly controlling family structure, in much wider circumstances than was previously enabled.

Commentators such as Wrennall[21] and Anderson *et al.*[22] argue that the current framework also furthers the government's e-Government agenda in relation to dataveillance via the Children Act 2004 Information Database (England) Regulations 2007[23] enabling data collection and retention in respect of all children in the form of databases, and by extensive and intrusive assessments. As a consequence, the 'net' referred to by Gibbons *et al.* in their 1995 government report on how the child protection system was operating[24] is now cast very widely, potentially causing unnecessary harm and distress to families in addition to the benefits of State interventions for a limited number of those referred.[25]

In addition to the obvious concern that a system overload causes some serious cases to be missed in a mass of referrals, there is also growing concern from a number of voluntary organisations, MPs[26] and Peers[27] that this is facilitating undesirable referrals including those that are simply mistaken, unfounded or malicious and which are being pursued to the detriment of families. This issue requires urgent review to ascertain the scale of the problem and the adequacy of redress and remedy for families in this situation.

A mix of intended and unintended results can therefore be identified from the complex strands that make up the nature and purpose of the legal framework.

By what mechanisms is the legislative and policy framework trying to achieve its purpose?

In attempting to prevent the most serious types of harm, the legislation has expanded to create an extreme of paternalistic surveillance and intervention, affecting all families. In 2007 Munro and Parton considered England was moving towards a highly intrusive system. Since then the position has become even more extreme:

> England is in the process of introducing a mandatory reporting system, not based on any notion of child abuse but on the basis of 'a cause for concern', which is not defined in the legislation. The new policy of 'safeguarding' children has a much wider remit than just 'protecting' children from abuse or

neglect. It aims to ensure all children reach the government's 'preferred out-comes' in terms of achievement at school, health, and behaviour.[28]

Taken together there are several important, linked legal issues that represent the key factors contributing to the loss of balance in the system:

- *The move from the concept of 'ownership' to the concept of parental responsibility and State duty:* Parents are *responsible for children* and the State is *responsible for policing parents* to ensure they discharge that responsibility. If, in the opinion of the local authority, they do not, the State has a duty towards children. A middle ground should be found to re-establish appropriate safeguards and controls to prevent unwarranted State intervention, whilst ensuring that cases of genuinely reasonably suspected significant harm are able to be robustly and quickly investigated and action taken.
- *The State's duty to police parental responsibility:* Policing is undertaken by mass surveillance of all families, including by all State agencies, most of whom are not experts in identifying any form of child abuse. Their training may be as minimal as completing an online training package bought from an unregulated private, profit-making provider. The use of personal data, including identification of 'signs' in children's behaviour and the inclusion of risk predictors on databases places all families under the surveillance umbrella. This creates a very low threshold for referral.
- *Public inquiries and serious case review findings, usually following a child fatality, have been used as evidence that the system should be strengthened:* This has translated into a policy drift towards more intrusive powers of surveillance and interference, but there is no evidence of critical analysis of the suitability of this policy response, to be applied to all children. This does not seem to be either resolving the problem of serious, fatal abuse or providing an appropriate framework for balanced social work response.

The issue of families harmed by State surveillance and assessment

The question of State harm gathered momentum as a serious issue in the millennium when several high profile child abuse criminal cases and concerns expressed to MPs prompted a House of Lords debate in 2001. A balance between protecting children and protecting families from harmful State intrusion was discussed.[29] Issues such as pressure put on children to corroborate suspicions of abuse and the interpretation of information by social workers in cases involving complex medical issues were raised.[30] A further issue of particular concern was the number of referrals in relation to middle class families on the grounds that their children had unexplained medical symptoms, for example Autism, ADD or CFS/ME,[31] described as analogous to 'the witch hunts of previous centuries'.[32]

One of the most uncomfortable points discussed highlighted the impact of referral and assessment upon children. It was noted that 'If there has been no abuse the child's world can still be torn apart. A child is damaged by a false accusation.'[33] This is an uncomfortable issue for proponents of the argument that the need to protect children should override concern for parents. Apart from direct trauma to a child, the evidence of the severity and longstanding nature of the harm to parents cannot be conducive to any notion of family stability. Children whose parents are traumatised and fearful will inevitably be affected. The Labour Government's response in the debate was expressed via the Parliamentary Under-Secretary of State, Department of Health (Lord Hunt of Kings Heath):

> We owe a great debt of gratitude to the noble Earl, Lord Howe. I can tell him that neither I nor the Government underestimate the impact of false accusations of child abuse on individuals, parents and the children concerned.[34]

What is particularly interesting about this debate is the simplicity of the issue that was raised, and the complexity of the responses to it. Earl Howe opened the debate thus:

> My concern can be summed up very simply. It is that alongside the worrying numbers of genuine child abuse cases there is a parallel cause for worry, which is that many innocent people are being wrongly accused of child abuse and whose lives in consequence are being turned upside down without due justification.[35]

His concerns were met with arguments that, rather than achieving a balance, there should be a prioritisation towards assessment and investigations over any harm caused to families:

> My Lords, the noble Earl, Lord Howe, is to be thanked for raising this important issue. There are, indeed, cases of false accusations of child abuse. They are distressing and they can be very damaging to families. We are therefore right to be concerned. Nevertheless, I am bound to say that we would do well to be even more concerned about our failure as a society to respond adequately to the issue of abuse itself. Adults can speak for themselves; children often cannot.[36]

The Bishop's response is an example of a common reaction to concerns over harm caused by unwarranted referral and assessment. Argument that the focus should be on preventing child abuse rather than supporting parents suggests an 'either/or' stance and inference that debate about the latter should not occur. Rather than seeing one type of harm as an inevitable by-product of attempts to prevent another type of harm, it seems more reasonable to balance the two positions, a position advocated by Lord Lucas in the same debate when he answered the Bishop of Birmingham by advocating a middle ground:

> I do not share the impression that I gained from the speech of the right reverend Prelate that, because of the horrendousness of the effects of child

abuse, we should pay any less attention to the horrendousness of the effects of false accusations of child abuse.[37]

A middle ground is appropriate to achieve a balance between State powers and private rights. There is need for an integrated debate about the State's role in protecting children on the one hand, and the State's role in harming families on the other. Whilst harm is acknowledged, its seriousness is minimised and considered to be a price worth paying to protect the vulnerable. However, the issue is important, and the debate necessary. If the outcome of debate is that harm may sometimes be an inevitable consequence the discussion should move naturally towards consideration of how the harm can and should be mitigated via remedies, with a view to ensuring sufficient remedy is available. If the outcome is that the balance should be reassessed, reform must be considered.

The concerns were triggered over the rise in the 1990s of controversy over MSBP[38] and SIDS.[39] These phenomena caught middle class families in the net of surveillance and referral. The system was not designed for such families. This was the first time that families who may have felt more empowered to complain spoke out about what they considered to be grave injustices. These phenomena were linked to the rise of medical theory in relation to child protection that led to the evidence of Professor Sir Roy Meadow in relation to cases such as those involving Sally Clark and Angela Cannings.[40] Once identified as leading to miscarriages of justice in the criminal justice system such evidence highlighted the more general concern about the trauma and harm caused to families in relation to cases that progressed to the family and criminal courts, and also those that did not progress beyond assessment.

Earl Howe's debate, in October 2001, followed Sally Clark's conviction and unsuccessful first appeal, but took place before her second successful appeal[41] so the House of Lords debate was timely. *R v Sally Clark* and other related cases concerned the conviction of mothers killing their infant children. The convictions were quashed on appeal following concerns about the quality of the prosecution's expert evidence. The objective of the debate was to point out the need for protection as far as possible from false accusations with reference to malicious and vindictive individuals who make false accusations, but many of the points raised would equally apply to families where no malice is intended but concerns are simply mistaken for whatever reason. Regardless of how or why they were referred, families were described as 'terribly hurt' by the experience.[42]

Despite the growing weight of evidence of harm, refocussing and the Lords' concerns about the effect of allegations on children and families, this evidence of harm to families remained a marginalised discourse. In 2002 Claire Curtis-Thomas MP, Chairwoman of the All Party Group on Abuse Investigations explained to the House of Commons why she set up a group:

> I had hoped that reasonable argument might persuade people that there was something amiss here, but I failed dismally, in terms of getting anybody, Ministers or civil servants, to be remotely interested in this subject. And

there was another issue as well, which is, I had spoken to a number of people who had been instrumental in trying to change the processes within the criminal justice system, and they said to me, 'If you don't handle this well, all you'll get is a backlash from various structures within the criminal justice system, and, instead of seeking to want to improve their processes, they will seek merely to defend the processes as they currently exist.'[43]

Although the discourse was marginalised, interest in the issue was not insignificant. Harm was noted by the medical and the legal professions as well as within the social sciences. It was variously construed as a psycho-medical problem, a social problem, a legal problem and a power relations problem. Once parliamentary interest had raised the profile of the issues opportunities for debate opened. Legal discourse expanded to include suggestion that a false allegation and investigation was tantamount to a miscarriage of justice. For example, in 2004 Wrennall gave evidence to the All Party Group on Abuse Investigations describing false allegations as miscarriages of justice;[44] also in 2004 Munby made a similar observation in *Re B*.[45]

The discourse was expanded by Davies.[46] Davies, a criminologist, found herself suspected of child abuse when she sought medical attention for her son after he hurt his head having rolled off a sofa and fallen onto a carpeted floor. Her account is both academic and personal. She locates her experience in the discourse of power relations and victimology, describing the wide devastation to family members, including wider family[47] and describes the impact of being under investigation being such that 'it caused me pain and made me and my family frightened, worried and scared. It made us and left us feeling vulnerable, undermined, disbelieved and threatened, all of which are symptoms of exclusion, marginalization and powerlessness.'[48] She reports that a collaborative working relationship with social workers did not prevent her family from suffering. Fundamentally she frames the experience through the lens of secondary victimization[49] and power imbalance.[50] Davies comments on the way in which discourse is given weight during assessment, which is dependent upon the person rather than what is said, explaining that her 'evidence was of a lower status than that of professionals and there were rankings of professional evidence too'.[51]

To address these issues, acknowledgment that harm can be caused to families is important alongside specific consideration of:

(a) the controls and conditions that might be feasible with respect to *initiating* investigations, with particular regard to the position of adults who are left in a continuing state of uncertainty;
(b) the controls and conditions with respect to the *conduct* of such investigations;
(c) what controls over the *conclusions* should exist, having completed an investigation, including a mechanism for exoneration where appropriate; and
(d) whether, *following a conclusion* that there is no evidence of child abuse, in what circumstances, and to what extent, there should be a clear process of exoneration and an appropriate remedy for harm caused.

Defining harm

'Harm' is a term that can be defined equally as widely as the term child abuse. It is important to establish what is meant by harm in this context, its criteria and its parameters. Within which discourse should harm caused by excessive or unnecessary State processes be primarily located? It could be considered a medical, psychological, social welfare, legal, economic or a power relations problem. The list may not be exhaustive. Harm may be wider than that simply caused by the mechanical process of referral and assessment if there is inference of parental insufficiency, even in referrals relating to families' need for support. Questions such as how widespread is harm, and its impact on individuals, families, the community, the economy and the State have not been adequately addressed in the legislation or policy. Does it, for example, include potential harm to children who are in real danger but for whom there are insufficient resources as a result of unnecessary and damaging assessments and investigations? Luza and Ortiz observe that:

> while unwarranted interventions occur, the lives of children who are in genuine need for intervention are endangered. As the overburdened child protective (CP) worker allocates time to investigate an unfounded case, a child in serious danger is left waiting. In addition unsubstantiated accusations, with the traumatic investigations that accompany them cause much harm to innocent families.[52]

Harm can be considered in a broad, contextual manner including consideration of harm to society as a result of social exclusion caused by State practices.[53] Foucault's description of genealogy in relation to bio-power had a similar genus; it emphasised that regardless of the *intention* of a system, it is the *effect* that needs to be measured, as well as how far the system has achieved the intended effect.[54]

There is a large body of literature considering harm caused by the tertiary and quaternary stages of the procedures. This area is less contentious: the potential for distress and trauma caused to parents and children by the forced removal of a child are obvious even where there has been some evidence of neglect or ill-treatment. There is less literature that focusses on harm caused by the referral and assessment processes. This does not mean that harm does not occur, although how and why it does may be less apparent.

The remainder of this chapter considers the issue of harm in relation to unsubstantiated allegations and unfounded concerns. It is, of course, the case that harm can occur even where allegations are substantiated and concerns are well founded. In such circumstances, however, the primary concern must be the welfare of the child. Even in these cases if the objective is anything short of permanent severance then the problem of State interventions potentially causing further damage must also be considered as a welfare issue that could adversely impact the child and his or her family.

Unsubstantiated allegations and unfounded concerns

Families where there is later shown to be no abuse, risk or need but who are nevertheless entered into the system and assessed can suffer adverse consequences.[55] This category of family merits separate consideration because they are not the families for whom the system was designed. As the referral threshold is now so low this category can also include families who may require a low level of specific support, for example support if a parent is unexpectedly seriously ill, but find themselves unable to access services without referral and assessment.

The State has given little consideration or guidance in relation to how such families cope with the short and long-term aftermath. *Working Together to Safeguard Children*[56] does not address the issue despite evidence that the psychological impact is potentially devastating if the process is non-consensual, or if parents feel they cannot withhold consent. Although there is a wealth of academic literature and anecdotal material looking at individual cases, small cohorts or the immediate aftermath, there is no substantive, longitudinal research into this phenomena, nor is there any systematic attempt to consider the nature of the harm itself. Is it an illness, a state of mind, a social difficulty or maybe a combination? Prosser, for example, considered that identifying the meaning of trauma in the context of investigation is necessary for balance to be achieved:

> It is prudent to consider that in order for investigators of child abuse to achieve a balance between protecting children and damaging families, they need to be aware of the meaning of trauma for abused children and families wrongly accused.[57]

It is possible that the type and level of trauma could be considered in the context of medical discourse. However, the reasons why a diagnosis might be important and whether it would prove exclusionary should also be considered in such instances. Harm arising from severely shocking and traumatising life events have been categorised as PTSD[58] but harm caused by referral and assessment has not been included in this category, despite reporting of similar symptomology.[59] If it is the case that referral and assessment causes the same symptoms, perhaps these should be considered in the context of traumatic events. If they are having the same impact, then it is an important issue for consideration.

The identification and consideration of harm caused by State processes of child welfare is not a new phenomenon. Commentators have observed and reported on it for decades. It has consistently been identified as an issue of importance but seems no nearer to thorough investigation, debate and redress than it was when the Children Act 1989 was enacted. Refocussing may have caused all referrals to be assessed under the *Framework for Assessment of Children in Need and their Families*,[60] but this approach may have exacerbated the problem by increasing the number of families affected by comprehensive assessment, including risk assessment. The new continuous assessment which removes the distinction between the types of assessment is likely to further exacerbate this problem.

Although the problem of harm is frequently raised and explored in the literature, the majority of the literature simply notes and describes the phenomena. Other literature involves research findings, usually following investigation of the problem by interviewing families and looking at file records. In 1986 Pride noted concern about harm and identified wide, non-specific definitions of 'child abuse' as a contributory problem to the issue of harm, concluding that definitions of 'abuse were as vague as inadequate parenting skills, educational neglect, unspecified neglect, lack of supervision, emotional abuse or neglect'.[61] In the same year Besharov, the first director of the USA's National Clearinghouse on Child Abuse and Neglect (NCCAN),[62] addressed the issue of unfounded allegations in the USA based on data he had observed. Within the data he identified what he described as a 'flood of unfounded reports' in an article that broadly outlined the development of child maltreatment as a social issue from relative obscurity in the 1950s.[63] Further American findings were referred to by Oellerich, who considered the findings of the San Diego Grand Jury[64] which described the American system as inherently biased and unable to detect or correct its errors.[65] Some of the professionals involved with child welfare were categorised as 'child savers', harming children in their zeal to protect them, and devastating the lives of families.[66]

In England the *Report of the Inquiry into Child Abuse in Cleveland 1987* highlighted the damage that can be done to families.[67] The Children Act 1989 was drafted during this period when concerns were emerging about over-intervention and its effects.[68] Griffiths, for example, commented on the impact of an allegation concluding that:

> Being incorrectly suspected of abuse is a frightening, demeaning and potentially destructive position for parents to be in. Where suspected abuse is discovered to be unfounded, counselling should be offered to parents to help them to recover from the distress of the investigation and its aftermath.[69]

Here, the existence of harm is placed in a psychological discourse with the suggestion that counselling is an appropriate intervention in relation to recovery. However, in such circumstances counselling may be seen as merely another coercive and interventionist technique imposed on parents who cannot trust State agencies, particularly if parents do not feel they have been exonerated of wrongdoing or parental insufficiency.[70] Counselling will not help alleviate the continued stigmatisation of having an unsubstantiated allegation recorded as the process of incorrect categorisation interrupts the 'tacit contract with the State' described by Donzelot.[71] Contract relies upon mutual co-operation; misapplication of tutelage can interrupt that process. Counselling is unlikely to be sufficient to resolve this issue and seems an inadequate way for the State to discharge an obligation to affected families if it does not address the underlying reasons for the trauma.

A systematic investigation of 100 unfounded cases of suspected child sexual abuse was reported by Schultz in 1989. He made a list of recommendations, including the need for further research and investigation into the phenomena: 'More refined measures of subjective distress and disability for those falsely charged should become a future research priority for the university community or responsible private organisations or private practitioners.'[72] Schultz also recommended that 'compensation for the falsely charged and/or convicted should be instituted or made a part of current victim compensation policy'.[73] Ultimately, Schultz's approach is to place harm into a medical and psychological discourse. Schultz also identified that 'Being labelled an abuser may produce the personality characteristics which are later called the causes of child abuse.'[74] This idea is not developed so it is unclear whether Schultz is suggesting that this leaves the falsely accused at future risk of further allegation as a result of these personality characteristics, or whether it is simply an observation that dysfunction and alteration to personality is a type of harm that tends to occur.

In 1990 Richardson cited Besharov's data as raising a cause for concern[75] and ranks the issue of false allegations and their impact as important as child abuse itself. He refers to the power imbalance between the State and families, considering State agencies have a 'grave responsibility' in relation to the public and investigated families. Richardson's findings are that the State is capable of 'thoroughly abusing' families and children through investigation.[76] Jones also conceptualises harm as 'system abuse' and 'iatrogenic harm'.[77] Luza and Ortiz described it as 'The dynamic of shame in interactions between child protective services and families falsely accused of child abuse.'[78] They describe shame as 'an internal, subjective experience. The shamed individual sees himself as inadequate, inferior, worthless and defective. It affects the whole self – emotional, mental and physical.'[79] Shame is recognised to have a negative impact on mental health.[80] Such findings reinforce the location of harm in psychological and medical discourse.

Wakefield and Underwager's findings also place harm in a medical and psychological discourse. Having conducted a study of thirty families for the support group Parents against Injustice (PAIN), where allegations of 'sexual abuse' had been made,[81] they conclude all suffered post-traumatic shock. Their report also suggests counselling, suggesting that the type of counselling required by these families is unique and the closest model is that offered to victims of violence.[82]

Although less prevalent, discourse considering harm in a wide context includes consideration of the 'cost to the child, the person accused and society.'[83] Prosser's empirical research using PAIN's data concerning families who had approached them for help strongly contends that children who are the subject of unnecessary investigation become victims 'in a way that can be more damaging to them than suffering sexual abuse'.[84] Prosser includes 'financial ruin and lost jobs, families and marriages' in his evaluation of harm.[85] Behaviour consistent with a state of lasting high anxiety was noted, including children's fear of strangers[86] and obsessive retention of information relating to the experience.[87] Identification of these indicators of high anxiety contributes to the insights into 'harm'. He describes a 'film loop' effect, and contributes to the medical and psychological discourse by also noting 'loss of sleep, loss of weight, loss of sexual relationships between parents, anxiety and depression, mental breakdown and the need to work with a psychiatrist'.[88] Robin also conducted an empirical study but collected his data from social services files rather than from parents' accounts. He also notes concern about harm that links the *outcome* of assessment with harm as well as the assessment itself. He reported that it was not routine to record the outcome of investigations, concluding that 'considering the trauma such investigations can cause this does not seem to be good practice'.[89] This may be indicative of a lack of awareness in social work practice of the impact of an allegation kept on file particularly where there is no clear outcome recorded.

Of particular note is that harm to children is highlighted by several researchers. Jack's research refers to the harm suffered by children, finding that older children regret having disclosed their situation, although it is noted that this refers to harm suffered by children who have been removed from their families following assessment.[90] Parton *et al.* also comment about the effect on children, observing that, as a result of an investigation, '[n]ot only did the parents become alienated, angry and bewildered, but the children were not helped'.[91] Although much of this research concerns events that occur further on in the process it cannot be assumed that the early stages do not contribute to the harm. Cooper *et al.* report, for example, that a high proportion of abused children regretted having disclosed abuse, finding that 'children and families drawn into the child protection process frequently find the whole experience traumatic, and sometimes more traumatic than the abuse itself'.[92] Prosser made observations about one case from his larger study of families who had faced allegations of sexual abuse. Specific reference is made to the harm suffered by the child who was the subject of the investigation. She is described as being the most profoundly adversely affected member of the family, and at 9 years old 'hates doctors', is isolated, pulls out sections of her hair and suffers from severe depression.[93] The father's relationship with his daughter suffered as he was left feeling 'bitter' towards his daughter as a consequence of the experience.[94] Prosser also reports that the official response to their trauma was 'severely underestimated'[95] and recommends that more awareness of the trauma is needed and notes that 'it remains a sad indictment of society that no support or therapy is available even to those severely traumatised by wrongful accusations and that there is only very limited redress or compensation for families'.[96] Again, therapy is implied to be a possible solution to the problem, but compensation is also mentioned drawing on both medical and legal discourses.

In theory, a system premised on support for families as envisaged in s.17 would avoid these problems. However, Jones and Novak found that 'social workers feel and act like besieged gatekeepers to an inadequate and crumbling system of support; they have been pushed remorselessly towards practices of surveillance, monitoring and control'.[97] The article was written before the refocussing debate took place in the mid-1990s warning of the dangers of a punitive model of social work. Much of their work focusses on critiquing policies advocating personal responsibility, claiming that the needs of social work 'service users' can be attributed to their inclusion in minority groups who have traditionally been oppressed and marginalised by society rather than by failure of personal responsibility, or a combination of both.[98]

By the mid-1990s sufficient attention had been drawn to the issue of harm for government research to acknowledge the problem. In the UK a systematic assessment of the 'child protection' system was undertaken and presented in *Child Protection: Messages from Research*,[99] which concludes that 'a suspicion of child abuse has traumatic effects upon families.'[100] This meta-analysis concluded that 'all the studies confirm the sense of shock, fear and anger felt at the point of confrontation and the lingering bitter aftertaste'.[101]

In this assessment, harm was considered in both a narrow and a wide sense; although the effect on parents and children stopped short of being conceptualised within a medical discourse, alienation, distress and hardship were reported in relation to the parents, and acknowledged as making life difficult for children.[102] Wider harm is described as 'worsening family relationships, leading to recrimination, marital breakdown, economic hardship and sometimes homelessness; all severe setbacks to the child's quality of life'.[103] Since then there has been an explicit refocus of social work response to referral away from a 'child protection' investigation towards assessment of 'need'. This is not on the face of it unreasonable, and was perhaps an inevitable response to the problems that had been identified.[104] However, it assumes the cause of harm is an allegation and investigation, rather than a trauma response to State interference *per se*. The change in social work response was challenged in research questioning whether 'partnership ideals' and 'service delivery principles of the child welfare model' would have a fundamentally different impact on families to the 'child protection model' of social work response.[105] Also the lack of distinction between 'protection' and 'support' could lead to perception that all social work interventions are potentially hostile and harmful rather than interventions being perceived as primarily supportive. This not only puts families in a very difficult position, it also makes the task of social workers to reconcile their policing and welfare role within the same process virtually impossible.

The refocussing debate identified that harm is caused by the punitive, investigative model of social work involved in child protection investigations. However, the issues are complex as although an allegation of child abuse obviously has strong negative connotations, a referral in respect of need also could, and frequently does, imply parental insufficiency. The modern threshold of 'safeguarding concern' expands referrals to include general concerns about a child which may be impossible to easily establish as being correctly categorised as need or abuse. This is a sensitive issue particularly as there is a blurred boundary between need, risk and neglect. Regardless of how it is described, any allegation of wrongdoing or insufficiency that would lower parents' standing in the community could have adverse consequences, so it is insufficient simply to assume that, unless a serious allegation of abuse is made, the process is benign. Where no well-founded concerns are found upon assessment parents may still feel distressed and traumatised at the suggestion they are considered to be inadequate parents, if not actual child abusers. A generic referral system does not remove negative connotations but possibly exacerbates the problem, leaving all referrals subject to being interpreted as a negative comment on the standard of parenting in a family. Fear of stigma and a punitive social work response are powerful disincentives for families when deciding whether to engage with social workers.

Research findings also note that systems attempting to incorporate investigations and support usually fail to meet the dual goals[106] because 'technical redefinition of cases at point of referral may not fundamentally change the nature of social work processes'.[107] In other words although the assessment framework resemble an assessment for a child in need, social work responses still resemble those in child protection cases.[108] Spratt and Callan conclude that 'whilst the refocussing debate has promoted a reconstitution of child protection work as child welfare work, the concept of risk has continued to preoccupy social workers in their practice in child welfare cases'.[109] These conclusions suggest the core issues of harm caused by referral and assessment did not disappear with refocussing but simply increased the numbers affected. Dumbrill, for example, found that parents viewed services as 'inhumane'. He draws on previous research noting that:

> in-depth qualitative studies of parental experience . . . reveal parents viewing services as 'inhumane' (Diorio, 1992; Drake, 1994, 1996), parents being afraid of worker power (Anderson, 1998; Cleaver & Freeman, 1995; Corby, Millar, & Young, 1996; Diorio, 1992; Howe,1989; McCullum, 1995), and parents claiming to be misunderstood by workers and unable to correct these misunderstandings (Corby *et al.*, 1996; Fisher, Marsh, & Phillips, 1986).[110]

On the other hand Millar and Corby conducted research into whether post-refocussing assessment could be termed therapeutic. The study reported mixed conclusions. There was some limited consensus that assessment may have been therapeutic (presumably because it forced reflection) amongst families who had sought social work contact in the first place or who agreed they had significant problems (e.g. alcohol or drug abuse problems). However, families where assessment did not seem to be consensual did not find the process therapeutic.[111]

Conclusion: power imbalance and individual harm

Discourses of power relations explain why an assessment which is apparently agreed by some to be 'therapeutic' would be seen by others as 'inhumane'. D'Cruz's theoretical evaluation for example considers how preferred versions of knowledge and meaning may override or dismiss alternative meanings with particular consequences for parents and children during assessments. D'Cruz's conclusion is that medical, social and legal practices in relation to child abuse suspicions are not neutral but embedded in power relations.[112] This is founded in Foucaultian theory and further reinforces the concern that refocussing did not solve the problems of harm if it is caused by imbalanced power relations rather than a specific allegation. Further post-refocussing studies[113] describe families as being often 'devastated' and 'bewildered, betrayed and powerless' in studies where following investigation there was held to be little, or no, 'risk' and no evidence of 'abuse'.[114]

The wealth of available evidence highlights the serious and significant nature of the problem, regardless of the lens through which it is considered or the discourse in which it is located. The most dominant is the psycho-medical discourse suggesting harm is an intra-psychic issue which can be identified and treated. The discourse of power relations understands harm in the context of powerless children and families unable to prevent State interference without possibly raising suspicion that there is 'something to hide'. Family members become victims whose narrative is marginalised in favour of professional discourse.

Regardless of approach, the common theme in the research is a conclusion that harm is severe, long-lasting and could result in symptoms analogous to or amounting to PTSD, possibly caused as much by the power imbalance as by an allegation. It is significant that there is no change in the conclusions of research following refocussing; indeed there seems to be no meaningful perception of this change by affected families. This supports the argument that, rather than solving problems, refocussing has simply widened the 'child protection net' described by Gibbons *et al.*[115]

Examination of harm through these different lenses and discourses raises questions over how this harm should be researched, understood, categorised and addressed. Failure to do so leaves families and family members bearing the burden of their individual harm. Society will also bear the burden of this harm in a wider sense, including the impact of the interruption to families' relationship with State agencies.

Notes

1 Devine, L. and Parker, S. (2015a) *Rethinking Child Protection Strategy: Learning from Trends*, Centre for Legal Research, Bristol Law School, UWE, Bristol. Online at: http://eprints.uwe.ac.uk/25258/ (Accessed 1 January 2016).
2 Ibid.
3 The history and development of this position is explored in Chapter 1.
4 Part I, Children Act 1989 c.41, ss.2, 3, 4, 4ZA and 4A, deal with parental responsibility. Historically children were considered to be analogous to possessions, particularly of their fathers. Historically wives were similarly considered to be chattels of their husbands and could not own property (or children) of their own.
5 See for example discussion in: Bainham, A., Day Sclater, S. and Richards, M. (eds) (1999) *What is a Parent? A Socio-Legal Analysis*, Hart Publishing, Oxford.
6 Ss.2 and 3 Children Act 1989 c.41.
7 Chief Secretary to the Treasury (2003) *Every Child Matters*, Green Paper Presented to Parliament in September, Cm 5860, TSO, London. Online at: www.gov.uk /government/uploads/system/uploads/attachment_data/file/272064/5860 .pdf (Accessed 4 May 2016).
8 Devine and Parker (2015b) *Safer Children? Evaluating Child Protection and Safeguarding Training in Schools: An Empirical Study*, Centre for Legal Research, Bristol Law School, UWE, Bristol.
9 Particularly psychology, where it is argued that the psychological effect of 'owning' engenders responsibility and care towards the owned person/object /situation. It is also recognised in adoption research where pre-adoption

placements have been shortened on the rationale that if a parent does not feel a sense of 'ownership' towards the child they emotionally distance themselves for fear of hurt if the child is removed. The psychology of 'ownership' has been discussed in, for example: Rudmin, F.W. and Berry, J.W. (1987) 'Semantics of Ownership: A Free-Recall Study of Property', *The Psychological Record* 37: 257, where it was noted that the legal concept of 'ownership' did not necessarily coincide with 'culturally and behaviourally grounded notions of ownership'.

10   Devine, L. (2015) 'Considering Social Work Assessment of Families', *Journal of Social Welfare & Family Law* 37(1): 70–83. Online at: http://dx.doi.org/10.1 080/09649069.2015.998005 (Accessed 28 February 2016).

11   Foucault, M. (1961) *Madness and Civilization: A History of Insanity in the Age of Reason*, Routledge, London.

12   See: Dame Brenda Hale (2000) 'In defence of the Children Act', *Archives of Disease in Childhood* 83: 463–7. Online at: http://adc.bmj.com/content/83/6/463.full.pdf (Accessed 5 February 2016).

13   See for example the principles in: *R (on the application of S) v Swindon Borough Council and another* [2001] EWHC Admin 334. This states that duties following the suspicion of sexual abuse, or the risk of sexual abuse, overrode both the need of the applicant for certainty over his status to a recognised evidential standard and the effect of the continued suspicion and State interference into private family life.

14   See for example the explanation given by Morgan, including statistics in: Morgan, P. (1999) *Adoption: The Continuing Debate, Choice in Welfare No. 53*, The Institute of Economic Affairs, London, p. 22.

15   Ibid., p. xiii.

16   See for example the Dennis O'Neill public inquiry findings in: Sir William Monckton (1945) *Report by Sir William Monckton KCMG KCVO MC KC on the Circumstances which Led to the Boarding Out of Dennis and Terence O'Neill at Bank Farm, Minsterly and the Steps Taken to Supervise their Welfare*, Cmd 6636, Home Office, HMSO, London. And mentioned in: Cretney, S. (2005) *Family Law in the Twentieth Century*, Oxford University Press, Oxford; Cretney, S. (1997) 'The Children Act 1948 – Lessons for Today?', *Child and Family Law Quarterly* 359. See also the numerous sexual, physical and emotional abuse cases that have emerged in relation to how children are treated whilst in the care of the State and particularly: Sir William Utting (1997) *People Like Us: The Report of the Review of the Safeguards for Children Living Away From Home*, HMSO, London; Levy, A. and Kahan, B. (1991) *The Pindown Experience and the Protection of Children: The Report of the Staffordshire Child Care Inquiry*, Staffordshire County Council, Stafford; and Brannan, C., Jones, J.R. and Murch, J.D. (1993) 'Lessons from a Residential Special School Enquiry: Reflections on the Castle Hill Report', *Child Abuse Review*, HMSO, London, pp. 271–5.

17   Parton, N. (2004) 'From Maria Colwell to Victoria Climbié: Reflections on a Generation of Public Inquiries into Child Abuse', *Child Abuse Review* 13(2): 80–94.

18   Wrennall reports that in the UK the 'Total gross expenditure on children in care in 2007–08 was £2.19 billion' and that in 'the US, the Child Protection expenditure is estimated to be $11.2 billion' (1998 figures); Wrennall, L. (2010) 'Surveillance and Child Protection: De-mystifying the Trojan Horse', *Surveillance and Society* 7(3/4): 304–24. Online at: http://library.queensu.ca/ojs/index.php/surveillance-and-society/article/view/4158 (Accessed 1 January 2016).

19   S.11(2)(a) Children Act 2004 c.31.

20   The Court of Human Rights has found that to arbitrarily database citizens breaches Article 8 of ECHR. See for examples: *Amann v Switzerland*

(27798/95) (2000) 30 EHRR 843; *S v UK* (30562/04) and *Marper v UK* (30566/04) (2009) 48 EHRR 50.

21 Wrennall (2010) (n. 18).

22 Anderson, R., Brown, I., Clayton, R., Dowty, T., Korff, D. and Munro, E. (2006) *Children's Databases: Safety and Privacy, A Report for the Information Commissioner*, 22 November, Foundation for Information Policy Research. Online at: www.fipr.org/press/061122kids.html (Accessed 1 January 2016).

23 Children Act 2004 Information Database (England) Regulations SI 2007/2182.

24 Gibbons, J., Conroy, S. and Bell, C. (1995) *Operating the Child Protection System: A Study of Child Protection Practices in English Local Authorities*, HMSO, London.

25 This is an important area for further research. There is a growing body of evidence to suggest surveillance and interference is causing distress of varying degrees to many families. See for example information presented by organisations such as: FASO (False Allegations Support Organisation). Online at: www.false-allegations.org.uk/ (Accessed 1 May 2016); Justice for Families. Online at: www.justice-for-families.org.uk/ (Accessed 1 May 2016); FACT. Online at: www.factuk.org/ (Accessed 1 May 2016); and also for example, papers such as: Robertson, B. (2002) 'The Harm Caused by False Allegations', April, paper submitted to the Home Affairs Committee Enquiry, Common Select Committee. Online at: www.coeffic.demon.co.uk/commons_select_committee.htm (Accessed 5 May 2016).

26 Notably John Hemmings MP: see for example John Hemmings MP, online at: www.unity-injustice.co.uk/john_hemming.htm (Accessed 5 July 2011) and http://johnhemming.blogspot.co.uk/ (Accessed 1 May 2016). It is noted that Hemming's stance is controversial.

27 For example, Earl Howe, Peer, when Shadow Minister for Health: '. . . many innocent people are being wrongly accused of child abuse and whose lives in consequence are being turned upside down without due justification . . . children are made to live in constant fear of being parted from their parents. The climate is like that of a witch hunt in which the voice of reason and all sense of proportion is lost.' From: Hansard (2001) *House of Lords Debate*, 17 October, Col. 646, Earl Howe. Online at: www.publications.parliament.uk/pa/ld200102/ldhansrd/vo011017/text/11017–06.htm#11017-06_head0 (Accessed 6 May 2016).

28 Munro, E. and Parton, N. (2007) 'How far is England in the process of introducing a mandatory reporting system?', *Child Abuse Review* 16: 5–16, 14.

29 Hansard (n. 27), Col. 667, Baroness Fookes: ' I do not think that we can leave things as they are. This is all much too serious . . . It is equally important [as detecting 'abuse'] that we support those who are innocent of any wrongdoing'.

30 Hansard (n. 27), Col. 656, Lord Eden of Winton. These issues were summed up by Lord Eden of Winton who stated that 'We must be warned by the growing weight of evidence that the experts in the social services, the medical profession and the police can get things tragically wrong. It arises either because they have been conditioned to believe that everything the child says has to be true or they fail to interpret correctly the physical symptoms they may be examining. What is most dangerous of all is that they might have a pre-conceived presumption that abuse has taken place. If so, the child is then subjected to suggestible questioning designed to substantiate that opinion. They appear to be too ready to jump to a conclusion on the flimsiest of evidence. In one or two cases I have heard about, when the police are brought in they sometimes trawl the neighbourhood to seek corroboration for that so-called evidence.'

31 ADD refers to attention deficit disorder. CFS/ME refers to chronic fatigue syndrome, or myalgic encephalomyelitis.

32 Hansard (n. 27), Col. 661, Countess of Mar.
33 Ibid., Col. 669, Lord Northborne.
34 Ibid., Col. 675, Lord Hunt.
35 Ibid., Col. 646, Earl Howe.
36 Ibid., Col. 652, The Bishop of Birmingham.
37 Ibid., Col. 663, Lord Lucas.
38 Munchausen syndrome by proxy, now known as fabricated or induced illness (FII).
39 This refers to sudden infant death syndrome which was formerly referred to as 'cot death'.
40 *R v Cannings (Angela)* [2004] 1 All ER 725; *R v Cannings* [2004] EWCA Crim 1; *R v Clark (Sally) (No.1)* 2000 WL 1421196; *R v Clark (Sally) (No.2)* [2003] EWCA Crim 1020.
41 *R v Clark (Sally) (No.2)* [2003] EWCA Crim 1020.
42 Hansard (n. 27), Col. 653.
43 House of Commons Select Committee on Home Affairs (2002) *Minutes of Evidence, Examination of Witnesses*, 20 June. Online at: www.publications.parlia ment.uk/pa/cm200102/cmselect/cmhaff/836/2062002.htm (Accessed 24 May 2016).
44 Wrennall, L. (2004) 'Miscarriages of Justice in Contemporary Child Protection: a brief history and proposals for change', Presentation by Dr Lynne Wrennall to the All Party Group on Abuse Investigations, Attlee Suite, Portcullis House, 2 December. Online at: http://ljmu.academia.edu/LynneWrennall/Papers/301109/Wrennall_L._2004_Miscarriages_of_Justice_in_Child _Protection_a_brief_history_and_proposals_for_change._Paper_presented _to_the_parliamentary_conference_held_by_the_All_Party_Group _on_Abuse_Investigations_Attlee_Suite_Portcullis_House_2_December (Accessed 18 February 2016).
45 Per Munby, J. in: *Re B (A Child) (Disclosure)* [2004] 2 FLR 142, para. 101.
46 Davies, P. (2011) 'The Impact of a Child Protection Investigation: A Personal Reflective Account', *Child & Family Social Work* 16: 201–9.
47 Ibid., 202.
48 Ibid., 207.
49 See: Doak, J. (2008) *Victims' Rights, Human Rights and Criminal Justice*, Hart, Portland, OR.
50 Davies, P. (n. 46), p. 202.
51 Ibid., p. 206.
52 Luza, S. and Ortiz, E. (1991) 'The Dynamic of Shame in Interactions Between Child Protective Services and Families Falsely Accused of Child Abuse', *Issues in Child Abuse Accusations* 3: 108–23. Online at: www.ipt-forensics.com/journal /volume3/j3_2_5.htm (Accessed 14 May 2016).
53 See discussion with respect to the criminal justice system by: Hillyard, P. and Tombs, S. (2004) 'Beyond Criminology?' in: Hillyard, P., Pantazis, C., Tombs, S. and Gordon, D. (eds) *Beyond Criminology: Taking Harm Seriously*, Pluto Press, London.
54 Foucault, M. (1998) *The History of Sexuality, Vol.1: The Will to Knowledge*, Penguin, London.
55 It is acknowledged that there are families who progress through the system as a result of social work and judicial error. This is outside the scope of this inquiry as *ipso facto* these families will suffer increased harm, and this is not disputed in literature, the point of contention being the justification for it. It is establishing the harm only at assessment and investigation stage that is of more relevance as there is less justification and more scepticism over damage caused by the early stages of the procedures.

56 HM Government (2015) *Working Together to Safeguard Children*, TSO, London.
57 Prosser, J. (1995) 'A Case Study of a UK Family Wrongly Accused of Child Abuse', *Issues in Child Abuse Accusations* 7: 1–12, 10. Online at: www.ipt-forensics.com/journal/volume7/j7_3_2.htm (Accessed 14 May 2016).
58 Post-traumatic stress disorder is described in Criterion A1, Section 309.81 of: American Psychiatric Association (1994) *Diagnostic and Statistical Manual of Mental Disorders*, 4th edn (DSM IV-TR), American Psychiatric Association, Washington, DC. The Association's website is at: www.psychiatry.org/practice/dsm/ (Accessed 13 May 2016).
59 The essential feature of PTSD is the development of characteristic symptoms following exposure to an extreme traumatic stressor involving either direct personal experience of an event that involves actual or threatened death or serious injury, or other threat to one's physical integrity. It extends to witnessing an event that involves death, injury or a threat to the physical integrity of another person, or learning about unexpected or violent death, serious harm, or threat of death or injury experienced by a family member or other close associate. As death, physical injury or threat to physical integrity is not relevant to referral and assessment the only part of the criteria that may apply is the 'serious harm' category. The remainder of the criteria rests on the response to the stressor. Literature describing the nature of individual harm strongly suggests that these criteria describe many of the symptoms reported by families, particularly by parents, including intense fear, helplessness or horror (or in children, the response must involve disorganised or agitated behaviour). The characteristic symptoms include persistent re-experiencing of the traumatic event, persistent avoidance of stimuli associated with the trauma and numbing of general responsiveness and persistent symptoms of increased arousal (hyper-vigilance). The full symptom picture must be present for more than one month, and the disturbance must cause clinically significant distress or impairment in social, occupational or other important areas of functioning.
60 Department of Health (2000) *Framework for Assessment of Children in Need and their Families*, TSO, London.
61 Pride, M. (1986) *The Child Abuse Industry*, Crossway Books, Illinois.
62 The National Clearinghouse on Child Abuse and Neglect is a national US resource for professionals seeking information on the prevention, identification and treatment of child abuse and neglect and related child welfare issues.
63 Besharov, D. (1986) 'Unfounded allegations: a new child abuse problem', *The Public Interest* 83(Spring): 18–33. Besharov notes (p. 22) that in 1984 65 per cent of all reports proved to be unfounded using the criteria that they were dismissed after an investigation by child protective agencies. These were allegations, not referrals.
64 In 1991–2 the San Diego USA County Grand Jury considered issues relating to 'sexual abuse' and allegations as a result of cases that had come before the courts. Although these reports relate to cases that have progressed to litigation the reports observed (p. 1) that 'allegations of in-home molest/abuse seem to cause the most severe conflict with the system'. This finding may be out of date; the rise of 'emotional abuse' as a difficult to prove and ill-defined category has arguably taken over the position of the most contentious area of 'child abuse' to investigate, but the issue of harm and trauma is nevertheless raised once again. See: San Diego County Grand Jury (1991–2) 'Child Sexual Abuse, Assault, and Molest Issues', Report No. 8, San Diego, CA.
65 Oellerich, T. (1998) 'Identifying and Dealing with Child Savers', *IPT* 10. Online at: www.ipt-forensics.com/journal/volume10/j10_1.htm (Accessed 12 May 2016).
66 Ibid.

67 See generally: Dame Elizabeth Butler-Sloss (1988) *Report of the Inquiry into Child Abuse in Cleveland 1987*, Cmd 412, HMSO, London.

68 Details of the Act's passage through Parliament and its implementation are set out in Chapter 2.

69 Griffiths, P. (1989) 'The Investigation of Suspected Child Abuse' in: Stainton Rogers, W., Hevey, D. and Ash, E. (eds) *Child Abuse and Neglect: Facing the Challenge*, Open University, London, p. 173.

70 See for example: Foucault, M. (1973) *The Birth of the Clinic: An Archaeology of Medical Perception*, Tavistock, London.

71 Donzelot, J. (1980) *The Policing of Families: Welfare versus the State*, Hutchinson, London, p. 91.

72 Schultz, L.G. (1989) 'One Hundred Cases of Unfounded Child Sexual Abuse: A survey and recommendations', *Issues in Child Abuse Accusations* 1(1): 29–38, 37.

73 Ibid.

74 Ibid., citing: Webb, C. (1986) *Forgive Me*, Berkeley, NY.

75 Richardson, D. (1990) 'The Effects of a False Allegation of Child Sexual Abuse on an Intact Middle Class Family', *Issues in Child Abuse Accusations, IPT* 2. Online at: www.ipt-forensics.com/journal/volume2/j2_4_7.htm (Accessed 12 May 2016).

76 Ibid., p. 19.

77 Jones, D.P. (1991) 'Professional and Clinical Challengers to Protection of Children', *Child Abuse & Neglect* 15: 57–66.

78 Luza and Ortiz (n. 52), p. 108.

79 Ibid., p. 111.

80 Kaufman, G. (2004 [1986]) *The Psychology of Shame: Theory and Treatment of Shame-Based Syndromes* (2nd edn), Springer Publishing Company, New York, describes the interrelation between shame and mental health in terms of object relations theory, interpersonal theory and Tompkins's affect theory to provide a powerful and multidimensional view of shame. Drawing on his own clinical experience he explains the application of affect theory to general classes of shame-based syndromes including compulsive; schizoid, depressive and paranoid; sexual dysfunction; splitting; and sociopathic disorders.

81 Wakefield, H. and Underwager, R. (1994) 'The Alleged Child Victim and Real Victims of Sexual Misuse' in: Krivacska, J. and Money, J. (eds) *The Handbook of Forensic Sexology*, Prometheus Books, Amherst, NY. Online at: www.ipt-forensics.com/library/alleged.htm (Accessed 14 May 2016). It cites the report produced by Westminster College, Oxford, partly funded by the BBC's Children in Need Appeal: *Child Abuse Investigations: The Families' Perspective*, Parents Against Injustice (PAIN), 3 Riverside Business Park, Stansted, Essex CM24 8PL.

82 Wakefield and Underwager (1994) (n. 81).

83 Prosser (n. 57), 10, drew on Wakefield and Underwager's earlier research: Wakefield, H. and Underwager, R. (1988) *Accusations of Child Sexual Abuse*, Springfield, Illinois, p. 327.

84 Prosser (n. 57), 10.

85 Prosser, J. and Lewis, I. (1992) *Child Abuse Investigations: The Families' Perspective*, Parents Against Injustice (PAIN), 3 Riverside Business Park, Stansted, Essex CM24 8PL. Prosser undertook an ethnographic case study involving families who had sought help from PAIN. In the study general and specific observations were made about the effects of investigation which were described as 'system abuse syndrome' (p. 20).

86 Ibid., p. 18.

87 Ibid., p. 20.

88 Ibid., p. 20.

89 Robin, M. (1991) *Assessing Child Maltreatment Reports*, Haworth Press, New York, pp. 47–8.
90 Jack, G. (1997) 'Discourses of Child Protection and Child Welfare', *British Journal of Social Work* 27: 659–78, 665.
91 Parton, N., Thorpe, D. and Wattam, C. (1997) *Child Protection, Risk and the Moral Order*, Palgrave Macmillan, Basingstoke, p. 14.
92 Cooper, A., Hetherington, R. and Katz, I. (2003) *The Risk Factor: Making the Child Protection System Work for Children*, DEMOS, London, p. 18.
93 Prosser, J. (n. 57).
94 Ibid., 10.
95 Ibid.
96 Ibid., 11.
97 Jones, C. and Novak, T. (1993) 'Social Work Today', *British Journal of Social Work* 23: 195–212, 196.
98 Ibid., 205.
99 Department of Health (1995) *Child Protection: Messages from Research*, HMSO, London.
100 Ibid., p. 44.
101 Ibid., p. 43.
102 Ibid.
103 Ibid., p. 44.
104 See for example: Spratt and Callan who concluded that: 'It is now regarded as axiomatic that there should be a re-focusing of social work practice, the debate having moved on from why this is necessary to how this may be achieved.' Spratt, T. and Callan, J. (2004) 'Parents' Views on Social Work Interventions in Child Welfare Cases', *British Journal of Social Work* 34(March): 199–224, 200. Research findings consistently linked suspicion and investigation as causing harm rather than the wider issues of power relations and state interference, although it is sometimes difficult to separate out the harm caused by assessment from harm which occurs later in the process. See for example: Dale, P., Green, R. and Fellows, R. (2005) *Child Protection Assessment following Serious Injuries to Infants: Fine Judgments*, NSPCC/Wiley series, Chichester. Other research identified false positive cases as causing 'great suffering'. See for example: Jones, D.P.H. (2001) 'Spotlight on Practice: Editorial – False Positives in the Field of Child Maltreatment', *Child Abuse & Neglect* 25: 1395–6.
105 Spratt and Callan (n. 104), p. 201.
106 Ibid.
107 Ibid., p. 209.
108 Ibid.
109 Ibid., p. 224.
110 Dumbrill, G. (2006) 'Parental Experience of Child Protection Intervention: A Qualitative Study', *Child Abuse and Neglect* 30: 27–37, 28.
111 Millar, M. and Corby, B. (2006) 'The Framework for the Assessment of Children in Need and their Families: A Basis for a 'Therapeutic' Encounter?', *British Journal of Social Work* 36: 887–99, 895. Online at: www.childcentredpractice. co.uk/Websites/ccp1/files/Content/1415052/Miller%20and%20Corby.pdf (Accessed 14 May 2016).
112 D'Cruz, H. (2004) 'The Social Construction of Child Maltreatment: The Role of Medical Practitioners', *Journal of Social Work* 4(1): 99–123.
113 See for example: Jack, G. (n. 90), who considered the discourses of 'child protection' and child welfare. He refers to Cleaver and Freeman's 1995 study of thirty families with experience of child protection investigation in four local authorities in the North-West of England.

114 Ibid., p. 664. These findings were within the context of the overall study where 'out of six hundred investigations less than ten were categorized as "dangerous" and in only 2 per cent of which did the children concerned require medical treatment'. With such a low incidence of 'significant harm' detected 'the researchers conclude by asking whether the disintegration of family relationships and the lingering suspicion and resentments are too high a price to pay when the majority of cases are minor'.
115 Gibbons *et al.* (1995), p. 51

7 The question of remedies

If harm caused by the State is to be taken seriously the question of remedies must be considered in tandem. Considering both together is particularly helpful in addressing the question of the appropriate balance between State powers and private rights, moving debate forward from either of the polemic positions described at the beginning of Chapter 1:

- that mass surveillance of children and their families, followed by targeted social work intervention is justified because it aims to protect children from abuse; or
- that it is not justified as it largely fails to achieve its aim to protect children from abuse, and harms families who are not abusing their children through unnecessary interference.

If a robust system to ensure that the State adequately discharges its duties is to operate successfully there must be recognition that in cases where inadvertent harm is caused an appropriate remedy and support for affected families must also be in place. The law needs to provide a framework for remedies in which the interests of both parents and children are recognised and protected.

Families need to feel protected from excessive State surveillance and interference and local authorities should be clear about the consequences of over-interference as well as the consequences of under-interference. The debate is not unique to this area of law. In many areas the law must balance competing interests in areas of conflict, particularly as English law must be European Convention compliant.[1] When legislating in such situations, consideration must be given to the power of the State and also the resources of the individual to challenge it.

Law involving competing interests of family members is particularly problematic. Although sociologists have considered what is meant by 'family'[2] in terms of human rights it has no status other than that described in Article 8 European Convention.[3] 'Family' now includes individuals including adults and children who, in the modern world, may or may not be biologically related.[4] When the potential rights and responsibilities of the individual family members conflict with each other it is difficult for legislation to draft law that represents all the interests equally. Similarly, the judiciary have to decide whose interests they are going to promote in relation to decisions where there are competing interests. There may be situations where the adults of the family have competing interests and these may conflict with the children of the family (whose interests may also conflict with each other), and any or all of these interests may conflict with those of the State. Consequently, a body of case law has evolved which has attempted to interpret the law and provide some guiding principles.

Complaints procedures and judicial review

An aggrieved family may initially turn to the complaints procedure, or seek judicial review of local authority decisions. Both are limited as a remedy and will not enable damages in respect of harm. Despite the limitations of complaint systems, it is a requirement under s.26 Children Act 1989 that:

> (3) Every local authority shall establish a procedure for considering any representations (including any complaint) . . . about the discharge by the authority of any of their qualifying functions in relation to the child.[5]

Internal, administrative remedies must be exhausted before an application for judicial review is allowed.[6] Dissatisfied claimants can refer unresolved complaints to the local authority Ombudsman in relation to issues of 'maladministration'.[7] Complaints procedures are a type of schema and are subject to the problems identified by Smith.[8] They have been subject to examination by Lloyd-Bostock who did not consider complainants had a high chance of satisfaction by following complaints procedures.[9] It is difficult to see how a family or its members, who are likely to be distressed and frightened are going to achieve satisfaction through such a procedure. The complaint system can be used in relation to Part V of the Children Act 1989[10] and can also be used in relation to the assessment stages.[11] Complaints systems have evolved in recent years and there are numerous government reports considering reforms but no substantive research to indicate that users of the system obtain satisfaction.[12] The complaints system only has to 'consider' not 'resolve'.

Judicial review is intended to be used in relation to *ultra vires* acts by public bodies either in relation to a decision or failure to make a decision. Illegality, irrationality and procedural impropriety are potential causes of action.[13] They are therefore available to families to use as a potential remedy. However, the very short three-month limitation period for commencing actions, coupled with the acknowledgement that applicants are likely to be traumatised, makes it unlikely to be an adequate method for families to obtain a remedy. In any event, the judicial review process only applies to procedural breaches not problems within the 'system' itself.

As the court cannot substitute a different decision because it is concerned with the *process* rather than the outcome, even a successful applicant may find a quashed decision sent back to the local authority for reconsideration. The local authority is then open to the possibility of reaching the same decision for a second time, this time using a different route. Given the wide drafting referred to above in relation to s.47 Children Act 1989 this route does not seem to offer much of a remedy to families. Even if successful, of the range of potential remedies[14] it is redetermination that is a possible outcome rather than overturning of a decision, making it an empty remedy for many families.[15]

R v Swindon Borough Council[16] concerned a Claimant S, a consultant gynaecologist, who sought judicial review of a local authority's decision over continued 'risk assessment'. His application was refused. He had been acquitted in the Crown Court of four counts of indecently assaulting the daughter, K, of the woman with whom he had been living. The jury was unable to agree on another three counts and the jury directed the prosecution that a retrial was not appropriate leading to a formal not guilty verdict. Despite his acquittal the claimant did not gain agreement from the local authority that they would not continue to 'risk assess' if he were to move in with his new girlfriend and her children. Scott-Baker, J. held that:

> If *Re H and others* governed the approach in cases such as the present the result would be to prevent local authorities from carrying out effective and timely risk assessments. They would be forced to take care proceedings to identify whether grounds for intervention were present. This would be completely contrary to the principle of non-intervention in children cases. I do not accept that a local authority has to be satisfied on balance of probability that a person is an abuser before intervention is justified.[17]

The judge expressed 'a good deal of sympathy for someone in the shoes of the defendant'[18] but drew the distinction between the need to establish facts on the balance of probabilities in relation to care or supervision orders, as in *Re H and others*[19] and the requirement to investigate if a local authority has 'reasonable cause to suspect a child is likely to suffer significant harm'.[20] In the former, evidence is adduced to prove on the balance of probabilities that there is a likelihood of 'significant harm' unless an order is made. In the latter the duty is on a local authority to investigate if they *suspect* there is a likelihood of significant harm. The distinction is important. Additionally there is a difference in objectives and the relevant standard of proof between a criminal prosecution and the duty of a local authority.

A 'not guilty' verdict in a criminal court leaves the accused innocent in the eyes of the criminal law. However, as Scott-Baker pointed out:

> Acquittal in criminal sexual abuse proceedings does not mean that a local authority is thereby absolved from further responsibility to protect the child who made the allegations or any other children who may in some way be at risk. Far from it, the various statutory duties under the Children Act must, if they are in play, be discharged.[21]

In other words, a criminal acquittal where the allegation is unable to be proved 'beyond reasonable doubt' does not preclude either civil proceedings being brought on the same issue where the standard of proof is on the balance of probabilities or the power of a local authority to investigate pursuant to s.47.

Given the different standards of proof and the differing underlying purposes of criminal prosecution and social work assessment it is not anomalous that following criminal acquittal, civil litigation or social work assessment could be justified. It seems, however, that one of the main tenets of argument by the applicant in *R v Swindon Borough Council*[22] is an objection to open-ended interference into private life without a clear process of resolution to bring it to an end. It is one thing for a local authority to investigate in order to establish whether or not to take further action, but quite another to suggest an ongoing and open-ended process of 'risk assessment' that does not enable exoneration or a clear outcome.

This is a key issue and the problem is exacerbated by the wording of s.47, which includes the requirement for a local authority to predict future risk. The process of assessment is not just an investigation to establish whether or not events have occurred which should trigger the local authority to take further action to protect a child, but also an exercise in predicting the 'risk' or 'likelihood' that something will happen in the future. The question of whether it is reasonable to be subjected to open-ended suspicion is, of course, a different question to that of whether it is reasonable for someone acquitted in a criminal court to be reinvestigated under a different process.

The 2013 judicial review in *AB and Anor, R (on the application of) v The London Borough of Haringey* set out a limit to State power.[23] This case concerned parents, both former social workers, against whom an anonymous referral was made. The referral was accepted by Haringey to be highly likely to be malicious. Before reaching this conclusion Haringey carried out extensive inquiries about the family, including sharing details before the parents were informed of the referral or the action taken. This included details about the nature of the referral (which referred to physical and emotional abuse) with *inter alia* the family GP, the child's school, a neighbour and an aunt.

When the parents complained, Haringey sought to rely on a purported decision that the inquiries were carried out under s.47, rendering the issue of consent irrelevant. This was challenged. The issues for the judicial review to address were:

(1) Was a s.47 enquiry decided upon?
(2) If so, was it unlawful?
(3) Was the data-gathering exercise before and during the Initial Assessment process unlawful?
(4) What remedies are the claimants entitled to?[24]

The outcome was to establish that it was insufficient for a local authority to claim they acted under the authority of s.47 to attempt to legitimise bypassing parental consent if they had not followed a recognised and legitimate procedure to do so:

> After this very lengthy analysis of the relevant events and documents, it is possible to refine the grounds for seeking judicial review. Essentially, it is contended by Ms Grey QC on behalf of AB and CD that Ms Chew's decision to abandon the initial assessment process and immediately to escalate SFR's response to the referral into a section 47 enquiry was unlawful. Firstly, the decision itself was not, either in substance or form, one that amounted to a decision to establish a section 47 enquiry at all so that, in truth, no section 47 decision was taken and no section 47 enquiry ever started. Secondly, if such a decision had in fact been taken, it was taken without there being any proper grounds to support it. The decision was, on analysis, so flawed procedurally and so fundamentally lacking in the essential minimum requirements of a guidance-compliant decision-making process that it was unlawful.[25]

It therefore followed that the data collection was also unlawful.

In summary it seems that the complaints system is unlikely to grasp the scale or complexities of the harm that can be caused, or provide an adequate and meaningful remedy for it. The judicial review decisions focus on whether procedures have been followed correctly which does not resolve the issue of harms caused by potentially excessive State powers and interferences with private family life.

Defamation

Defamation as a remedy is not generally available in relation to statements made in relation to child protection and safeguarding processes. Statements made in the course of local authority assessments and case conferences are covered by qualified privilege. It has been contended, however, that this does not go far enough and absolute privilege should apply, leaving parents without even this limited opportunity to be afforded a remedy.[26]

Although this has not been accepted by the courts, primarily on the grounds that it is not necessary, it demonstrates the prevailing view of the State that parents and children should have no remedy in defamation no matter what the circumstance. The deciding case was *W v Westminster City Council and Anca Marks and James Thomas*,[27] where it was held that absolute privilege in defamation cases did not extend to statements made by a social worker in a child protection conference.[28] The court had to balance the Article 8 rights of the child against the parents' rights under Article 8 to a reputation. The evidential hurdles parents would have to overcome to succeed in such an application would be high. That children may be defamed is not considered.

In this case the test in relation to the comments that were complained about was whether they provided evidence from which malice could be inferred. It was contended unsuccessfully by the claimant that the recklessness of the social workers was of a kind which might be evidence that the communication was made for some motive other than a desire to perform the duty in question.[29] In other words, the claimant objected to the comments and claimed they were made maliciously. The court did not agree there was sufficient evidence to establish malice as a motive.

The State argued for absolute privilege in relation to such statements as, previously, *Taylor v Director of Serious Fraud Office*[30] had established that courts could in principle extend absolute privilege at common law to new circumstances if the test of necessity was satisfied.[31] Although Taylor was referred to in *W v Westminster City Council and Anca Marks and James Thomas*,[32] it failed as it was considered that the test of necessity did not apply in this case. Had they been successful, the question of malice would have been irrelevant.

Unless malice can be shown, the common law appears to have maintained the restricted ability of parents or children to use defamation as a remedy. However, it is the 'truth' of a statement in relation to a child or their parent that is central to whether the system is able to claim to be effective or efficient not why it is made. Decision making on false or inaccurate statements cannot lead to reasonable outcomes. Regardless of malice, untruthful and inaccurate statements can cause harm.

The flaw in the current approach is that it not only fails to consider the truth as central to the issue of child welfare, it also fails to consider the consequences and impact of things said about children and parents that may not be true. For example, a child may also want to claim a remedy in defamation if they do not agree they have been a victim of abuse. It is regrettable that children, in whose interests the system claims to operate, are not independently advised of a remedy as the system is seen as acting in a welfare capacity.

The European Convention on Human Rights 1950 and the Human Rights Act 1998

Article 3 ECHR

The possibility for family members other than a child to bring a successful action under Article 3 in respect of torture or inhuman or degrading treatment or punishment through over-interference seems unfeasible. However, an action in relation to under-interference which left children unprotected from harm was successful in *Z and Others v United Kingdom* which found in favour of the applicant children in respect of a breach of Article 3.[33]

The principle is therefore yet to be tested in relation to the referral and assessment process. However, if the argument were advanced that the effect of the procedures is potentially punitive, that harm must be balanced against the potential benefits in cases where parents have not harmed their children when deciding whether it is possible for an action to be brought.[34] The possibility for an action therefore exists, although its prospects of success may not be high.

Article 6 ECHR

Article 6 concerns the right to a fair trial. In relation to determining civil rights at the referral and assessment stages the question is whether the local authority is determining civil rights this early on, in which case Article 6 applies and may demand external scrutiny before a court:

> In the determination of his civil rights and obligations or of any criminal charge against him, everyone is entitled to a fair and public hearing within a reasonable time by an independent and impartial tribunal established by law.[35]

Whereas 'the appropriate balance of power between courts and local authorities in "care cases" has long been debated'[36] it is less clear that the 'appropriate balance of power' between parents and local authorities in relation to the assessment schema has been similarly considered. Although there is no case law specifically in relation to Article 6 and assessments, there is evidence that local authorities are concerned that the assessment process may give rise to challenge using Article 6 in the future.[37]

Its use as a remedy is therefore limited. In contrast, if a criminal charge is brought there may be some protection as the matter transfers to the criminal jurisdiction, and the right to a fair trial is a relevant consideration in the proceedings, as it is in care proceedings. However, this is not directly relevant to referral and assessment as there is no trial, although it is possible that criminal allegations and suspicions will be discussed and recorded about the family.

Article 8 ECHR

The discussion concerning Article 8 is divided into two parts: the first part concerns potential remedies in relation to harm caused by surveillance and the second concerns potential remedies in relation to harm caused by assessments.

Although the use of Articles 3 and 6 seem remote, the emerging jurisprudence from the European Court of Human Rights (ECtHR) in relation to the effect of the European Convention on Human Rights 1950 (ECHR) and the Human Rights Act 1998 is intended to provide potential remedies. It does so by providing a framework to theoretically ensure actions of State bodies are proportionate and reasonable. The most obvious remedy is Article 8 which concerns the right to respect for private and family life.

Article 8, however, is a qualified right and there is a short limitation period. The remedy is not absolute because of its qualified nature, the 'paramountcy principle'[38] and the lack of agreement over what 'family life' constitutes. However, the ECtHR[39] now clearly recognises that the collection of information on an individual by officials of the State without consent constitutes interference with that individual's right to respect for his or her private life, which is guaranteed by Article 8(1) of the European Convention on Human Rights.[40] In *Amann v Switzerland*[41] the ECtHR gives guidance on the retention of personal information for longer than is necessary. The ECtHR found that the storing of information in relation to a citizen's private life by the State amounted to an interference with that private life. In this case, the ECtHR held that the Swiss authorities should have destroyed the stored information 'when it emerged that no offence was being prepared'. Under Article 8 any interference must be 'necessary in a democratic society'. It must also be proportionate to a legitimate aim.[42] European jurisprudence may therefore have relevance as a remedy for both surveillance and interference particularly as it has already been noted in case law that surveillance itself constitutes interference.[43]

Article 8 ECHR: a remedy for mass and targeted surveillance?

Article 8 gives a citizen the 'right to respect for his private and family life, his home and his correspondence'.[44] Under Article 8(2) interference with privacy and family life is permitted provided it:

* is 'in accordance with the law';
* serves one of the legitimate aims e.g. national security, public safety, the economic wellbeing of the country, prevention of disorder or crime, protection of health or morals, or the protection of the rights and freedoms of others; and
* is 'necessary in a democratic society' for the purpose in question.

In addition to the statutory provision there is case law establishing that there are two requirements over and above the requirement that interference must have some basis in domestic law:

* The law must be adequately accessible: citizens must be able to have an adequate indication of the legal rules applicable to a given case. Secondly, a practice cannot be regarded as lawful unless it is formulated with sufficient precision to enable the citizen to regulate his or her conduct: he or she must be able to foresee, to a degree that is reasonable in the circumstances, the consequences which a given action may entail. These are principles of 'fair labelling'.[45]
* Any law invoked as a basis for an interference with a Convention right must be 'compatible with the rule of law, which is expressly mentioned in the preamble to the Convention'.[46] The legal rules in question must not allow for arbitrariness as this is contrary to rule of law. This in turn relates back to the question of how precisely a legal rule is phrased.[47]

The principles apply generally to local authorities and government secret surveillance powers. Legislation granting authorities the power to interfere with fundamental rights must be formulated with sufficient precision:

* to allow individuals who might be affected to foresee, to a reasonable extent, how the rules will be applied in specific cases; and
* to prevent the authorities in question from applying the rules arbitrarily.

If authorities are granted discretionary powers, that discretion must be fettered: it must be made clear when it is appropriate to use the discretionary powers and when it is not. In addition, there should be appropriate procedures to ensure that the rules are properly applied, to which citizens should have access, and there should be adequate remedy.[48] The requirements are set out in Malone:

> The degree of precision required of the law in this connection will depend upon the particular subject matter . . . Since the implementation in practice of measures of secret surveillance of communications is not open to scrutiny by the individuals concerned or the public at large, it would be contrary to the rule of law for the legal discretion granted to the executive to be expressed in terms of an unfettered power. Consequently, the law must indicate the scope of any such discretion conferred on the competent authorities and the manner of its exercise with sufficient clarity, having regard to the legitimate aim of the measure in question, to give the individual adequate protection against arbitrary interference.[49]

These statutory and case decisions would, on the face of it, provide some remedy for all UK families whose private data has been collected and used without their consent for mass surveillance. However, s.47 Children Act 1989 is not the only statutory provision conferring power on local authorities to interfere into the private lives of citizens. S.2 Local Government Act 2000, for example, allows local authorities to do 'anything which they consider is likely to promote or improve [the economic, social or environmental] well-being of their area'[50] although this is restricted in s.3. Similarly to s.47[51] the precise boundary of legitimacy for State interference is not clear, but as Anderson *et al.* observed this is one of the main provisions on which government and local authorities base the sharing of sensitive data on children and their families.[52]

The Department for Constitutional Affairs (now obsolete) guidance on databases paved the way for data sharing in relation to child and family surveillance in support of child protection and safeguarding,[53] but it mistakenly relied on *Peck v the United Kingdom*[54] in respect of allowing personal data exchanges on the basis of wide statutory provisions. In *Peck* personal data on a CCTV tape on which the applicant could be identified was disclosed by a local authority to the press, acting *inter alia* under s.111 Local Government Act 1972, a previous provision similar to s.2 Local Government Act 2000.[55] This was not a correct interpretation, however, as *Peck* should have been interpreted to be restricting rather than enabling. In addition to this, the main provision the Department for Constitutional Affairs relied on was s.163 Criminal Justice and Public Order Act 1994,[56] which allowed local authorities to establish CCTV systems in order to *inter alia* 'promote the prevention of crime'. It was held that even these combined provisions provided only a sufficient legal basis for the disclosure of non-identifiable data without the consent of the data subject.[57]

Although it was considered by the Department for Constitutional Affairs that the above-mentioned provisions, read together, were a sufficient legal basis for the disclosure of non-identifiable data without the consent of the data subject, it cannot be assumed to provide a sufficient basis for the disclosure of personal data, nor can it be said that the broadest provision, s.111 of the 1972 Act,[58] is sufficient on its own. Indeed, it is clear that the collecting of personal data (and especially of sensitive data) constitutes:

> an interference with the data subject's private life, and that the disclosure of such data will constitute a serious interference if it can have serious consequences for the data subject, and (ii) that such interferences must be authorized in clear and specific legal rules relating to the particular processing.[59]

Also, in a case in which the HIV status of a citizen had been revealed it was held that 'any State measures compelling disclosure of such information without the consent of the patient and any safeguards designed to secure an effective protection call[s] for the most careful scrutiny on the part of the Court'.[60] Despite this, the guidance provides that:

> If there are no relevant statutory restrictions it may then be possible for local authorities to share data either internally or externally in reliance on Section 111(1) of the Local Government Act 1972 or section 2 of the Local Government Act 2000. The power that is contained in section 2 of the Local Government Act 2000 is of particular relevance as it is designed to ensure that service delivery is coordinated in ways which minimise duplication and maximise effectiveness.[61]

They consider open-ended provisions can apply specifically to children's databases such as s.2 Local Government Act 2000 or s.111 Local Government Act 1972, and are sufficient for data disclosure and data sharing, including sensitive data. However, Anderson *et al.* deem this guidance to be:

> not compatible with the EC Framework Directive on data protection. The guidance is therefore mistaken in terms of EC, and thus (under the ECA) UK law. At the very least, those conditions should be extremely restrictively applied, subject to special rules and special safeguards.[62]

Surveillance is therefore potentially a breach of Article 8. The extensive sharing of highly sensitive data about children and their families, wider families and friends clearly involves:

> serious interferences with the rights of those children under Article 8 ECHR. Under the Convention, such interferences must be based on legal provisions that are clear, precise, foreseeable in their application and compatible with the rule of law. The same applies to the sharing of data on parents, siblings and friends. Vague and open-ended provisions such as (again) section 2 of the Local Government Act 2000 or section 111 of the Local Government

Act 1972 do not meet these requirements and cannot therefore legitimise the data sharing in question.[63]

It is unfortunate that despite the warnings over illegality issues by Anderson *et al.* in their 2006 report to the Information Commissioner,[64] the Labour Government continued with its plans regardless. There has not been any significant legal challenge to the lawfulness of the databases and information sharing. It is likely that the reason for this is the cost jeopardy of bringing such an action together with the uncertainty of outcome. It is not clear why the Information Commissioner, having received this report, did not exercise powers to insist the government acted in accordance with both domestic and European provisions to protect citizens from mass surveillance.

Article 8 ECHR: a remedy for harm caused by assessment

Demonstrating a breach of Article 8 seems to provide the most obvious potential remedy in relation to the interference into private family life caused by assessment. However, the qualified nature of the right removes from parents and children the right to claim a breach under Article 8 in relation to local authority assessment *per se.*[65] An Article 8 breach may, however, be held to have occurred if the assessment process can be demonstrated to be flawed or inadequate; it is thus the way in which the process is carried out that could amount to a breach of Article 8, not the intrusion and its consequences itself.

Discussion of some of the relevant case law is included in the common law negligence section as it flows from cases that began as negligence actions and proceeded to the European court. *AD and OD*[66] illustrates some of the important issues. The case concerned an action brought by a mother and her child in relation to lack of adequate risk assessment as the child's *osteogenesis imperfecta* (brittle bone disease) was not initially detected, leaving the parents open to suspicion in relation to the child's injuries. The methods of assessment used by the local authority were protracted, intrusive and resulted in the child's placement in foster care whilst the local authority prepared to apply for a s.31 care order. This was only halted and the child returned to his parents when an X-ray showed the underlying medical condition following the child's fall and admission to hospital whilst in foster care. The mother contended that she had separated from the father as a result of the experience and that she and the child had suffered damage as a result.

At the time of the claim in the UK courts, the Human Rights Act 1998 was not in force. The mother also did not have a cause of action in negligence as no duty of care was owed to her.[67] The child's claim in negligence failed as no recognised psychiatric damage was found to have occurred. The ECtHR case was brought on the basis that mother and child had both suffered a violation of their human rights under Article 13 read in conjunction with Article 8.[68] The Convention demands that parents have an effective remedy for any breach of their Article 8 rights. The Human Rights Act 1998 s.7 now provides a remedy for any breach of these rights. In this case there was a breach of Article 13 because the Human Rights Act 1998 was not in force at the time the events occurred. The Human Rights Act 1998 is now deemed to supply that remedy and the claim was successful in relation to a breach of Article 8 rights.

It was held that:

> The [UK] Government . . . accepted that it was arguably obliged to ensure that an enforceable right to compensation was made available for such damage as could have been proved to have been suffered as a result of any violation of art. 8 and that this complaint should be declared admissible. As the applicants acknowledged, there was now an effective remedy provided under the Human Rights Act 1998.[69]

Given the amount of trauma and distress suffered by the family, and the long-term consequences of it, it is questionable whether these remedies under the Human Rights Act 1998 are effective or adequate in relation to addressing this type of harm suffered by families when their private life is so completely interfered with by the State. This relates back to the question of who should bear the consequences of damage caused by surveillance and interference if it does not progress beyond the assessment stage, is not negligent within the common law framework but causes a family and its members acute and potentially long-term trauma and distress.

In addition to the question over the adequacy of Article 8 as a remedy its use may be very restricted. For example, Article 8 may provide a potential remedy only if an existing family relationship can be shown.[70] The meaning of 'family life' is relevant to establishing whether an applicant has *locus standi*. This issue was considered in *Marckx v Belgium*[71] in relation to illegitimate children, establishing they held the same position as a legitimate child in relation to their relationship with their mother. The position, however, is not the same for a father, who has to demonstrate the existence of family life between himself, the child and the mother.[72]

In addition to the negative requirement that Article 8 confers, *Marckx* established that there is also a positive duty on the State to:

> act in a manner calculated to allow those concerned to lead a normal family life. As envisaged by Article 8, respect for family life implies in particular, in the court's view, the existence in domestic law of legal safeguards as to render possible as from the moment of birth the child's integration in his family . . . a law that fails to satisfy this requirement violates paragraph 1 of Article 8 without there being any call to examine it under paragraph 2.[73]

However, even if a breach of Article 8 can be established, the breach may be claimed to be justified by arguing the action or violation to be 'in accordance with the law', 'that it pursued a legitimate aim' and was 'necessary in a democratic society'.

An additional bar to success is the welfare principle and its 'paramount' status. There is, however, at least an argument to suggest that, unless there is judicial reinterpretation of the meaning of 'paramount', there could be grounds for a declaration of incompatibility under the Human Rights Act 1998 provisions.[74]

The reluctance of the judiciary to critically challenge the orthodoxy in relation to the paramountcy principle is derived partly from the use of expert evidence in relation to welfare issues. The reliance on social welfare discourse in relation to children has created a perhaps uncritical approach by the judiciary to issues concerning children. This includes reluctance to consider any erosion of the welfare approach, considering it to be compatible with the rights approach in placing the child subject ahead of their parents, and potentially other children.[75] Herring, however, identified fundamental differences between the welfare and the rights approaches.[76] Despite this, there seems to have been an assumption that decisions informed by the 'best interests' of the child will automatically conform to the requirements of Article 8.[77]

Common law negligence

Negligence has been established as a potential remedy in some circumstances. Case law has established a set of principles surrounding:

- when and why a duty of care is owed to a child; and
- when and why (not) a duty of care is owed to the child's parents and other adults.

Most case law involving families and social work related actions consider situations that have progressed beyond the assessment and investigation stage. However, there are some cases that exemplify the dilemma of parents, children and the State in situations of over-interference. Conversely there are also cases of under-interference where child abuse is evident but the local authority has failed to take robust action.

In relation to under-interference, *X and Others (Minors) v Bedfordshire County Council*[78] concerned an interlocutory appeal against the striking out of a negligence action on the grounds that the local authority *inter alia* failed to take action under ss.17 and 47 to assess and investigate, and, having done so, to take appropriate action. It was struck out as having failed to disclose a cause of action. The negligence case was brought by five sibling claimants aged between 3 and 1 on the grounds that the local authority had failed to investigate notifications to them that they were at risk. Various professionals had reported the children to the local authority and had made recommendations but no action was taken other than a case conference, despite both parents requesting removal of the children. Following the mother's threat that she would 'batter them' if they were not removed the children were placed with foster carers and were eventually placed on the Child Protection Register in relation to neglect and emotional abuse. No application was made in respect of a care order at that time despite the fact that the local authority accepted the children should not return to the care of their parents. Some months later the local authority did apply for care orders which were successfully granted. The children's case was that the local authority should have acted more quickly and effectively. It was struck out by the House of Lords who did not want to impose a duty of care on social workers and local authorities.

Four of the five siblings pursued the action as *Z and Others v United Kingdom in the ECtHR in 2001*.[79] It was held there were breaches under Articles 3 and 13 of the Convention, although there was no breach of Article 6. In relation to Article 3 there was a positive obligation on the government to protect children from inhuman or degrading treatment. The authorities had been aware of the abuse over a period of years, and had failed to bring this to an end. In relation to Article 13 there should be available to the victim or the victim's family, a mechanism for establishing liability of State officials or bodies for acts or omissions involving the breach of their rights under the Convention, and that would include compensation for non-pecuniary damage.

M (A Minor) v Newham Borough Council[80] was heard together with *X and Others (Minors) v Bedfordshire County Council* in 1995 and concerned over-interference. The legal issue, if not the factual issue, was the same: that of establishing whether a duty of care exists between a local authority, children and/or parents. The Claimants were mother and daughter. The daughter was separated from her mother following allegations that she had been abused by the mother's boyfriend. The allegations proved to be incorrect. The claim was also struck out on the grounds that no duty of care should be held to exist between social workers and children or parents. *M (A Minor) v Newham Borough Council*[81] progressed to Strasbourg as *TP v UK*.[82] The Applicants contended that there had been a breach of their rights under Articles 6, 8 and 13. The claim under Article 6 was dismissed but it was found there had been a breach of Article 8. It further found that the Applicants had been denied an effective remedy, contrary to Article 13 as the possibility of applying to the Ombudsman and to the Secretary of State did not provide the Applicants with any enforceable right to compensation. The European Court awarded damages on the basis that the Applicants suffered distress and anxiety, and, in the case of the first Applicant, feelings of frustration and injustice.

This decision laid the groundwork for the establishment of a duty of care in relation to social work decisions and children and resulted in UK negligence cases being reconsidered. This established that a duty of care could exist in relation to children, but not in relation to their parents and other adults. Following those European judgments further cases were brought in the UK in 2003 claiming negligence which prompted the judiciary to reconsider the issues together with the related academic commentary.[83]

The watershed cases in the UK were *JD v East Berkshire Community Health NHS Trust, MAK and RK v Dewsbury Healthcare NHS Trust and another, RK and another v Oldham NHS Trust and another*.[84] These cases occurred before October 2000, so no claim could be brought under the Human Rights Act 1998, although in the judgment Lord Phillips said that it was necessary to consider whether the introduction of the 1998 Act had affected the common law principles of the law of negligence. The three cases concerned instances of over-interference.[85] Each case involved accusations of child abuse made against a parent and in each case the accusations proved to be unfounded. The decision established that children who suffer harm as a consequence of negligent medical diagnosis and social work interference do have a duty of care owed to them. These decisions represent a significant shift in judicial policy.

In the first case D claimed for acute anxiety and distress that she suffered as a result of being incorrectly accused of suffering from Munchausen syndrome by proxy. In the second case MAK was accused of sexually abusing R, his daughter, which led to his being denied access to her for a short period. The girl suffered from Schamberg's disease, which produces discoloured patches on the skin and which was misdiagnosed as bruising and evidence of sexual abuse. In the third case the parents RK and another were accused of having inflicted injuries on their daughter, which led to the child being separated from them for nearly a year following an X-ray of her left thigh which showed an oblique displaced fracture. It was eventually agreed that she suffered from *osteogenesis imperfecta* (brittle bone disease) rendering M particularly susceptible to fractures. All three cases were turned down at first instance on the grounds that no duty of care was owed.

The Claimants appealed to the Court of Appeal where Lord Phillips identified a number of issues including: whether the position in *X and others (Minors) v Bedfordshire CC*,[86] and *M (A Minor) v Newham London BC, E (A Minor) v Dorset CC*[87] had developed since then, and whether more recent authority had varied those principles; whether *X and Others (Minors) v Bedfordshire CC*[88] could be distinguished on the facts; and whether a duty of care was owed to both the children and the parents in each case. Lord Phillips concluded that the effect of other decisions was to significantly restrict the effect of *X and Others (Minors) v Bedfordshire CC*[89] to the core proposition that decisions by a local authority whether or not to take a child into care were not reviewable by way of a claim in negligence.[90] This left the possibility for a different outcome, which proved to be the case.

As far as the position of the child was concerned, Lord Phillips considered that the decision in *X and Others (Minors) v Bedfordshire CC*[91] could not survive the Human Rights Act 1998, i.e. it could not be used as a precedent after HRA1998 came into force in October 2000; further, HRA1998 would have no effect on claims for wrongful acts or omissions which occurred before October 2000 (i.e. it could not be used to make such claims). It would therefore no longer be legitimate to rule that, as a matter of law, no common law duty of care was owed to a child in relation to the investigation of suspected child abuse. It was possible that there would be situations where it was not fair, just or reasonable to impose a duty of care, but each case would fall to be determined on its own facts.

Having established the position in relation to children, the judgment turned to the position of the parents. Although the position of the child in a common law negligence action had developed under the Human Rights Act 1998 the position in relation to parents was very different. It was held there were cogent reasons of public policy for concluding that, where child welfare decisions were being taken, no common law duty of care should be owed to them. Although decisions in relation to Article 13 established that parents and other adults must have a remedy, it did not follow that they would establish the same rights as children in relation to common law negligence. Parents could establish a breach of Article 8, and there were other remedies available to them in relation to specific situations, for example defamation. The rationale for the decision was that the duty owed to children was in potential conflict with the interests of parents. It was considered essential that professionals should not be inhibited in acting in the child's best interests by concerns that they might be in breach of a duty owed to parents as it would always be in the parents' interests that the child should not be removed, thus the child's interests may be in conflict with the interests of the parents.

In these cases the Claimants' counsel had tried to distinguish the cases from *X and Others (Minors) v Bedfordshire CC*[92] by arguing that there was a duty of care owed by the doctor who made the misdiagnosis to the child and the parents. This argument was rejected and was held to be unrealistic because the initial diagnosis of the doctor simply set in train the multidisciplinary approach. The moment the doctor suspected that the child had been abused, his duty to the child was in potential conflict with the parents.

Although the position in relation to remedies has developed in favour of children who now have a remedy in common law negligence, the current position is that their parents and other adults do not. The difficult balancing act that the courts were faced with has left parents in an unsatisfactory position despite their apparent right to an effective remedy and case law indicating success in relation to breaches of Article 8.

Conclusion: remedies – an inadequate position

Remedies are available in specific and limited circumstances, ranging from using the complaint system at one end of the spectrum, through to taking a case to the ECtHR at the other. However, the remedies do not adequately address the question of harm, and are severely restricted to certain types of litigants, particularly in the case of negligence where children have a cause of action but parents do not.

The courts' decisions have attempted to resolve some of the difficulties surrounding whether, and in what circumstances, a claim could succeed against a local authority or an assessing professional. Such claims could arise through over- or under-interference in relation to child abuse investigations, or a failure to act on the part of a local authority. The reasoning and decisions seem to provide some remedy in very restricted circumstances, but certain classes of claimant are excluded. The decisions do not adequately address some of the issues that arise, particularly in relation to the dilemmas of parents and the position of claimants such as that in *R v Swindon Borough Council*[93] who could not bring an end to the suspicion surrounding him. The decisions also do not help parents such as those in *M (A Minor) v Newham BC*[94] who were left distressed and traumatised by the situation despite not being either the child, or the alleged perpetrator of abuse.

This leaves parents in a difficult position although it has enabled children to claim damages. Some of the reasons for the distinction between children and parents do not stand up to scrutiny. Arguments that establishing a duty of care would create a conflict of interest for social workers and may cause them to act defensively are weak: a social worker acting in accordance with their statutory duty in a reasonable and proportionate way would have no reason to fear a negligence action. Furthermore, the notion that a local authority should have immunity from accountability regardless of the actions of their social workers seems to tacitly admit that social workers can behave in a damaging manner but need to be protected from the consequences. In addition, government has been keen to promote accountability in relation to social work mistakes if the issue is a lack of interference and this presumably also fuels defensive social work practice, creating an imbalance between the consequences for over- and under-interference.

The principle underpinning the remaining local authority and government immunity in relation to harm to parents caused by child protection and safeguarding processes of referral and assessment is that local authority social services departments have to be free to carry out their functions without the possibility of an action for negligence. However, simply denying the right to a remedy at common law does not address the issue of the harm caused to and the impact on parents, children and society. Ultimately it is not reasonable to deny a remedy to citizens harmed by negligent State interference, particularly where citizens are powerless to stop such interference. This entrenched position is enabling a power imbalance between State and family. If fault-based negligence is not available as a remedy to all harmed parties, then discussion of remedies must include the possibility of a means of compensating a wider class of harmed family members than children. The important principle here must be to promote family support.

In conclusion, there are numerous hurdles that must be overcome in order to obtain any form of remedy. Time limits are strict, particularly in relation to judicial review actions. The cost of bringing an action may be prohibitive. Finding a lawyer willing and able to bring an action on complex grounds with an uncertain chance of success is another challenge. Even if successful, damages are limited and remedies do not include important questions such as the support damaged families may need post-referral and assessment, or the importance of exoneration so families do not live with stigma.

If State powers and processes, particularly those involving a power imbalance are not acknowledged to be damaging then there will be insufficient remedy to deal with harm caused. There is no statutory remedy to counter the powers of the State in relation to referral and assessment, partly as the extent of the paternalistic drift of policy was not envisaged at the time of the Children Act 1989. Consequently the common law has had to develop piecemeal remedies as best it can. The time is right for a more fundamental review of remedies in light of the extent of modern State powers in order to re-establish the balance on a statutory footing. This would also clarify and control the extent of the powers, and of the adequacy of the associated remedies.

Notes

1   Reasonableness is embodied in the common law; *Associated Provincial Picture Houses Ltd v Wednesbury Corp* [1948] 1 K.B. 223. Proportionality has been imported and developed in the common law from Human Rights and European Union jurisprudence and is set out by Lord Steyn in: *R (Daly) v The Secretary of State for the Home Department* [2001] 2 AC 532, paras 25–8.

2   For example see: Murdock, G.P. (1949) *Social Structure*, Macmillan, New York, p. 1, which considers family to be a social group characterised by common residence, economic co-operation and reproduction. It includes adults of both sexes, at least two of whom maintain a socially approved relationship, and one or more children, own or adopted, of the sexually cohabiting adults.

3   Article 8, Human Rights Act 1998 c.42 concerns the right to private family life but 'family' is not restricted to biological family. European Court of Human Rights, Convention for the Protection of Human Rights and Fundamental Freedoms, as amended by Protocols Nos 11 and 14. Online at: www.echr.coe.int /Pages/home.aspx?p=home&c (Accessed 20 May 2016).

4   This is a consequence of the rise of modern families with step-parents, step-families, adopted members and same sex relationships.

5   The 'qualifying functions' were originally complaints relating to Part III issues but were extended in 2002 to include complaints under Parts IV and V. The complaint procedure is set out in the Children Act 1989 Representations Procedure (England) Regulations 2006 SI 2006/1783.

6   For example see: *R v London Borough of Barnet, ex parte B* [1994] 1 FLR 592 and *R v Royal Borough of Kingston-Upon-Thames, ex parte T* [1994] 1 FLR 798.

7   In: Murphy, J. (2003) 'Children in Need: The Limits of Local Authority Accountability', *Legal Studies* 23(1): 103–34, 130–2, Murphy explains that s.84 Children Act 1989 allows complaints to be referred to the Secretary of State for Health, but this is limited to an alleged failure of the local authority complying with its statutory duties under the Children Act 1989 c.41.

8   Smith, D.E (1990) *Facts, Texts and Femininity: Exploring the Relations of Ruling*, Routledge, London.

9   Lloyd-Bostock, S. (2007) 'The Jubilee Line Jurors: Does Their Experience Strengthen the Argument for Judge-only Trial in Long and Complex Fraud Cases?', *Criminal Law Review* (April): 255–73.

10 c.41. Part V of the Children Act 1989 deals with matters relating to the 'protection of children'.

11 For example, one of the reasons social workers failed to complete an Initial Assessment in relation to Khyra Ishaq was because, following their visit, Khyra's mother lodged a complaint with the local authority about the visit and the proposed assessment. See: Radford, J. (2010) *Serious Case Review Under Chapter VIII 'Working Together to Safeguard Children' In respect of the Death of a Child Case Number 14*, 26 April, Birmingham Safeguarding Children Board, p. 167. Online at: http://northumberlandlscb.proceduresonline.com/pdfs/kyhra_ishaq _scr.pdf (Accessed 1 May 2016).

12 The complaints system in relation to social services has evolved as part of the Department of Health's complaint system which includes NHS complaints procedures. The Local Authority Social Services and National Health Service Complaints (England) Regulations SI 2009/1768 was introduced with the implementation of joint complaints procedures from April 2009. See the following in relation to complaint system research and policy documentation: Simons, K. (1995) *I'm Not Complaining But . . . Complaints Procedures in Social Services Departments*, Joseph Rowntree Foundation; Department of Health (2006a)

Our Health, Our Say, Our Care, TSO, London; Health Service Ombudsman (2005) *Making Things Better? A Report on Reform of the NHS Complaints Procedure in England*, National Audit Office, HMSO, London; Healthcare Commission (2006) *Spotlight on Complaints*, TSO, London; Department of Health (2006b) *Learning from Complaints: Social Services Complaints Procedure for Adults*, Care Services Directorate, TSO, London; Department of Health (2006) *Supporting Staff, Improving Services: Guidance to Support Implementation of the National Health Service (Complaints) Amendment Regulations 2006*, TSO, London; Department of Health (2007) *Making Experiences Count: A New Approach to Responding to Complaints: A Document for Information and Comment*, TSO, London; Health Service Ombudsman (2008) *Feeding Back? A Report on Reform of the NHS Complaints Procedure in England*, National Audit Office, TSO, London; Healthcare Commission (2009) *Spotlight on Complaints*, TSO, London.

13 As laid down by Lord Diplock in: *Council for Civil Service Unions v Minister for the Civil Service* [1985] 1 AC 374. The reason for a judicial review is that the body's decision was based on either 'illegality, irrationality or procedural impropriety.' The proportionality of decisions is also grounds for review under EU law and the European Convention on Human Rights.

14 Under the Civil Procedure Rules, Part 54, Rule 54.19, the courts may quash decisions of public bodies, and either refer the matter back to the public body and 'direct it to reconsider the matter and reach a decision in accordance with the judgment of the court', or 'in so far as any enactment permits, substitute its own decision for the decision to which the claim relates'. Judicial review decisions are limited by s.31(1) Senior Courts Act 1981 c.54. Although redetermination is the most likely outcome there are other potential remedies: Quashing Order, Prohibiting Order, Mandatory Order, Declaration, Injunction and damages.

15 Although, see the comprehensive research paper: House of Commons Library (2006) *Judicial Review: A Short Guide to Claims in the Administrative Court*, Research Paper 06/44, 28 September 2006, HMSO, London. Online at: http://researchbriefings.files.parliament.uk/documents/RP06–44/RP06–44.pdf (Accessed 4 May 2016).

16 [2001] EWHC Admin 334.

17 Ibid., para. 35.

18 Ibid., para. 37.

19 [1996] AC 563.

20 [2001] EWHC Admin 334, para. 34.

21 Ibid., para. 37.

22 Ibid.

23 [2013] EWHC 416 (Admin) (13 March 2013).

24 Ibid., para. 69.

25 Ibid., para. 67.

26 *W v Westminster City Council and Anca Marks and James Thomas* [2004] EWHC 2866.

27 Ibid.

28 Ibid.

29 [2004] EWHC 2866.

30 [1998] UKHL 39; [1999] 2 AC 177.

31 [1998] UKHL 39, para. 214.

32 [2004] EWHC 2866, paras 25–60.

33 *X (Minors) v Bedford CC* [1995] 2 AC 663, which was heard in Strasbourg as: *Z and Others v United Kingdom* [2001] 2 FCR 246; (2002) 34 EHRR 3, found in favour of the applicant children in respect of a breach of Article 3.

34 See, for example the discussion in: Wrennall, L. (2010) 'Surveillance and Child Protection: De-mystifying the Trojan Horse', *Surveillance and Society* 7(3/4): 304–24, 309.
35 Article 6, Human Rights Act 1998 c.42.
36 Miles, J. (2002) 'Mind the Gap . . . Child Protection, Statutory Interpretation and the Human Rights Act', *Cambridge Law Journal* 61(3): 533–7, 533.
37 For example, Devon County Council considers that Article 6 'is likely to affect' Initial Assessments. See: Devon County Council (2004) *Multi-Agency Child Protection Procedures: Plymouth, Torbay & Devon, Area Child Protection Committees*, 22 December, Devon County Council, Section 5.1. Online at: www.devon.gov.uk/multi-agency-child-protection-procedures-2001.pdf (Accessed 1 May 2016).
38 S.1(1) Children Act 1989 c.41.
39 See 'Paper No. 4: The Legal Framework: An Analysis of the "Constitutional" European Approach to Issues of Data Protection and Law Enforcement' in: Brown, I. and Korff, D. (2004) *Privacy & Law Enforcement: Study for the Information Commissioner*, ICO, London.
40 See: *Amann v Switzerland (Application No 27798/95)* (2000) 30 EHRR 843.
41 Ibid.
42 Ibid., para. 78.
43 Ibid., para. 292.
44 Article 8(1) ECHR.
45 For example: *Sunday Times v United Kingdom* (A/30) (1979–80) 2 EHRR 245, para. 49.
46 See for example: *Malone v United Kingdom* (A/82) (1985) 7 EHRR 14, para. 67, which cites *Silver and Others v United Kingdom* (A/161) (1981) 3 EHRR 475, para. 90, and *Golder v United Kingdom* (A/18) (1979–80) 1 EHRR 524, para. 34.
47 Ibid.
48 This procedural aspect of the rights protected by the Convention is increasingly acknowledged in case law. This is consistent with Article 13 of the Convention (notably the only substantive provision in the ECHR that has not been included in the Human Rights Act 1998 c.42).
49 *Malone v United Kingdom* (A/82) (1985) 7 EHRR 14, paras 67–8.
50 Local Government Act 2000 c.22 s.2(1).
51 Children Act 1989 c.41.
52 See: Anderson, R., Brown, I., Clayton, R., Dowty, T., Korff, D. and Munro, E. (2006) *Children's Databases: Safety and Privacy, A Report for the Information Commissioner*, Foundation for Information Policy Research, Bedfordshire, p. 105. Online at: www.fipr.org/press/061122kids.html (Accessed 1 January 2016).
53 Department for Constitutional Affairs (2003) *Public Sector Data Sharing Guidance on the Law – November 2003*. Online at: http://webarchive.nationalarchives.gov.uk/+/http://www.justice.gov.uk/guidance/docs/data_sharing_legal_guidance.pdf (Accessed 5 May 2016).
54 *Peck v United Kingdom (Application No 44647/98)* (2003) 36 EHRR 41.
55 Department for Constitutional Affairs (n. 53), para. 3.26, referring to *Peck v The United Kingdom*, European Court of Human Rights Judgment, 28 January 2003. S.111 states 'a local authority shall have the power to do anything . . . which is calculated to facilitate, or is conducive or incidental to the discharge of any of their functions.' For a detailed description of *Peck* see: 'Paper No. 4', in Brown and Korff (2004) *Privacy & Law Enforcement*.
56 Criminal Justice and Public Order Act 1994 c.33.

57 Ibid., see paras 80, 85 and 87 of the judgment for the court's assessment of this issue.
58 Local Government Act 1972 c.70.
59 Anderson *et al.* (n. 52), p. 105.
60 Ibid., p. 106, from the judgment in *Z v Finland (Application No 22009/93)* [1997] ECHR 10.
61 Children Act 1989 c.41, s.3.30.
62 Anderson *et al.* (n. 52), para. 7.3(6).
63 Ibid., para. 7.3(7).
64 Anderson *et al.* (n. 52), p. 118.
65 Established in: *K v United Kingdom* (2009) 48 EHRR 29, para. 36, and reiterated in: *AD and OD v United Kingdom (Application No 28680/06)* [2010] ECHR 340, paras 68 and 84.
66 *AD and OD v United Kingdom (Application No 28680/06)* [2010] ECHR 340.
67 Ibid., para. 99.
68 Ibid., para. 95.
69 Ibid., para. 97.
70 See for example: *Frette v France (Application No 36515/97)* [2003] 2 FCR 39, para. 32.
71 *Marckx v Belgium* (A/31)(1979–80) 2 EHRR 330.
72 *Lebbink v Netherlands (Application No 45582/99)* [2004] 3 FCR 59; (2005) 40 EHRR 18.
73 *Marckx v Belgium*, para. 31.
74 Paramountcy in favour of children over adults and over other children is arguably incompatible with equality of rights under ECHR: Article 14 – Prohibition of discrimination. The enjoyment of the rights and freedoms set forth in this Convention shall be secured without discrimination on any ground such as sex, race, colour, language, religion, political or other opinion, national or social origin, association with a national minority, property, birth or other status. Convention for the Protection of Human Rights and Fundamental Freedoms, 1950, Rome, 4.XI.1950, Registry of the European Court of Human Rights. Online at: www.echr.coe.int/Documents/Convention_ENG.pdf (Accessed 7 May 2016). Following the Lisbon Treaty the Convention is now part of EU Law and the supremacy of EU Law over national law (for EU member States) makes this a General Principle of Law.
75 See: *Re KD (A Minor) (Ward: Termination of Access)* [1988] 1 AC 896, 820 and *J, P v Miss C, S County Council (Case No: IP33/03)* [2005] EWHC 1016 (Fam).
76 Herring, J. (1999) 'The Human Rights Act and the Welfare Principle in Family Law: Conflicting or Complementary?', 11 *Child and Family Law Quarterly* 223–31.
77 See for example: *Re H (Children)(Contact Order)(No.2)* [2001] 3 FCR 385 (FamDiv) and *Re B (A Minor) (Adoption: Natural Parent)* [2001] UKHL 70.
78 [1995] 2 AC 663.
79 [2001] 2 FCR 246, (2002) 34 EHRR 3.
80 [1995] 2 AC 663.
81 Ibid.
82 [2001] 2 FLR 549.
83 The issues these cases raise have been considered extensively in academic literature. For example: Johnson, M. (2004) 'Public Authority Liability in Child Abuse Compensation Claims – the *X v Bedfordshire CC* Case Undergoes a Re-examination by the Court of Appeal', *Journal of Personal Injury Law* 1: 28–38; Mildred, M. (2004) 'Personal Injury – Psychiatric Harm – Parents – Children', *Journal of Personal Injury Law* 1: 9–12; Williams, K. (2005)

'Abusing Parents and Children: Negligence Remedy Not Afforded to Parents', *Journal of Professional Negligence* 21: 196–203; Case, P. (2005) 'The Accused Strikes Back: The Negligence Action and Erroneous Allegations of Child Abuse', *Professional Negligence* 21(4): 214–32; Gumbel, E., Scorer, R., Johnson, M. (2006) 'Recent Developments in Child Abuse Compensation Claims', *Journal of Personal Injury Law* 1: 21–8; Inglis, A. (2009) 'Personal Injury Claims for Child Protection Failures', *Scots Law Times* 29: 173–6.

84 [2003] EWCA CIV 1151.
85 Ibid. In: *JD v East Berkshire* JD, the mother, had been incorrectly diagnosed with Munchausen syndrome by proxy by Professor Southall before it was discovered that in fact her son, M, was suffering from extensive and severe allergies. In: *K and another v Dewsbury Healthcare NHS Trust and another*, the Appellants were R, a 9-year-old girl and her father, K. The trial judge had held that R had an arguable claim for clinical negligence against the doctor who made the incorrect diagnosis. The NHS trust did not appeal from that finding. However, R also claimed against the local authority (whose social services initiated the child protection investigation). The trial judge applied the policy considerations in *X v Bedfordshire CC*. As far as the father was concerned, his claim could only be attributed to the child protection investigation itself. Again the trial judge had applied the policy considerations in *X v Bedfordshire CC*. In: *K and another v Oldham and another* a nine-month-old child had *osteogenesis imperfecta* (brittle bone disease). The parents were suspected of injuring her before the condition was discovered.
86 [1995] 2 AC 663.
87 [1995] 3 All ER 353.
88 [1995] 2 AC 663.
89 Ibid.
90 Lord Phillips also considered two New Zealand cases: *AG v Prince* [1998] 1 NZLR 262 and *B v A-G of New Zealand* [2003] UKPC 61. In the latter case a claim by a child was allowed, but rejected in relation to the father on the grounds that no duty of care was owed because he was the alleged perpetrator: the statutory duty on social services was not imposed for the benefit of alleged perpetrators.
91 [1995] 2 AC 663.
92 Ibid.
93 [2001] EWHC Admin 334.
94 [1995] 2 AC 663.

8   Reforming policy
The politics of change

The question of reform

✸ The examination in this book points to a conclusion that the balance of State power and private rights is weighted in favour of the State. The rationale is that it provides a robust system of welfare interventions prioritising a risk avoidant approach in relation to children. However, the approach does not take account of:

- the plight of non-abusing families 'caught' in a system which many find very damaging;
- an overloaded system that risks missing serious cases; or
- the statistical evidence showing the failure of current policy to identify more child abuse in proportion to the increased number of referrals.

The intention of any legislation is to create a regulatory framework to solve or avoid a problem that would occur should the legislation not exist. In the case of s.47 Children Act 1989, the problem the legislation intended to resolve was that of severe maltreatment of children resulting in significant harm, particularly when inflicted by parents or care givers. Neither s.17 or s.47 were designed as a general panacea for government strategies of early intervention, nor a gateway to interference into parental autonomy in an attempt to achieve optimum child welfare, no matter how robust the social welfare claims. The policy drift away from this intention towards early intervention when 'signs' are noted and 'concerns' are raised indicates the need to provide a remedy in the cases where, following referral and assessment, there is little or no evidence to support that children are being harmed, but families are left distressed and frightened. There is need to restore balance to a system of increasingly interventionist and intrusive State processes of surveillance and interference, should they cause harm, whilst providing a framework to protect children from significant harm where possible.

The intention of the Children Act 1989 was to reduce unnecessary State interference, whilst allowing the State to act to protect a child where there was significant danger to them in their home circumstances. Specific remedy for families harmed by local authorities fulfilling their duty under s.47 to make inquiries was not considered necessary: the intention was to reduce interference, not increase it and harm families in the process. Despite this intention, policy has introduced an unprecedented level of State surveillance and interference via the inclusion of safeguarding processes, enabled by s.11 Children Act 2004 and *Working Together to Safeguard Children*.[1] Taken together, they embed a drift towards mass surveillance of all families and targeted early intervention as soon as a pre-determined risk factor is noted and reported by any agency with whom children have contact. Children and parents have few rights to stop or prevent these processes.

There is a need for a reconceptualised and more balanced legal framework to be put into place in order to reduce the largely unfettered State powers, and to provide protection and remedy for parents and children caught 'in the system' unable to be exonerated and suffering harm. In the current policy and legislative framework these issues are not given adequate consideration. The consequence for families is that there is no mechanism for adequate remedy for harm caused by the suspicion of child abuse and the mechanisms of State investigation of it. The current position is not satisfactory for social workers or for families. From a family's perspective the most serious adverse impacts are long-term family fear and stress, potential serious distress, illness and severely damaged relationships between families and the State.[2] From a local authority's perspective the most serious issues are the large number of families referred to them who are potentially harmed by investigative processes, those families' potential unwillingness to have any further contact with State agencies, and the mass of data potentially masking some of the rare but real cases that end in a fatality and increasing burden on local authorities and individual social workers. A policy rethink and a specifically drafted framework of controls and remedies is indicated.

The question of how best to address these issues is complex and sensitive, but it is worth bearing in mind that the current system does not work well from a welfare or a justice perspective. Serious cases are missed. Judicial decisions are made on the balance of probabilities, which leaves respondents in contested proceedings vulnerable, but with fewer due process rights than in the criminal justice system. Continual surveillance and continuous assessment leaves children and families living with long-term uncertainty, a position known to cause stress. For children who are removed from their families, the future is uncertain and historically in such situations their life chances have been badly compromised.

In child welfare legislation there are frequently competing and unequal interests involved, with the State championing those of the child, whose interests are paramount.[3] Consequently, parents' interests are *de facto* subordinate. Conversely, so are the child's views unless they are synonymous with those of the State. Children cannot stop the State acting in what it considers to be their best interests during the referral and assessment process. For cases that progress to litigation power transfers from the local authority to the courts: it is a moot point whether it is a frequent occurrence for courts to disagree with local authority findings. The data is not readily available. This is a question of growing importance as there is increasing judicial reliance on expert evidence from the instigators of the proceedings.[4] This is directly at odds with the underpinning theories surrounding the use of expert evidence, which should be impartial.[5] Consequently, although children are not owned by the State or by parents, they are nevertheless at high risk of being State-controlled if the State considers their parents have not adequately discharged their parental responsibilities. This has the potential to cause harm to both parents and children, particularly when families are simply seeking the provision of services under s.17. When this happens children have a limited right to a remedy in certain circumstances at common law, but parents do not.[6]

Family support and the enforcement of children's rights are not analogous and are frequently incompatible. Global approaches to child protection tend to fall into either the family support model or the children's rights model but not both together.[7] Although there are policy variations between England, Scotland, Wales and Northern Ireland, the overall policy approach of the UK has prioritised children's rights over provision of family support, even in s.17 cases. There is no mechanism for families requiring support to extricate themselves from this quasi-consensual process without potential fear of escalation into the s.47 coercive framework. There is also no mechanism for children to have an absolute right to stop the State acting in their 'best interests' (decided by the State), whether *Gillick*[8] competent or otherwise, once things are escalated. The question of consent is contentious under this framework. Children may not be in any meaningful sense able to give informed consent to this complex process, may not be asked or may be too young. Any child (or adult) may be unable to fully grasp how their data will be processed and stored, or understand the adverse inferences that could be drawn from it. Regardless of the evidence demonstrating that the vast majority of referrals amount to no more than a s.17 outcome,[9] these significant intrusions into their privacy have adverse consequences into their adult lives. Children, even when they reach adulthood, are unable to protect themselves against these consequences. The phrase 'known to social services' is a risk factor and is a stigmatising data identity which, as noted above, forms part of the questioning of parents in a social work assessment. This means that an adult child's status as having been subjected to interventions as a child will be seen as a risk factor in relation to their own parenting.

This has moved a long way from the intention of the legislation relating to the investigation of families under s.47, which was intended to be used where *significant harm was reasonably suspected*. This does not mean 'any harm', 'non-significant harm' or child-rearing practices that deviate from norms but are not causing significant harm. The use of the assessment framework under s.17 to assess families who would like to access rationed social services was intended to be used consensually. It was to encourage social workers and families to 'work together' to gain a detailed insight into their family's circumstances, not to be used to gather evidence for future non-consensual interventions and potential litigation.

Child protection and safeguarding has thus expanded from a genuine attempt for the State to fulfil its statutory obligations in relation to children who have suffered non-accidental injury, to a paternalistic programme of surveillance and interference into private family life. This has enabled the system to be used for parental non-compliance with State ideals in relation to child rearing. It is particularly evident in the massive expansion of what is understood to be meant by 'child abuse' and 'safeguarding', particularly in relation to areas that are either very hard to precisely define[10] or have been held unreliable in criminal appeals.[11] There are several reasons why this has not been recognised as a serious issue requiring urgent review. Fundamentally, these reasons stem from the perception that the need to protect children overrides other considerations, together with a perception that there is a high prevalence of undetected abused children and dangerous parents.[12] When viewed through the lens of protecting children as the paramount consideration, issues of due process[13] can be seen as subordinate to this overriding aim. As a consequence, balance is lost.

Framework for a new approach

The following are suggestions to contribute to the formation of a new policy framework, offering a starting point for policy reform within the existing legislation. The question of reform is complex, but, as a general rule, a starting premise must be to ensure there is a system in place that works so as to minimise harm to all involved. This is preferable to continuing with a system that largely identifies and deals with s.17 cases but treats them as part of an integrated system together with s.47 and providing inadequate remedies once the State withdraws. The literature concerning harm caused by State processes is sufficiently extensive to indicate that procedural reform is needed in cases where parents have not caused significant harm to their children but are harmed by State processes of investigation. The aim of this section is to consider how this procedural reform might be structured.

Any new framework needs to focus on the critical points in the current system where there is the most potential for State harm, either from false positives or false negatives entering and travelling through the referral and assessment system. The following areas are the critical points where change is most needed:

(1) *Privacy, data and consent.* This thread should run through the whole of the process, taking account of the Anderson *et al.* recommendations. It is suggested that the highest level of control over State practices recommended by Anderson *et al.* is adopted in relation to all stages of child protection and safeguarding processes. This would involve:
   • introduction of a Code of Practice;
   • rebalancing rationed and unrationed family services; and
   • pulling back government spending on profit-making child protection activities (in the public and private sectors), particularly in relation to curtailing the introduction of new, privately commissioned and costly IT systems and risk assessment tools.

(2) *Referrals.* This would include the manner of making, recording and acting on them. The focus for reform would be:
   • separating out referrals into s.17 and s.47 categories at the first point of contact, with the caveat that referrals could fall into both categories;
   • providing greater clarity for referrers in relation to what is, and is not, appropriate to refer in the categories of 'need' and 'harm';

- dismantling the policy interpretation of s.11 as a mandatory reporting gateway; and
- and legal advice to be offered at the point where a referral is accepted by a local authority.

(3) *Assessments.* This would be specifically:

- introduction of a Code of Practice surrounding the management of referrals and assessments;
- introduction of forensically led investigations in cases of reasonably suspected significant harm in order to ascertain factual circumstances. This would be carried out via a bespoke investigatory local authority body and the police working as one investigatory unit to ascertain whether there is sufficient evidence to reach the welfare threshold and/or the criminal threshold for further action to be taken;
- establishment of an independent decision-making body analogous to the Crown Prosecution Service (CPS);
- s.17 assessments to be carried out by professional social workers working within local authorities who would refer s.47 matters to the new investigatory joint social work and police investigating body. This body would have a framework taking account of the need to undertake evidence gathering within a framework that balances crime (and abuse) control with due process. This would operate alongside increased provision of universal and means-tested services for all families at a lower level, available without assessment; and
- requirement for local authority data to be collected so as to enable local and national data to be annually independently audited and evaluated.

(4) *Outcomes and redress.* This would include:

- clear outcomes from the new investigatory body establishing whether there is sufficient evidence for:
  - o a criminal action – in which case evidence would be referred to the CPS;
  - o a public law action – in which case evidence would be referred to the new equivalent of the CPS;
  - o both;
  - o whether a child 'in need' has been identified; or
  - o whether a family should be exonerated or not; and
- no fault compensation should be available in circumstances where families are harmed by State practices of child protection and safeguarding referrals and assessments.

Privacy, data and consent: taking the Anderson recommendations seriously

Anderson *et al.*'s two major research publications in 2006 and 2009 concerned children's and families' data with emphasis on questions of information sharing, decision making and privacy.[14] Both reports contained robust recommendations to protect privacy without compromising child safety. In the 2006 Report the point was made that European countries tended to have a widespread agreement over their approach:

> We believe that the law and practice in other countries . . . can help the Information Commissioner to formulate and support his own position on the matters discussed in this report. In particular, there appears to be widespread agreement between the data protection authorities on the Continent . . . .[15]

This widespread agreement related to the following important issues:

- Data protection laws and principles should be applied with *extra force* to data on minors. It is particularly important to avoid stigmatising children by computer.
- Special care should be taken in seeking consent from minors.
- Involving parents in decisions on under-age children (except in special circumstances) is to be encouraged; failing to involve parents may render the consent of a minor invalid and/or the processing unfair.[16]

Anderson *et al.* stressed that confidentiality is crucially important and considered that 'professional duties of confidence should therefore not be easily overridden'.[17] The rationale was that current data protection legislation already allows for data to be shared and disclosed under certain circumstances of risk. For example, if there is a reasonable suspicion of significant harm and an identifiable, actual risk is being assessed, there is an existing gateway for data sharing. They pointed out that 'the data protection laws do not stand in the way of such disclosures anywhere.'[18]

However, a general wish to assess because a family has certain characteristics or there is a low level of general 'concern' where following child protection training, leading professionals working with children to spot 'risk characteristics' and 'signs of abuse' do not fall into this category. This type of data trawling amounts to a fishing expedition. Consequently, the Report highlighted concerns about disclosing and sharing data for reasons of rationed social welfare or general concerns, rather than for specific events and precise reasons. The authors considered this type of data collecting and sharing should be 'strictly limited – and require clear and specific legal authority, preferably in primary legislation'.[19]

These recommendations make the point that a general welfare argument cannot simply override protections and controls that are already in place, not just in the UK but across Europe, to protect the rights of citizens to be free from unnecessary State interference. Adherence to these principles is necessary if adequate balance is to be maintained between privacy and interference. However, the current collecting and sharing of data about families in the UK particularly following the refocussing debate is based on a dominant welfare discourse which is out of balance with concerns for privacy. Reform ensuring that policy and practice in relation to referral and assessment adheres to privacy guidelines is essential.

Anderson *et al.* also recommend curtailing the use of automated systems in relation to decision making. This is another area where caution needs to be exercised in relation to welfare policies. Risk assessments have an extremely high false positive rate even when not automated.[20] Decision making on the basis of such information is tantamount to profiling, or 'predicting abuse'. This creates a scenario where no concerns need to exist, other than the data profile. Anderson *et al.* consider that:

> the law should not seek to take away from the professional his or her proper job to decide what is in the best interest of a child . . . Automated systems tend to do precisely that, even if initially supposedly limited to the generating of indicative 'alerts' only. Reliance on automatically generated indicators and 'profiles' in the taking of important decisions on children violates their human dignity, identity and personality.[21]

They recommend *inter alia* that the Information Commissioner should:

* confirm the importance of strict data protection for children;
* clarify the requirements for valid consent by minors, and the need to involve parents whenever possible; and
* stress that disclosures and sharing of data on minors can be based only on specific, clear statutory provisions that reflect the principle of proportionality and respect professional competence and discretion.[22]

To reflect the Anderson *et al.* recommendations, the introduction of a Code of Practice analogous to PACE to regulate child protection and safeguarding referrals and assessments is one way to ensure that these issues are taken seriously and have been addressed. It should also ensure the UK's policies are in line with policies elsewhere in the EU which focus on strict data protection for children with emphasis on consent and parental involvement.

In the 2009 report *Database State*,[23] further recommendations were made in relation to how data should be collected, held and managed by government, indicating the position was still unsatisfactory. *Database State* was written by a team from the Foundation for Information Policy Research that included some of Britain's foremost experts in information systems and human rights. An important focus of the Report was on consent: 'Sensitive personal information should normally only be collected and shared with the subject's consent – and where practical people should opt in rather than opting out.'[24] This reverts to the point made earlier that, unless s.47 procedures are invoked on a more clearly defined notion of 'core abuse',[25] consent should be fundamental to the processes.

Anderson *et al.* recommend in relation to breaches that 'Individuals should be able to enforce their privacy in court on human-rights grounds without being liable for costs – the State has massive resources to contest cases while the individual does not.'[26] This attempt to address this power imbalance between citizens and the State is important, and is a necessary reform. The burden should be shifted away from individuals in cases where parents have not harmed their children. The State should bear the cost of unwarranted intrusion if it has caused harm via a specific framework of no-fault remedies, discussed later in this chapter.

Database State also makes the point that there has been a policy of collecting increasingly large amounts of personal data from users of public services. Unless private data is disclosed, services are denied or the denial can act as a trigger for referral.[27] The report advocates the return to the position where citizens can anonymously use services without offering their data in return for permission to access them:

> Citizens should have the right to access most public services anonymously. We have been moving from a world in which departments had to take a positive decision to collect data, to one where they have to take a positive decision not to. This needs to be challenged.[28]

An important aspect of policy reform would be to rebalance the use of universal and rationed services more appropriately. The loss of privacy in exchange for services for children in need is a high price for families to pay; the rationed services are 'paid for' by non-pecuniary means: the relinquishing of family privacy and the gathering of extensive data on the family.

Database State also makes a further set of recommendations on how government should go about developing and building IT systems more effectively in the future, which include specific changes to the way in which IT projects are commissioned, managed and understood in relation to government services for the public. One consideration is that 'the procurement and development of new database systems should be subject to much greater public scrutiny and openness'.[29] This would arguably prompt debate about policies, particularly non-consensual policies that affect families. Its conclusion in relation to the power that has been allowed to vest in private, profit-making companies to develop systems in relation to government policy is that '[t]here should never again be a government IT project – merely projects for business change that may be supported by IT. Computer companies must never again drive policy.'[30] These recommendations should be adopted. Introducing these three privacy-, data- and consent-related reforms would provide a foundation for rethinking the precise mechanisms of referral and assessment. A Code of Practice, a rebalancing of early intervention services to remove the need for intrusive assessment from families simply requesting services, and the scaling back of government expenditure on the 'child protection industry' provides the basis of a more robust framework. Consent should be at the centre of policy and practice unless there is clear justification for s.47 to be invoked. The following sections set out an example of what a new framework could look like. It is a starting point to address the issues identified as areas of priority for change.

Referrals: improving methods of making and recording referrals

The referral of a child to a local authority is the moment when the use of State mass surveillance of all families moves to targeted intervention. The most obviously indicated reform is to improve the methods and rationale for making and record-ing referrals. The data shows that the vast majority of referrals are not assessed at all, or are assessed and found to fit the s.17 criteria, or require no further action. In addition, research studies looking at the impact on families indicates that the refo-cussing debate has not resolved the problems flagged in *Messages from Research*,[31] but seems to have compounded them. This is not the fault of the debate, it is sim-ply that its interpretation has enabled policy to drift further towards embedding coercive practices into consensual areas.

These issues have not been acknowledged as a serious problem. The govern-ment does not adequately audit any adverse impact caused by their own policies, or adequately evaluate how effective or efficient, or even how lawful they are. Centrally held data differs from year to year making comparative analysis time consuming and difficult.[32] A rigorous recording of data at the point of referral and at every point of decision making, both at local and national level, is indi-cated. Additionally, the flood of low-level risk-related 'concerns' based on identi-fication in the community of highly speculative 'signs' interpreted from children's behaviour has the potential to mask serious cases whilst creating a very large num-ber of false positives. It also creates an increased danger of categorisation errors which are inadequately addressed via Serious Case Reviews, leading to an endless cycle of missed cases and repeated reviews.[33]

Policy has widened the net via the drive towards assessment as a means of being eligible for early intervention. Early intervention extends far further than the services envisaged under s.17, leaving the emphasis increasingly on assessing risk. The holistic assessment that takes place may be described as having extended so far so as to be tantamount to imposing a kind of child protection inquiry on children about whom there has been no allegation of abuse or neglect.[34]

The fundamental reform required to address these issues is to separate out notifications to local authority social services departments at the outset and to categorise them as requiring an initial s.17 social work response, a s.47 social work and criminal investigative response delivered via co-investigation, or both responses in tandem but carried out separately. This necessitates moving away from both the pre- and post-refocussing 'trawling' response, both of which notionally treat all referrals at the outset in the same manner. The two extremes of the pendulum swing, from treating all referrals as allegations of child abuse to treating all referrals as a notification of a child in need, have now been tested. This has led to a third way which encompasses the least clear of both: all referrals are now subject to a continuous assessment and it is difficult to separate out the precise boundaries of ss.17 and 47.

In addition to creating the welfare/policing dichotomy this approach does not heed the warnings from social work commentators such as L. Davies who advo-cates moving away from the post-refocussing preventative approach, arguing that:

> The rationale for a prevention approach as presented in the mid-90s was to challenge over-zealous professionals, excessive State intrusion into family life, a reactive incident-led forensic approach and financial resources deemed to be

wasted on 'unrequired' investigations (Horwath 2002, Cleaver and Walker 2004). However, it was exactly these features which, by 2009, emerged as a result of policies supposedly designed to achieve the opposite. The prevention agenda had progressed to mark the destruction of child protection systems (Munro and Calder 2005, House of Commons 2009), a devaluing of professional investigative skills (Lonne et al., 2009:60), punitive, pathologising approaches to child victims (Parton 2006:144) and to those professionals who represented the voices of vulnerable children (Fairweather 2008a, Ahmed 2007, Waugh 2007).[35]

If consensual notifications of potential need and consensual and non-consensual referrals of reasonably suspected significant harm were separated out at the outset the system would be considerably simplified. It would enable any suggestion of maltreatment to be swiftly dealt with, leaving questions of need, and questions of significant harm, to be addressed by separate specialist social workers who are working within the framework of either s.17 or s.47, and therefore do not have the complications of a dual role. It is also recommended that risk-only-based 'concerns', particularly those based on characteristics, should concurrently be reduced via a rebalancing towards non-rationed services, with an additional layer of means- and need-tested early intervention services. A similar model operates in relation to services to care for the elderly.

Where there is a 'reasonable suspicion of significant harm' (which is not the same as 'any suspicion'), s.47 referrals should be treated as a separate and immediate priority, forensically investigated by police officers and s.47 social workers. Under their separate remits, the members of the unit would consider separately the s.47 thresholds as well as criminal thresholds with reference to the different standards of proof. Knowledge and good forensic practice could be shared under this model. It is, of course, the case that 'significant harm' to a child is also quite likely to amount to a criminal offence in many circumstances, albeit to a different evidential standard. Not only would it be easier to collect and analyse data in order to see how the system is working, but the response to referrals could be more targeted to address the reasons for it.

Within this framework, professional social work within the traditional local authority framework could specialise in referrals categorised as s.17 and focus on providing support and services for families classed as being 'in need' and who fall above the threshold for the rebalanced increased universal and means-tested service model. If during the course of delivering those services a s.47 or a criminal suspicion arose this would be referred on. The judgment in *F v Cumbria County Council, M, The Children (by their Children's Guardian)*[36] exemplifies the reasons why this approach is desirable. In this case Mr Justice Jackson found on the balance of probabilities that Poppi Worthington's father had sexually abused her before her death. No criminal charges had been brought against the father, who was the applicant in this case. The father brought the action as his surviving children were made subject to a s.31 care order and he wanted to appeal an earlier finding that it was in their best interests for the care order to be made.

The resultant public outcry led to the father apparently receiving death threats and leaving the country. The outcry centred around the perceived investigative anomalies of a criminal justice system and a social work welfare system that did not operate coherently together where there was an allegation of a criminal act against a child. Whilst it is the case that different standards of proof apply in the criminal justice and the public family systems, the same evidence should be available to both. Although the procedural arrangements for sharing information and investigating undoubtedly are already linked, the entrenched adherence of ss.17 and 47 to each other still underpins procedural ideology. Rethinking and understanding s.47 as a potentially coercive, investigative process in cases of reasonably suspected significant harm to children locates it towards a model where procedural fairness, justice and strength of evidence must play an important part.

This approach would necessitate careful thought about the number of referrals classified as s.47 at the outset. Cases would by necessity be able to be considered concurrently s.17 and s.47 if both were evident in the referral information, but with the assessment and investigation remaining separate. The s.47 investigation has the statutory gateway needed to obtain information from those carrying out the s.17 assessment, in addition to the usual gateways enabling information transfer from other agencies. This would provide a clearer evidential pathway and separation through the process of the Public Law Outline 2014[37] and would remove the fundamental problems of the welfare/policing dichotomy.[38] It would more accurately reflect the information provided by government statistics on the eventual outcome showing most cases are ultimately cases of need. This structure would not be a bar to cases categorised as s.17 being able to be investigated under s.47, nor would it prevent families initially investigated under s.47 being offered s.17 services from the local authority if they were requested via the separate process. Categorisation errors are a major concern under the current system. This new approach would make the separations explicit and able to be easily audited. The rebalancing of universal services with emphasis on family support, and on a layer of means-tested services, preserves the integrity of families' privacy and data without compromising the ability for referrals to be made if genuinely necessary.[39]

There is no evidence that treating all referrals as either s.17 or s.47 at the outset has resolved the problems consistently highlighted since the Children Act 1989. It is costly, overloading social workers and potentially masking very serious cases of abuse whilst concurrently causing unnecessary damage to frightened families who have not abused their children. It could be described as the worst of both worlds. There are numerous examples from Serious Case Reviews highlighting the problem. A high profile example is the tragic death of Peter Connolly, known as 'Baby P'. In Peter Connolly's case a s.17 approach was found to have dominated social work response, which focussed on supporting Peter's mother.[40] Professional response to publicity surrounding Peter's death (the publicity occurred some considerable time after the event and was triggered by the subsequent criminal proceedings) has been termed the 'Baby P effect' and is likely to have triggered an increase in routing of referrals towards s.47 and s.31 proceedings, and an increased number of families travelling through the system to litigation.[41]

Neither universal response to referrals takes sufficient account of the underlying categorisation issues, and both run the risk of high profile problems and public and professional response to them. L. Davies notes that '[t]he universal approach has led to incidents becoming lost amongst numbers of low-level referrals, leading to the tragic consequences now apparent from analysis of serious case reviews (Munro 2008).'[42] Although rarely described as such there has been a system of mandatory reporting in place in England since the implementation of the s.11 Children Act 2004. This was introduced by policy makers to interpret the appropriate professional response to s.11. Munro and Parton note that since 2004, when the effect of refocussing could be seen, a system that 'is far more inclusive and wide-ranging than any other system in the world' has been revealed.[43] The authors conclude that:

> England is in the process of introducing a mandatory reporting system not based on any notion of child abuse but on the basis of 'a cause for concern', which is not defined in the legislation. The new policy of 'safeguarding' children has a much wider remit than just 'protecting' children from abuse or neglect. It aims to ensure all children reach the government's 'preferred outcomes' in terms of achievement at school, health, and behaviour.[44]

This system requires mandatory reporting for many professionals working with children under the provisions of s.11. It is quite correct to state that this is far more intrusive than simply a mandate to report suspected abuse; it includes the legal requirement to report suspected need and children showing suspected 'signs of abuse', which means a broad spectrum of behaviours in children which may or may not be significant. This is carried out under the guise of 'safeguarding', but its extension to 'promoting welfare' has widened the net. In addition policy enforces referral of 'concerns' based on risk models with a very low evidence base and high error rate. The quality of training for professionals caught in the s.11 requirement reinforces this problem.[45] This is the most intrusive statutory system that could be envisaged. In addition to system overload and increased risk of categorisation errors, mandatory reporting can also discourage children trusting adults and disempower them in relation to decision making. Consequently the current requirement in the statutory guidance for s.11's 'safeguarding and promoting welfare' duty to equate to mandatory reporting should be dismantled.

Justification for this suggestion can be drawn from the numeric consequence of rationed early intervention and the s.11 mandatory reporting requirement. The ratio of referred cases to cases of detected abuse has dramatically fallen since the Children Act 1989 was implemented, from 24 per cent to 7 per cent, leaving the system inefficient and error prone.[46] The large number of Serious Case Reviews provides further evidence of the adverse effect of mandatory reporting of low-level 'safeguarding' and 'welfare' concerns into a system whose legislative framework is to deal with reasonably suspected significant harm. Social workers are compromised as a consequence of their dual roles of professional social service assessors and providers, and forensic investigators.

Refocussing may not only have eroded privacy and freedom and failed to protect more children, it may have increased the danger to some children. Taken in the context of what is now known about the harm such interference causes, this is unsatisfactory. L. Davies concludes strongly that:

> A devaluing of professional knowledge and a 'squandering of the collective intelligence about how to protect children' (Campbell 2008) has led both to the unnecessary removal of children (false positives) and to inadequate intervention to protect abused children (false negatives) (Lonne et al. 2009:176, Waldfogel 2000b:315).[47]

Assessments: a bespoke investigatory body and Code of Practice

One of the key issues in relation to the current system of referral and 'holistic investigation' is the lack of boundary in social work assessment. Another important issue is the problem of social workers carrying out the intrusive and risk-based 'holistic assessments' whilst also trying to 'work with' families. This mixed assessment approach creates the welfare/policing dichotomy, previously identified and described by the author as a consequence of current policy.[48] This is a particular issue in cases where the referral itself was not disputed as the family want s.17 services, but the resultant quasi-coercive assessment creates conflict and fear of escalation should consent be withdrawn. This problem is well noted in literature but has not been addressed in practice. Dumbrill, for example, notes that 'Separation into policing and helping cases may be possible from the perspective of those delivering service, but not from the perspective of parents on the receiving end of service.'[49] In relation to disputed, non-consensual referrals, an investigatory body whereby the criminal and public family issues can be investigated by professionals skilled in obtaining evidence to the relevant thresholds would bring the investigative nature of child abuse allegations into a framework that could more closely align with the approach taken in the criminal justice system. It would enable a swifter, more evidence-focussed, forensic aim with clearer outcomes and protections for children, parents and any accused third parties. This would apply in cases where families do not agree to the reasons for the referral, particularly where it relates to an allegation of parental neglect, abuse or insufficiency.

Such an investigatory body could comprise specialist police officers and specialist social workers. The body would have a separate remit from social work practitioners providing professional, s.17 services to families. Social workers are not principally forensic investigators and in addition are not being given an appropriate framework to do this type of investigation. The separate body of specialist social workers and police, with expertise in law and evidence gathering and analysis, could conduct an accountable, transparent single assessment which would establish whether there is sufficient evidence for criminal and/or public family proceedings to be brought, whether there is no evidence of 'significant harm' but there is a 'need' to be addressed by s.17 social work or whether there is simply no evidence which would justify State interference. This investigative approach addresses issues such as 'A lack of joint investigation of child abuse allegations risks flawed judgments in the context of both over- and under-intervention with consequential breaches of the right of children to protection.'[50] By keeping coercive interventions to a minimum but applying them where necessary, it would also align with more historic approaches to the investigation and control of child maltreatment within the criminal justice framework. It would also rebalance the system towards the intention of the Children Act 1989 to keep coercive and non-coercive interventions separate. Introducing a national body akin to the CPS for public family law cases under s.31 would provide a further layer of procedural justice, indicated for the same reasons the CPS was implemented in 1984.

The new investigatory body would work under a statutory Code of Practice, which would be similar to PACE. An analogy can be drawn with the arguments surrounding the need for PACE: vulnerable members of society need to be protected from crime, and this aim has to be balanced against the need for rights of citizens suspected of committing crime to be protected from excessive or unjust State practices. This is the key plank of due process and is particularly important in the UK's adversarial legal system. The PACE Codes of Practice[51] provide a statement of the rights of the individual and the powers of the police. Police powers of arrest are wide and are not without criticism, but at least afford some level of statutory framework protecting the accused and setting out the conduct of investigation. Cape, however, notes that the ability of the police to arrest upon 'suspicion' gives them 'almost unlimited powers'.[52] Sanders supports this conclusion and also expresses concerns that the balance between the rights of individual citizens to be free from unwarranted State interference and the right of the State to prevent and detect crime is weighted too far in favour of the State.[53] The same threshold for non-consensual State interference, 'reasonable suspicion', is evident in s.47 itself, but the drive towards referral of any 'concern' about a child in child protection and safeguarding training leaves all referred families vulnerable to excessive or unnecessary interventions but without the same protection of a Code of Practice. Although PACE may be argued to be inadequate to prevent miscarriages of justice in the criminal system, a citizen suspected of a serious crime against a stranger is protected by a Code of Practice, whereas a parent suspected of having a child either 'in need' or 'at risk' is not. As the aim of both systems is intended to protect vulnerable citizens it seems unreasonable in a socially just society to accept that a Code of Practice is necessary in one situation but not the other.

The Code of Practice would clearly set out the controls and conditions that are feasible with respect to initiating and conducting assessments and investigations. The focus would be on where consent is or is not necessary, and evidence-based practice in relation to fact finding. The evidence basis for seeking information would be clearly defined and justified. The issue of consent within this framework would be addressed at each stage of assessment, and clear guidelines set out to separate consensual from non-consensual assessment. The circumstances in which assessment is undertaken in relation to 'need' and in relation to whether 'significant harm has occurred or is likely to occur' could be more clearly defined.

This would necessitate a move away from the drift towards increasingly coercive interventions on the strength of theoretical future risk towards a forensic evidence-based practice where there are reasonable grounds to invoke it. Reliance on hearsay would be minimised, as would intrusive questions such as whether parents were themselves abused as children.

Although the refocussing debate considered that an integrated approach to assessment with need as a starting point would give a fuller picture of a family's life, this does not take account of the precise nature of consent and the purpose of the inquiries undertaken as part of each stage of assessment. It has failed to resolve issues of stigma and distress: arguably it has added to them by increasing the number of families subject to the processes. Assessment is based on an extremely intrusive framework from which inferences are made not just about what services might be needed but about what might happen in the future in relation to risk, leaving families subjected to extensive and ongoing assessment. This approach is contentious.

The proposed restructuring would acknowledge a clearer focus on identifying (in relation to allegations) whether specific events have occurred. Non-contested cases and issues of neglect and emotional abuse could use a modified and less-intrusive version of the more systems-based, 'holistic' Initial Assessment framework, which originated in the *Framework for the Assessment of Children in Need and their Families*.[54] The issue of consent would have to be very carefully considered and the threshold of 'reasonable suspicion of significant harm' could be more precisely conceptualised.

As part of a Code of Practice, the extent to which someone cleared of wrongdoing in a criminal court can be subject to ongoing non-consensual assessment and investigation should be more clearly defined, such as the position highlighted by the applicant in *R v Swindon BC*.[55] In contested situations, the proposed police and social work forensic investigative model with clearly recorded outcomes could assist. The different standards of proof required for a criminal prosecution and civil proceedings do not indicate that forensic evidence-based practice cannot be employed for both types of inquiry. To the contrary, the evidence for the lower civil standard and higher criminal standard could be clearly articulated and set out with decisions made in light of analysis of where on the continuum the evidence sits.

It is worth noting that criminal proceedings are necessarily backward looking whereas social work assessments are necessarily forward looking, with past acts only relevant insofar as they provide a basis for an assessment of future 'risk'. A specialist, joint investigation would contribute to both of these elements. Such an approach could solve many of the current problems of uncertainty and the 'grey areas'.

On balance, the stigma that inevitably attaches to a family assessed in relation to an accusation of suspected significant harm, or in relation to parental insufficiency, could be better addressed by separating out the reasons for referral at the outset, with disputed referrals investigated by a joint body controlled by a Code of Practice. The key issue in relation to an allegation has to be establishing whether it is founded or unfounded to an appropriate evidential standard, using a Code of Practice which protects both investigator and families under investigation. The feeling that families cannot 'clear their names' and escape the stigma of referral and unwanted social work interference could, at least in part, be addressed by adopting stricter controls of this nature.

Outcomes: issues of exoneration and redress in unsubstantiated cases

In contrast to the wealth of literature that exists in relation to the issue of harm caused by State processes, there is very little in relation to the question of how to mitigate it. Effects on families (including children) identified from research is the shock, stigma and ongoing distress following allegations and suspicions. Where parents have significantly harmed their children these concerns may be able to be justifiably overridden, but in cases where they have not a solution needs to be found. It is known that it is not simply the acts of referral and assessment that are the cause: an additional layer of distress in unsubstantiated cases is lasting records which leave damaging allegations and lingering suspicions. These must all be considered to be contributory factors to family stress and harm. It is therefore important that consideration is given to these issues, even though they run counter to prevailing policies of increasing information gathering, retaining and sharing. Two suggestions are exoneration and the notion that records should be expunged where child abuse is alleged but not proved on the balance of probabilities. P. Davies explains that:

> The lack of exoneration or total closure that featured in our case only serves to prolong the agonies of the experience. Although of a different magnitude, there are parallels with notorious cases. Even when freed on appeal, Farrall reports how Sally Clark and Angela Cannings said 'Because of the way the legal system works, appeal judges do not say "we proclaim Sally Clark innocent of all crimes". They just say "her convictions are unsafe", no one used the word "innocent"', they were both robbed of 'the feeling they had been fully vindicated' (Farrall 2009, p. 189).[56]

The following extract from a 2003 House of Lords debate summarises the opposing positions. In this debate the Countess of Mar asked a question of the government:

> Whether the refusal of social services officials to expunge from their child abuse registers allegations against individuals of Munchausen's Syndrome by Proxy, which prove to be false, is an abuse of the human rights of the individuals concerned.[57]

The response given by the Parliamentary Under-Secretary of State, Department for Education and Skills (Baroness Ashton of Upholland) was unequivocal:

> My Lords, well-kept records provide an essential underpinning to good child protection practice. To expunge allegations of child abuse or neglect,

including those which subsequently prove to be unfounded, from local authority records would undermine the proper function of social services' recording and the effectiveness of the area child protection committee. Provided that a social services department complies with legislative requirements in the way that it records and discloses information, it would not breach the human rights of an individual.[58]

These comments encapsulate the opposing views, and their fundamentally different approaches. The issues can thus be summarised as:

- the 'welfare position', which advocates a bar on exoneration as it sees child abuse on a continuum of escalating need. This approach justifies keeping long term, extensive records, described as a 'picture' of a family. This approach is seen as a means of helping to protect children; and
- the 'justice position', which views the lack of ability for exoneration unacceptable, and the extensive record keeping as a gateway for future intervention as an unnecessarily stigmatising and damaging label that creates injustice, does not significantly benefit children and may harm them through unnecessarily controlling low-level interventions.

The two positions are not easily reconcilable. However, it is important to note that there is a significant difference between exoneration and expunging of records. Exoneration refers to a process by which lingering suspicion is removed whereas expunging records 'whitewashes' the event from records completely. There may be argument in favour of exoneration as an outcome, but expunging records may not help a harmed family. Without clear records reflecting an outcome that no evidence of abuse has been found, they may be left vulnerable to continued suspicion or assumptions of parental insufficiency. Robust privacy controls in line with the Anderson *et al.* recommendations together with clear recorded outcomes, including exoneration unless there is evidence to the contrary, is more realistic. This leads to the possibility of a specific remedy, for example no-fault compensation where harm to families is caused by these State processes. It is, of course, the case that records should eventually be destroyed in line with Data Protection Act principles after a specified period of time, and in this regard expunging the records is no different from the removal of data from any system once it is no longer relevant. The point of contention seems to be that, in a welfare framework, there is no agreed point at which the records are no longer relevant, whereas using the justice discourse the records are no longer relevant when there is insufficient evidence to pursue an allegation. Reform must take account of these views and create a 'middle ground' position which is reasonable in both circumstances.

To enable this, the new investigatory social work and police response to referrals involving allegations of suspected significant harm and suspected criminal conduct would control the investigatory data in relation to these referrals and their outcomes. This approach provides additional control over storage of the data and supports arguments that, although exoneration can be suggested as an outcome if no evidence to support the reason for a referral is found, expunging the record as if no investigation took place is not recommended. However, a requirement for the investigating body to keep records confidential with a clearly recorded outcome is needed to ensure that damaging allegations and suspicions do not continue to harm a family. This information should not transfer out to other organisations other than a simple record that an investigation took place (but not the grounds) and that the family were exonerated or otherwise. At the very least a clear finding should be made over whether any reliable evidence has been found to support an allegation and, if so, what that evidence is. Although this does not resolve all the issues it goes some way to achieving a fair outcome for families.

It is well established in cases that have travelled further through the system than investigation that there is potential for miscarriages of justice to occur. These are usually assumed to be the tragic cases where children have been harmed or killed when action could have been taken to remove them from a dangerous environment, whether their family home or a State placement. However, they may also describe cases of unnecessary and forcible removal of a child from their families where evidence is later adduced to suggest this decision was mistaken, or that due process was not followed. It also applies to cases that have led to criminal convictions of parents, overturned on appeal. Litigation in family and criminal courts following 'child protection' investigations in England and Wales[59] has given rise to judicial comment describing some of these cases as miscarriages of justice. Munby identified in *Re B (A Child) (Disclosure)* that 'it would be complacent of us to assume that miscarriages of justice do not occur in the family justice system'.[60] An individual who is arrested and interviewed regarding a criminal offence but is later released without charge would not be able to claim he was a victim of a miscarriage of justice, but such an experience would nevertheless be traumatic and distressing. Analogy can be drawn in relation to referral and assessment, but in this process there are fewer controls as a result of the lack of a Code of Practice. In cases of arrest and release without charge there is also no process of exoneration but there is a presumption of an 'entitlement to be presumed innocent'. The extent to which this is evident is questionable but there is at least a notional framework. For those suspected of child abuse, or who have 'risk characteristics' which are outside their control, there is no framework upon which they can rely. These parents are effectively in a limbo of suspicion.

Specific remedies in unsubstantiated cases

Given the issues concerning existing *ad hoc* remedies described in Chapter 7, specific provision for remedy should be drafted into the policy framework. Introduction of a non-fault regime specific to referrals, assessments and their outcomes would be preferable to the current reliance on remedies available on the basis of fault and blame via the diverse and confusing combination of potential statutory and common law remedies. Eligibility should be at the end of the assessment stage in cases where no further action is taken, or if further action is taken unsuccessfully. This question is connected to the issue of how unfounded allegations and suspicions following referral should be framed: are they inevitable consequences of a proportionate system, or should they be considered to be tantamount to a miscarriage of justice? If it is accepted that harm arises from the process of assessment to try to establish whether a child is 'in need' or 'at risk', then a method of addressing this harm must at least be considered. The key questions in relation to damages are:

- the appropriate parameters for damages to be paid at all, including clear guidelines on who is owed a duty of care by the State; and
- the basis on which they should be paid. Should they be based on negligent practice (fault-based) or based on evidence of harm, regardless of wrongdoing?

Arguments relating to State liability for damages have been comprehensively debated in relation to health care, particularly in relation to clinical negligence. There is a large body of literature from this field relating to both no-fault and fault-based compensation.[61] Many of the issues are similar to the issues of concern here.

The principle of an available remedy is well established in cases of harm caused by negligent State practice in relation to children, but it is fault-based. Negligence is a general common law area, and is not specific to cases of State harm. It has been held that no duty of care is owed to parents, leaving them unable to claim a remedy in negligence.[62] Whether or not parents give their consent to assessment it could be argued that, in the case of State practices where non-compliance carries the risk of measures being taken to force compliance, the duty of care should be higher rather than lower, although this does raise difficult issues in relation to what should happen if the parents' and the child's interests conflict and who should make that decision. This reasoning is the opposite of that adopted in *D v East Berkshire Community NHS Trust & another; M A K & another v Dewsbury Healthcare NHS Trust; R K & another v Oldham NHS Trust & another*[63] where no duty of care was held to exist between parents and those carrying out assessments.[64]

As the issues have been widely debated in relation to medical accidents and harmful practices, this literature provides useful insights into the debate about the State's liability towards those harmed by its practices. Harm can occur in relation to health care for a variety of reasons, frequently through errors. A fault-based system of compensation, based on negligence principles of establishing a duty of care and a breach of that duty as well as consequential loss, compensates some victims of errors. However, it does not compensate for harm caused by the system if its processes are working as intended. The fault model seeks to establish error through practice that falls below an acceptable standard[65] but does not address harm caused by damaging processes. This leaves the question of who should bear the burden of harm. If it is not the perpetrator, it must be the victim and the wider society. This is the basis for the widespread criticism of the 'fault'-based system. The concept of no-fault compensation is widely mooted as a possible solution in relation to health care and has already been adopted *inter alia* in Sweden and New Zealand.[66]

In the 1960s an early concept of no-fault compensation was mooted in the UK, recommending compensation for all patients with untoward and unexpected medical outcomes. It was not implemented. In the 1970s this was refined to consider whether it was possible for adverse outcomes to be avoided. This led to two models of remedy for harm caused by medical practices, with a focus on State-provided services. A. Davies, in his critique of compensatory models for health identifies the two models of regulation. The first focusses on blame and deterrence:

> One is the government's attempt to implement more fully a *punitive* model of regulation. Doctors in the NHS have traditionally been regulated through a set of liability regimes: complaints, disciplinary procedures (conducted by the NHS or by the General Medical Council (GMC), the profession's regulatory body) and negligence litigation. These regimes punish doctors who make mistakes, and seek to prevent future mistakes through deterrence.[67]

Whereas the second model is educative:

> The second facet of the reforms is very different in character. The government has been persuaded by evidence from other sectors, notably the aviation industry that the rate of error is likely to be reduced by encouraging people to learn from their mistakes. As a result, it also wants to implement an *educational* model of accountability. This will involve, for example, putting in place systems through which doctors can report mistakes, and providing feedback on how to avoid those mistakes in the future.[68]

Arguments balancing deterrence against educative priorities have focussed on whether it is desirable for a 'blame culture' to exist, or whether the focus should move from acts and omissions of individuals towards a systems-centred approach that seeks to improve through understanding why a problem occurred and how to prevent it in the future. In order to achieve this, there is a need for honesty and accuracy in the systems supporting and regulating decision making. The creation of a Code of Practice for referrals and assessments would strengthen the systems themselves in providing a clear account of the rights and restrictions of social workers. However, a robust system of individual and system error reporting is also necessary. In a 'blame culture' of deterrence, self-reporting of adverse events is not encouraged particularly if it is not mandatory. In the sensitive area of child abuse, a fault-based system is counterproductive and undesirable if it is accepted that the aim of any State system of child welfare is to improve family stability and wellbeing, not create a system whose actors have good reason to avoid admitting to mistakes and failures.

It is known that a punitive model of fault-based compensation is characterised by low levels of trust and high levels of enforcement.[69] At its heart is the establishment of minimum standards of competence, below which fault will be found and blame attributed. Where performance has fallen below the minimum acceptable standards sanctions are imposed and the victim can sue for compensation. There are adverse implications for State organisations if fault is found, which could take the form of damaging media publicity, management accountability and the possibility of inquiry. It is thus a deterrence model. A. Davies observes that:

> The classic law and economics justification for tort law, the Learned Hand formula, expresses this idea most clearly. A person should be found liable in negligence where the cost of avoiding the accident is less than the 'expected cost' of the accident, in other words, the cost of the accident multiplied by the probability of its occurrence. The fear of being held liable and required to pay a large sum of money in compensation will encourage that person to take all reasonable steps to prevent the accident.[70]

The punitive model clearly has its limitations. Its focus is on individual, not systemic, error and has thus been subject to debate and critique, particularly in comparison with the educative model. This model is similar to the use of Serious Case Reviews following severe, adverse incidents involving children who have usually had previous contact with social services. The punitive model does not acknowledge that systemic errors do not occur in isolation. Acts and omissions form part of a complex and interrelating chain of events. Therefore, in many cases that result in damage to the patient (in medical cases) or a family (in social work cases) it may not be possible to show that an individual acted in a way that directly caused the harm. This does not equate to a finding that no harm has occurred. In such circumstances it may be the acts or omissions of the individual that were the cause of the harm or the underlying system. The punitive model is thus not only arguably unfair to the blamed individual but fails to address an underlying flawed system, necessary to prevent such situations repeating.

In an attempt to address some of the issues identified in relation to the punitive model of compensation, the educative model adopts a different approach based on trust and education, rather than blame. The rationale is to encourage systems and the workers within those systems to aspire to a model of 'best practice'. Defining and communicating what is understood to be best practice is an important component of this model, which links into the notion of a Code of Practice in relation to assessments and a mechanism for remedies that gives prominence to questions of harm to families to balance the prominence given to cases meriting a Serious Case Review.

The educative model operates with an aim of continuous assessment and improvement. Feedback and self-reporting are a part of the continuous improvement process. Mistakes are seen as an opportunity to learn for the future, rather than an opportunity to attach blame to individuals, thus creating the opportunity for systemic failure to be addressed and balanced policy improvements to be made. Proponents of the educative model argue three advantages in the context of preventing future harm:[71]

- Positive recommendations can be made for making systems safer. By removing adverse consequences which occur under a punitive regime a learning environment is encouraged and avoidant behaviours on the part of the workers avoided.[72]
- More information about mistakes and harm becomes available by removing the punitive model as there is theoretically no reason to cover up, so the organisation can 'learn lessons'. The punitive model provides incentive to deny, cover up and conceal mistakes and errors. As well as measuring actual harm, this model encourages reporting of 'near misses' so that they can be analysed and avoided in the future.
- Mistakes and systemic errors can be analysed without the goal being the identification of individuals who are at fault. This may encourage a deeper and more meaningful analysis.

The educative model, however, has also attracted criticism and could be difficult and costly to implement in practice. Importantly it requires a cultural change within organisations from blame to learning which may be unfeasible.[73] This culture has been defined as 'the willingness and the competence to draw the right conclusions from [the organisation's] safety information system, and the will to implement major reforms when their need is indicated'.[74] A weakness of the educative model is its reliance on open and transparent self-reporting by staff working within the organisations. In order to achieve this, reports must be quick and simple, their impact on change must be visible and the culture of the organisation must allow workers to admit to mistakes.[75] However, there were shortcomings with the educational model that may result in an external appearance of 'learning lessons' from mistakes:

> At the organisational level, the desire to shield the organisation from being blamed by outsiders may impede the internal learning process. Staff may create a 'good story' to tell outsiders, and come to believe it themselves: as Sagan explains, 'committed individuals and organizations can turn the experience of failure into the memory of success'. No lessons are learned because the failure is covered up.[76]

This could entrench problems. It could encourage social workers to 'find something' because a finding of 'no further action' may have adverse consequences. Any family under intense scrutiny could be written up by social workers as exhibiting something that could be used to justify assessment. A 'no blame culture' that finds no fault may make it difficult for 'cover ups' to be identified and addressed.

Analysis and comparison of the punitive and educative models of compensation highlights their feasibility and their impact on an organisation.

Regardless of which approach is, on balance, preferable, the fundamental question remains: who should bear the cost of harm caused by State processes? If a State practice inherently causes harm the question must be whether it is reasonable that those harmed should bear their own loss, particularly in circumstances where they have not wanted or needed the State's intervention in the first place.

Unless specific provision is drafted into policy, parents who suffer harm are left with inadequate redress. No-fault, educative compensation may therefore be a better route to address this harm than leaving increasing numbers of families in this position. It must be acknowledged, however, that damages can never reasonably be sufficient to mitigate this type of harm. Damages may serve to validate a litigant's sense of being acknowledged, but it does not restore the victim to his or her former position. It is a moot point whether monetary damages would 'mend' the harm caused by assessment, and, if not, the question is what should be done, and whether this should be done as well as, or instead of, a monetary acknowledgement. The notion of severely traumatised family members left to cope does not seem to be in the best interests of children, their parents or society. It also does not seem reasonable that parents have to accept they bear the brunt of this damage when they have done nothing wrong.

Taking all the issues discussed above into consideration a no-fault scheme drafted into policy as a specific remedy based around support seems most appropriate. It allows prompt investigation and compensation without the need for the claimant to prove negligence. It attempts to convert a culture of blame to one of 'open disclosure', which is believed to facilitate clinical quality improvement. It also removes the right to sue, precluding any occurrence of a legal dispute, since it focusses only on compensating the injured party without apportioning blame. Such a scheme should acknowledge it is not only negligent practice that should prompt a remedy for harmed families. Alongside the scheme should be robust procedures for how a family in this circumstance should be treated by State agencies in order to re-establish trust and wellbeing, thus responding to the consistent findings that families can be damaged and frightened.

The threshold criteria for compensation would have to be established: is it dependent upon individual or system fault, whether accidental or deliberate, or is it assessed with reference to the impact on the victim regardless of any failure on the part of the State? Tan addresses the question of individual and systemic errors, and points out that:

> The underlying philosophy of no-fault compensation in health care is that clinical injury may not result from the fault of any individual, but rather from system errors. Furthermore, the complexity of medical practice makes it difficult to determine fault when errors occur.[77]

Compensation for harm caused by assessment must therefore take account of system errors as well as individual fault and bad practice. This would, at least in theory, provide a feedback mechanism for continuous policy improvement.

Conclusion: rebalancing – the basis for reform

Current policy places emphasis on increasing the number of families referred for assessment, but gives inadequate mechanisms for informed consent in cases where consent is necessary. Consequently, there is insufficient remedy for wrong decisions, which include decisions early in the process of referral and assessment.[78] Such cases are not generally high profile and attract little attention to the plight of harmed family members. Although high profile criminal cases highlighted the issues in relation to criminal convictions, there are a number of stages earlier in the system where harm occurs, including the referral and assessment stages. The high profile cases in the 2000s of Sally Clark,[79] Angela Cannings[80] and Trupti Patel[81] raised the profile of the question of justice in relation to welfare assessment where wrong conclusions about child welfare led to criminal convictions that were later overturned on appeal. However, cases that do not progress beyond assessment are not involved with the criminal justice system and there is no finding of 'guilt' that can be appealed.[82]

Cases arising from social work referrals and assessments occupy a unique position. However, despite the plethora of decision-making stages, the fundamental issue of whether the underlying reasons for the referral have actually occurred is often left undecided.[83] Social workers are less controlled than the police in relation to the lack of a Code of Practice to regulate their methods of investigation.[84] Additionally, there are competing and unequal interests involved: the State's welfare agenda championing the interests of the child, whose interests are 'paramount'.[85] Children cannot stop the State acting 'in their best interests'. The assessments themselves may be non-consensual or consent may be assumed.

It could be argued that, as referral and assessment are at the heart of cases that continue on to the courts, improvements to the referral and assessment process should help to prevent further miscarriages of justice in the family courts where 'innocent' parents may find it extremely difficult to challenge the increasingly expert and legal discourse. Mr Justice Ryder describes the plight of such parents:

> An 'innocent' parent caught in the glare of accusation and without knowledge or support is in a difficult position. Their attempts to find anything that might explain what had happened will inevitably have had something of the character of desperation if not hopeless medical conjecture. There is little that even an experienced judge can do other than to remind himself or herself of this possibility when considering the credibility of their evidence in this difficult context.[86]

If investigations themselves were controlled in the manner suggested above, and were carried out by a specialist investigative body led by local authority specialist social workers and the police, then evidence collected in relation to a criminal trial would be available for both the criminal and welfare issues. Assessment would be evidence-based, and, although the standard for the welfare issues would be lower (on the balance of probabilities), it would be a robust standard for which evidence would have to be obtained to proceed to litigation. This suggestion is not analogous to the current drift towards multi-agency assessments, carried out by bodies such as MASH (Multi-Agency Safeguarding Hubs). These do not separate out investigations, and their practices do not adhere to the Anderson *et al.* guidelines. Recent case law suggests their approach may be unlawful, which was the precise problem Anderson *et al.* identified.[87]

The suggestions and framework for reform runs counter to prevailing ideology and policy to locate ss.17 and 47 together outside the justice framework, but the evidence of systemic harm and lack of effective remedy do not fit comfortably into this welfare framework. Current policy and outcomes do not suggest that the system is working particularly effectively or is without harm. A redesigned system with clearer delineations of welfare and justice would enable the greatest dedicated focus on the cases where children are significantly harmed and delivered in a more robust framework. Where families need provision of services, this should operate as a genuinely non-coercive service. A clearer framework is needed of due process and evidence thresholds where allegations are made, in tandem with the ability for professional social workers to focus on non-blame-focussed, supportive social work where it is needed. Social workers themselves are under immense pressure from their dual welfare/policing role, and risk blame and public and professional censure when an adverse event occurs.

Individual harm and the wider harm to society will not be recognised and addressed unless referral and assessment are considered in the 'justice discourse' as well as the 'welfare discourse'. The system needs to be rebalanced back to evidence-based practice with skilled investigation of fact and clear outcomes, including a mechanism for removing lingering suspicion from parents where indicated. Issues of the difficulties of exoneration following referral and assessment are analogous to the early stages of a criminal investigation. In such investigations the position on record keeping as regards criminal allegations where prosecution and conviction do not follow are more precisely defined and controlled.

The suggestion of these policy changes is a step in a new direction; there is a pressing need for a rebalancing to take place in order for the system to work as it was intended. These suggestions do not take away any of the current abilities of the State to fulfil its statutory duties towards families and children, but enable a more precisely defined framework with clear accountabilities. The reduction of funds spent on the outlined areas of the child protection industry could be redirected towards the rebalancing of rationed early intervention. This needs to be refocussed away from assessed need at a very low threshold involving extremely intrusive loss of privacy for a family, towards greater universal services and an additional layer of subsidised universally available services for families that need and want them. The relentless collection of data collected to identify low-level concerns, and collected in order for families to check their eligibility for children in need services, is indeed a high price for families to pay for basic welfare services.

Notes

1 Department of Health (1999) *Working Together to Safeguard Children*, TSO, London; HM Government (2010) *Working Together to Safeguard Children*, TSO, London; HM Government (2013) *Working Together to Safeguard Children*, TSO, London; HM Government (2015) *Working Together to Safeguard Children*, TSO, London.
2 Earl Howe, Peer, the then Shadow Minister for Health. See for example: Hansard (2001) *House of Lords Debate*, 17 October, Col. 646, Earl Howe:

> many innocent people are being wrongly accused of child abuse and whose lives in consequence are being turned upside down without due justification . . . children are made to live in constant fear of being parted from their parents. The climate is like that of a witch hunt in which the voice of reason and all sense of proportion is lost.

Online at: www.publications.parliament.uk/pa/ld200102/ldhansrd/vo011017 /text/11017-06.htm#11017-06_head0 (Accessed 6 May 2016).
3 S.1(1) Children Act 1989 c.41.
4 See: Munby LJ, Sir James (2013) 'View from the President's Chambers: Expert Evidence', *Family Law* 43(7): 816–20. Online at: www.judiciary.gov.uk/wp-content /uploads/JCO/Documents/FJC/Publications/VIEW+President+Expert(3).pdf (Accessed 1 May 2016).
5 *Family Procedure Rules*, Part 25, Ministry of Justice, London. Online at www.justice.gov.uk/courts/procedure-rules/family/parts/part_25 (Accessed 1 May 2016).

> Rule 25.3 Experts' overriding duty to the court
> (1) It is the duty of experts to help the court on matters within their expertise.
> (2) This duty overrides any obligation to the person from whom experts have received instructions or by whom they are paid.

6 See discussion in Chapter 7.
7 Devine, L. (2015) 'Considering Social Work Assessment of Families', *Journal of Social Welfare and Family Law* 37(1): 70–83. Online at: http://dx.doi.org/10. 1080/09649069.2015.998005 (Accessed 28 February 2016).
8 *Gillick v West Norfolk and Wisbech Area Health Authority* [1986] AC 112.
9 Devine, L. and Parker, S. (2015a) 'Rethinking Child Protection Strategy: Learning from Trends'. Working Paper. Centre for Legal Research, University of the West of England. Online at: http://eprints.uwe.ac.uk/25258 (Accessed 28 February 2016).
10 For example: the categories of 'emotional abuse' and 'sexual abuse'.
11 For example: the 'Munchausen syndrome by proxy' or 'FII cases', 'cot' or 'SIDS' death cases and, more recently, the debate concerning 'shaken baby syndrome' or 'SBS' cases. All of these involve disputed expert theory giving rise to circumstantial 'evidence' against parents, generally mothers, although a recent case heard in 2011 involving a father, Mark Bruton-Young, was heard in Gloucester Crown Court where the prosecution expert was Professor Peter Fleming, who instigated the unreliable evidence given by Sir Professor Roy Meadow in the FII appeals. The defendant was acquitted. Unreported (i.e. no law report), but BBC News report available: BBC News (2011) 'Gloucester Man Cleared of Murdering Baby Daughter', 24 May, *BBC News Online*. Online

at: www.bbc.co.uk/news/uk-england-gloucestershire-13469941 (Accessed 28 February 2016).

12 Cawson, P., Wattam, C., Brooker, S. and Kelly, G. (2000) *Child Maltreatment in the United Kingdom: A Study of the Prevalence of Child Abuse and Neglect*, NSPCC, London; Radford, L., Corral, S., Bradley, C., Fisher, H., Bassett, C., Howat, N. and Collishaw, S. (2011) *Child Abuse and Neglect in the UK Today*, NSPCC, London. Online at: www.nspcc.org.uk/Inform/research/findings/child_abuse _neglect_research_PDF_wdf84181.pdf (Accessed 25 November 2011).

13 In the sense identified and described by Herbert Packer in relation to the criminal justice system. See: Packer, H.L. (1968) *Two Models of the Criminal Process, from The Limits of the Criminal Sanction*, Stanford University Press, Stanford, CA.

14 Anderson, R., Brown, I., Clayton, R., Dowty, T., Korff, D. and Munro, E. (2006) *Children's Databases: Safety and Privacy, A Report for the Information Commissioner*, Foundation for Information Policy Research, Bedfordshire. Online at: www.fipr.org/press/061122kids.html (Accessed 1 January 2016); Anderson, R., Brown, I., Dowty, T., Inglesant, P., Heath, W. and Sasse, A. (2009) *The Database State*, The Joseph Rowntree Reform Trust, York. Online at: www.jrrt.org.uk/publications/database-state-full-report (Accessed 1 January 2016).

15 Anderson *et al.* (2006) (n. 14), p. 191.

16 Ibid.

17 Ibid.

18 Ibid.

19 Ibid.

20 See the discussion in Chapter 2, Tables 2.2 and 2.3 and associated text considering the risk prediction numbers in Browne, K. and Saqi, S. 'Approaches to Screening for Child Abuse and Neglect', in Browne, K., Hanks, H., Stratton, P. and Hamilton, C. (eds) (1988) *Early Prediction and Prevention of Child Abuse*, Wiley, Chichester, pp. 57–85.

21 Anderson *et al.* (2006) (n. 14), pp. 191–2.

22 Ibid., p. 192.

23 Anderson *et al.* (2009) (n. 14).

24 Ibid., p. 7.

25 Defined by Creighton for the NSPCC to comprise physical abuse and sexual abuse. Emotional abuse and neglect were intended to be largely considered via s.17 processes unless neglect was 'wilful' in which case it is a criminal offence.

26 Anderson *et al.* (2009) (n. 14), p. 7.

27 For example, maternity services, health visiting services, GP health care, A&E care.

28 Anderson *et al.* (2009) (n. 14), p. 7.

29 Ibid.

30 Ibid.

31 Department of Health (1995) *Child Protection: Messages from Research*, HMSO, London.

32 Devine and Parker (2015a) (n. 9), p. 7.

33 See for example: Khyra Ishaq, Daniel Pelka and Peter Connelly (Baby P).

34 For example, the Initial Assessment form that is used by social workers when completing an Initial Assessment: Department of Health (2002) *Initial Assessment Record*, v.0, particularly, pp. 4, 6 and 7 and the assessment framework in *Working Together*.

35 Davies, L. (2010) 'Protecting Children: A Critical Contribution to Policy and Practice Development', PhD thesis (unpublished), p. 7. Online at: https://lizdavies.net/academia/publications/%20phd-thesis/ (Accessed 12 May 2016).

36 [2016] EWHC 14 (Fam).

37 Ministry of Justice (2008) *The Public Law Outline Guide to Case Management in Public Law Proceedings*, TSO, London. Online at: www.familylaw.co.uk/system/uploads/attachments/0000/2168/public_law_outline.pdf (Accessed 25 January 2016).

38 Devine, L. (n. 7).

39 Sure Start was an attempt at this model, although it had an agenda that went beyond what is proposed here in relation to surveillance of service users.

40 Lord Laming (2009) *The Protection of Children in England: A Progress Report*, HC 330, March 2009, The Stationary Office, London. Online at: www.cscb.org.uk/downloads/policies_guidance/national/The%20Protection%20of%20Children%20in%20England%20-%20%20a%20progress%20report%20by%20Lord%20Laming,%202009.pdf (Accessed 1 January 2016).

41 See: BBC News (2008) 'Care Cases "soaring after Baby P"', 24 November, *BBC News*. Online at: http://newsvote.bbc.co.uk/1/hi/uk/7745497.stm, (Accessed 4 May 2016). Also see for example: Bennett, R. (2009) 'Why Britain is Failing the Victims of Child Cruelty', 6 April, *The Times*, London.

42 Davies, L. (n. 35), p. 8.

43 Munro, E. and Parton, N. (2007) 'How Far is England in the Process of Introducing a Mandatory Reporting System?', *Child Abuse Review* 16(1): 5–16, 5.

44 Ibid., p. 14.

45 See: Devine, L. and Parker, S. (2015b) *Safer Children? Evaluating Child Protection and Safeguarding Training in Schools: An Empirical Study*, Centre for Legal Research, Bristol Law School, UWE, Bristol.

46 Devine and Parker (2015a) (n. 9), p. 45.

47 Davies, L. (n. 35), p. 8.

48 Devine (n. 7), p. 71.

49 Dumbrill, G. (2006) 'Parental Experience of Child Protection Intervention: A Qualitative Study', *Child Abuse and Neglect* 30(2006): 27–37, 35.

50 Davies, L. (n. 35), p. 21.

51 See: Police and Criminal Evidence Act 1984 c.60 and accompanying codes of practice: Home Office (2016) *Police and Criminal Evidence Act 1984 (PACE) Codes of Practice*. Online at: www.homeoffice.gov.uk/police/powers/pacecodes/ (Accessed 21 May 2016).

52 Cape, E. (2006) 'Arresting Developments: Increased Police Powers of Arrest', *Legal Action*, LAG Education and Service Trust, London, pp. 24–7, p. 24.

53 See: Sanders, A. and Young, R. (2007) *Criminal Justice*, 3rd edn, Oxford University Press, Oxford, pp. 164–5.

54 See: Department of Health (2000) *Framework for the Assessment of Children in Need and their Families*, TSO, London, Chapter 2, particularly Section 2.2.

55 [2001] EWHC Admin 334.

56 Davies, P. (2011) 'The Impact of a Child Protection Investigation: A Personal Reflective Account', *Child & Family Social Work* 16: 201–9, 208.

57 Hansard (2003) *House of Lords Debate*, 2 July, Vol. 650, Cols 874–7. Online at: http://hansard.millbanksystems.com/lords/2003/jul/02/child-abuse (Accessed 6 May 2016).

58 Ibid.

59 There is a separate and distinct system in operation in Scotland.

60 Per Ryder, J. in *Oldham MBC v GW and Ors* [2007] EWHC 136 (Fam), para. 75, quoting Munby, J. in *Re B (A Child) (Disclosure)* [2004] 2FLR 142, para 101.

61 See for example: National Health Service Litigation Authority (2010) *Reports and Accounts 2010*, HC 52, TSO, London; Bismark, M. and Dauer, E. (2006) 'Motivations for Medico-Legal Action: Lessons From New Zealand', *The Journal*

of Legal Medicine 27(1): 55–70; Farrell, A.-M., Devaney, S. and Dar, A. (2010) *No Fault Compensation Schemes for Medical Injury, A Review: Interim Report,* Scottish Government Social Research, TSO, Edinburgh; Chief Medical Officer (2003) *Making Amends: A Consultation Paper Setting Out Proposals for Reforming the Approach to Clinical Negligence in the NHS,* Department of Health, London; Farrell, A. and Devaney, S. (2007) 'Making Amends or Making Things Worse? Clinical Negligence Reform and Patient Redress in England', *Legal Studies* 27(4): 630; Constitutional Affairs Committee (2006) *Compensation Culture: Third Report of Session 2005–06,* TSO, London; Oliphant, K., Lewis, R. and Morris, A. (2006) 'Tort Personal Injury Claims Statistics: Is There a Compensation Culture in the United Kingdom?', *Torts Law Journal* 14: 158; Morris, A. (2011) 'Common Sense Common Safety: The Compensation Culture Perspective', *Journal of Professional Negligence* 27(2): 82; Wright, J. and Opperman, G. (2008) 'The Disclosure of Medical Errors: A Catalyst for Litigation or the Way Forward for Better Patient Management?', *Clinical Risk* 14: 193; Keren-Paz, T. (2010) 'Liability Regimes, Reputation Loss and Defensive Medicine', *Medical Law Review* 18(3): 363; and Dingwall, R. (2003) 'No Fault is No Panacea', *British Medical Journal* 326: 997.
62 See the case law discussion earlier in Chapter 7.
63 [2003] EWCA Civ. 1151.
64 See the reasoning in: *JD (FC) (Appellant) v East Berkshire Community Health NHS Trust and others (Respondents) and two other actions (FC)* [2005] 2 AC 373, para. 379.
65 See: *Bolam v Friern Hospital Management Committee* [1957] 1WLR 582, and *Sidaway v Board of Governors of Bethlem Royal Hospital and the Maudsley Hospital* [1985] AC 871.
66 For the position in New Zealand see for example Oliphant, K. (2007) 'Beyond Misadventure: Compensation for Medical Injuries in New Zealand', *Medical Law Review* 15(3): 357; in Scotland the No Fault Compensation Review Group chaired by Professor Sheila McLean recommended that in conjunction with improved social welfare provisions the Scottish Government should implement a no-fault system similar to that which operates in Sweden. See: McLean, S.A.M. (2011) *No Fault Compensation Review Group: Report and Recommendations,* Vol. I, Scottish Government, Edinburgh, p. 5. Online at: www.gov.scot/Topics /Health/Policy/No-Fault-Compensation/ReviewGroupVol1 (Accessed 1 May 2016).
67 Davies, A. (2002) 'Mixed Signals: Using Educational and Punitive approaches to Regulate the Medical Profession', *Public Law* Winter: 703–23, 703.
68 Ibid., 704.
69 Ibid., for example 703–5.
70 Ibid., 705.
71 See for example: Johnston, A.N. (1996) 'Blame, Punishment and Risk Management' in: Hood, C. and Jones, D. (eds) *Accident and Design: Contemporary Debates in Risk Management,* UCL Press, London, p. 83; and Reason, J. (2000) 'Human Error: Models and Management', *British Medical Journal* 320: 768.
72 See: Kirby, M. (2001) 'Tort System Reforms: Causes, Options, Outcomes', *Journal of Law & Medicine* 8: 380.
73 For example see: Sagan, S.D. (1993) *The Limits of Safety: Organizations, Accidents, and Nuclear Weapons,* Princeton University Press, Princeton, pp. 41–3.
74 Reason, J. (1997) *Managing the Risks of Organizational Accidents,* Ashgate, Aldershot, p. 196.
75 Ibid., Chapter 9.

76 Sagan, S.D. (n. 73), p. 258.
77 Tan, H. (2009) 'Minimising Medical Litigation: A Review of Key Tort and Legal Reforms', *International Journal of Law in Context* 5(2): 179–233, 179, 201.
78 See for example the discussion in: Harris-Short, S. and Miles, J. (2007) *Family Law: Text, Cases, and Materials*, Oxford University Press, Oxford, Chapter 12, pp. 899–984.
79 *R v Clark (Sally) (No.1)* 2000 WL 1421196 and *R v Clark (Sally) (No.2)* [2003] EWCA Crim 1020.
80 *R v Cannings (Angela)* [2004] 1 All ER 725 and *R v Cannings* [2004] EWCA Crim 1.
81 *R v Patel* (2003) (Unreported). References in the media include: BBC News (2003) 'Trupti Patel Says "no more children"', *BBC News Online*, 11 June. Online at: http://news.bbc.co.uk/1/hi/england/berkshire/3009134.stm (Accessed 4 May 2016); and BBC News (2003) 'Patel Mother Suffers Child Ban', *BBC News Online*, 13 June. Online at: http://news.bbc.co.uk/1/hi/england/berkshire/2987390.stm (Accessed 4 May 2016).
82 Over the past decade there has been an increase in 'child protection'-related criminal prosecutions, for example: Munchausen syndrome by proxy cases including: *R. v Cannings (Angela)* [2004] 1 All E.R. 725; *R. v Clark (Sally) (No.2)* 2003 EWCA Crim 1020; *R. v Clark (Sally) (No.1)* 2000 WL 1421196 and the shaken baby syndrome line of cases including for example: *Harris, Rock, Cherry and Faulder* [2005] EWCA Crim 1980. These prompted the recent Law Commission review (see: Law Commission (2009) *The Admissibility of Expert Evidence in Criminal Proceedings in England and Wales: A New Approach to the Determination of Evidentiary Reliability*, CP190, TSO, London; and Law Commission (2011) *Expert Evidence in Criminal Proceedings in England and Wales*, LC325, HC 829, TSO, London. Online at: www.lawcom.gov.uk/wp-content/uploads/2015/03/lc325_Expert_Evidence_Report.pdf (Accessed 1 May 2016)) and their recommendations for change to the way in which expert evidence is given and evaluated.
83 Parton, N., Thorpe, D. and Wattam, C. (1997) *Child Protection, Risk and the Moral Order*, Macmillan Press, Basingstoke, p. 196.
84 Police powers are regulated by the Police and Criminal Evidence Act 1984 c.60 (PACE). There is no similar Code of Practice in relation to the regulation of social work assessments; see discussion above in relation to the arguments for introducing a Code of Practice.
85 S.1(1) Children Act 1989 c.41.
86 Per Mr Justice Ryder in: *Oldham Metropolitan Borough Council v GW, PW, KPW (A Child) (by his children's guardian, Jacqueline Coultridge)* [2007] EWHC 136 (Fam), para. 39.
87 See: Anderson *et al.* (2006) (n. 14) and *AB and Anor, R (on the application of) v The London Borough of Haringey* [2013] EWHC 416 (Admin) (13 March 2013).

Conclusion

The book has examined the balance between State powers and private rights, concluding the balance is weighted heavily in favour of State power. The examination has included specific issues surrounding the legal framework, policy and system operation as well as the wider issues of theory and principle. It can be concluded that, whilst State powers are extensive, families and individual family members have limited rights, and restricted circumstances in which they can be exercised. Although in its infancy, the measures introduced by the Labour Government from its election in May 1997 in relation to mass surveillance, databasing, increased referrals and the mandate to agencies to respond on a statutory level to safeguarding has decreased the efficiency of the system. However, it has also enabled the start of a more critical debate to emerge.[1] The aim of this book is to contribute to this debate.

The rationale for State powers to intervene into private family life to investigate suspected significant harm is based on sound welfare principles. Historically, real dangers existed for children who had no overt protection. Children died as a result of poverty,[2] neglect,[3] cultural practices[4] and deliberate cruelty.[5] The notion of child welfare as a public responsibility grew from social and political concern over the plight of children as a disadvantaged group. Consequently, the argument supporting a level of State interference into private autonomy is strong. However, the ongoing critical debate is crucial to determine the appropriate level and limits of that interference, and the appropriate balance with private rights.

Practices of State intervention follow a generally accepted principle that there is a necessary level of interference with individual liberty in order to protect society and individual citizens. For example, the police will investigate crime. It is generally accepted, at least as a theoretical concept, that the police should have certain powers to not only detect crime but also to take steps to prevent it.[6] However, there is debate about the precise level at which citizens should be policed in their private lives outside the criminal justice system.[7] Child protection and safeguarding systems and processes exemplify the issues. A comparison can be drawn between the rationale for interference with personal liberty in a criminal matter and the rationale for interference following safeguarding or child protection concerns. The ideology for both is the notion the State has a duty to 'police' in order to protect others from harm. However, the role of the police is restricted to investigating suspected crime, whereas the role of the local authority is to investigate every aspect of private family life. This is where the interface, and thus the conflict, between the welfare and policing agendas are most evident.[8] Assessment does not only investigate the reason for the referral, but assesses every aspect of a family's private life. It is arguable that local authority social services departments operate the most powerful methods of surveillance and interference in the UK, without being constrained by the same safeguards and controls provided by PACE.[9] It is difficult, therefore, to see precisely where the limits of local authority powers lie. Conversely, private rights are limited and those that exist are only able to be exercised in restricted circumstances. The lack of private rights derives from the origins of the system in welfare ideology. However, the rise of the policing and surveillance ideology has not triggered appropriate safeguards and protections for families caught within its net. Consequently, the argument that there is an appropriate balance between State powers and private rights is weak. In cases that initially fall below the threshold of significant harm the right of a parent or child to refuse assessment may be seen as grounds to escalate matters into a non-consensual process, or parents and children consent because they do not know they have a choice. In either scenario the family are disempowered from the outset. One of the central questions in the book was to consider how a different system might look which does not leave abused children disempowered whilst rebalancing family justice.

State powers of surveillance, referral and assessment in relation to child welfare are demonstrably extensive. Although families can theoretically refuse to consent to assessment, an assessment could be escalated to take place under s.47 in order to justify it being non-consensual. It is possible that, before parents are asked for their consent, a form of investigation has already started via inter-agency inquiries and information sharing about the family. The wording of s.47 does not place specific restrictions on the powers of local authorities to investigate, nor does it dictate what form the investigation will take.[10] Once a family has been referred into the system, the assessment schema set out in *Working Together to Safeguard Children*[11] operates. A decision about whether to assess will be made. Once assessment begins, the family moves through stages of the schema which will only discard those that fail to meet the criteria for progression.[12] Once cast as a 'case' the discourse of the family carries little weight. The schema serves to mediate and control the subject's discourse and evaluate that of the professional: once 'in the system' subjects have little opportunity to be heard. The best outcome they can hope for is to be discarded either with or without services should they need them. Consequently, even if no evidence of child abuse is found, an allegation is at best considered 'unsubstantiated'. Opinion can legitimately be recorded regardless of whether the foundation on which it is based is accurate or not. A 'concern' presumably amounts to an opinion and therefore cannot be overridden. A finding of need is not officially considered contentious, although families may be offended, intimidated and demeaned by a suggestion that they are deficient, or conversely may feel they have needs that the local authority does not recognise.

Consent is a key issue for productive working relations between families and the State. There are serious deficiencies in the dispensing of consent in relation to surveillance, referring and assessing at a level of need, without clear and specific grounds to reasonably suspect significant harm. In fact, the precise boundaries of consent, and circumstances where it is needed, are unclear as a consequence of the drift towards a mix of welfare and policing ideology delivered within the same framework. This approach is a serious problem with a system which aims to address a welfare issue via policing processes without regard for due process.

The notion of children's welfare being the responsibility of the State as well as of parents has mirrored the erosion of privacy. The original intention in the Children Act 1989 that State powers would only be used coercively where necessary has been supplanted by subsequent legislation and the policy framework. These have caused an unprecedented level of State paternalism and surveillance of families. The claim that this rise in State powers and erosion of private rights is justified by the need to protect large numbers of abused children from their parents is weak. The argument is diminished by the uncertainty surrounding child prevalence estimates, and the longitudinal data, which demonstrates that, despite the policy drive to increase referrals, no corresponding increase in substantiated cases of significant harm are reported.[13] As a policy for detecting high levels of child abuse, increased State power is not yielding strong evidence that it is successful. Successive prevalence studies do not suggest the level of undetected child abuse is falling; despite the uncertainty over the accuracy of the estimates, there is little of substance to indicate the current policy is making a significant difference.

Another factor contributing to lack of balance is the lack of consensus of *what* is being measured and *how* it can be measured. This uncertainty has stifled effective cross-discipline debate. Whilst development of a civilised system of child protection suggests a multidisciplinary approach, it has not resulted in cross-discipline critique taking place. There has been an assumption that there is a need for the dominant discourse from each discipline to *inform* rather than critique the other. Questioning the orthodoxy in child protection could be criticised as an attempt to undermine children's welfare. This is a powerful disincentive but leaves excesses of State power unchecked.

In cases of suspected child abuse, and increasingly in cases of low-level concerns about children, there is a natural fear of making errors that result in a failure to protect children. The most extreme examples concern errors of under-interference that result in a child dying as a result of abuse. This concern is very legitimate but should not override equally legitimate critical examination of whether there is sufficient protection afforded for referred families, of whom the vast majority are not harming, let alone killing, their children.

The evidence points to a conclusion that State power is excessive and not adequately balanced with private rights. This is not to say that the system and the rationale for it is wrong, but it operates on a dominant series of presumptions about child welfare that embeds a family policing agenda within a welfare framework. The result is a system which does not take adequate account of the needs of the family to have protection against excessive State power and appropriate remedies for harm caused.

Additional adverse consequences of increased surveillance, referral and assessment may be that children who do pass the threshold of significant harm and face life threatening situations are still in danger. They may be lost in the excess of data that is generated by the expansion of child protection into safeguarding, creating one process tasked with identifying need and risk on a continuum. This creates difficulties and complexities around the relationship of social workers with families. Forcing families to 'work with' a social worker who is also policing them can be construed as coercive and controlling. It is not an easy partnership for either the social worker or the family. Conversely, the rare but invariably shocking fatal cases that occur and emerge into public consciousness are used to reinforce the paradigm as opposed to prompting debate. Public inquiries and Serious Case Reviews have been criticised for being a mechanism for reinforcing surveillance and intervention agendas rather than providing a prompt for re-evaluation.[14] On the other hand, the plight of children and their parents encountering severe stress and adverse outcomes once in the system are not prioritised. The current imbalance between State powers and private rights leaves children and families vulnerable to both over- and under-interference.

A system of State power which does not adequately balance the interests of those affected by it is open to criticism that it infringes civil liberties and is opressive. It is ironic that a principled ideology intended to protect some of the most vulnerable members of society has become open to criticism for its excessive use of State power. It is hoped that this book will contribute to the case for rethinking child protection strategy.

Notes

1 See for example: Anderson, R., Brown, I., Clayton, R., Dowty, T., Korff, D. and Munro, E. (2006) *Children's Databases: Safety and Privacy, A Report for the Information Commissioner*, Foundation for Information Policy Research, Bedfordshire. Online at: www.fipr.org/press/061122kids.html (Accessed 1 January 2016); and Wrennall, L. (2010) 'Surveillance and Child Protection: De-mystifying the Trojan Horse', *Surveillance and Society* 7(3/4): 304–24. Online at: http://library.queensu.ca/ojs/index.php/surveillance-and-society/article/view/4158 (Accessed 1 January 2016).
2 See for example: Spencer, N. (2000) *Poverty and Child Health*, Radcliffe Medical Press, NJ; Spencer, N. (1996) 'Race and Ethnicity as Determinants of Child Health: A Personal View', *Child Care Health & Development* 22: 327–46; Marmot, M. (1996) 'The Social Pattern of Health and Disease' in: Blane, D., Brunner, E. and Wilkinson, R. (eds) *Health and Social Organisation: Towards a Health Policy for the 21st Century*, Routledge, London, pp. 42–67; Power, C., Manor, O. and Fox, J. (1991) *Health and Class: The Early Years*, Chapman and Hall, London; Reading, R. (1997) 'Social Disadvantage and Infection in Childhood', *Sociology of Health & Illness* 19: 395–414; Sidebotham, P., Heron, J., Golding, J. and the ALSPAC study team (2002) 'Child Maltreatment in the "Children of the Nineties": Deprivation, Class, and Social Networks in a UK Sample', *Child Abuse & Neglect* 26(12): 1243–59; and Spencer, N. (2008) *Health Consequences of Poverty for Children*, End Child Poverty, End Child

Poverty, End Child Poverty, London. Online at: www.endchildpoverty.org.uk/
files/Health_consequences_of_Poverty_for_children.pdf (Accessed 4 August 2011).
3 See for example: Nagler, J. (2002) 'Child Abuse and Neglect', *Current Opinion
in Pediatrics* 14(2): 251–4; Benziman, G. (2011) *Narratives of Child Neglect
in Romantic and Victorian Culture*, Palgrave Macmillan, London; Greenwood,
G. (1869) *The Seven Curses of London*, Blackwell, Oxford; Pinchbeck, I. and
Hewitt, M. (1973) *Children in English Society*, 2 vols: (1969) *From Tudor Times
to the Eighteenth Century*; (1973) *From the Eighteenth Century to the Children
Act 1948*, Routledge, London; and Behlmer, G. (1982) *Child Abuse and Moral
Reform in England 1870–1908*, Stanford University Press, Stanford, CA.
4 See for example: *Factsheet No. 23: Harmful Traditional Practices affecting the
Health of Women and Children*, Office of the High Commission for Human
Rights. Online at: www.ohchr.org/Documents/Publications/FactSheet23en.
pdf (Accessed 4 May 2016).
5 For example: Margaret Waters in 1870 who murdered children boarded out
into her care. Mentioned in Eekelaar, J. and Maclean, M. (1994) *A Reader on
Family Law*, Oxford University Press, Oxford. For an interesting account of the
practice of baby farming, see: Haller, D. (1989) *Bastardy and Baby Farming
in Victorian England*. Online at: www.loyno.edu/~history/journal/1989-0
/haller.htm (Accessed 4 May 2016).
6 For debate concerning State paternalism in a moral sense, see for example the
Hart–Devlin debate which focussed upon the tensions between individual liberty
and government controls over citizens' behaviour. Hart questioned the con-
ventional morality that objections by a few members of the population should
be justification for preventing people doing what they wanted to do (as long
as it did not harm others). See: Hart, H.L.A. (1963) *Law, Liberty, and Morality*, Stanford University Press, Stanford, CA. Devlin, however, considered that
any category of behaviour was capable of posing a threat to social cohesion.
Therefore, morals laws are justified to protect society against the disintegrating
effects of actions that undermine the morality of a society: society has the right
to defend its own existence. See: Devlin, P. (1965) *The Enforcement of Morals*,
Oxford University Press, Oxford. For specific controls over the extent of the
power of the police to investigate citizens suspected of a crime see: Police and
Criminal Evidence Act 1984 c.60 (PACE).
7 For example, contentious areas such as the rights of citizens when investigated
by the police or the rights of suspected terrorists have been the focus of much
debate and critique. In relation to citizens' rights and suspected terrorism the
controversy over the Anti-terrorism, Crime and Security Act 2001 c.24 illustrates
the tension between the government's assertion that draconian measures are necessary to protect the public against terrorism, which must be balanced against the
rights of citizens not to be deprived of their human rights. This Act was intended
to make it easier for law enforcement agencies to track terrorist funds, share information and detail suspects as the Act grants the Home Secretary the power to
detain suspected international terrorists without trial if deportation is not possible, because it would endanger the suspects' lives. Article 5, Human Rights Act
1998, guarantees the right to liberty and grants protection against detention
without charge. Since this provision violates Article 5 the Home Secretary has
to assert that the UK is in a 'state of public emergency'. This introduction of
anti-terror legislation in the UK in the wake of 9/11 attacks adds to a significant
debate in relation to citizens' rights when suspected of a crime, which had previously led to the introduction of the Police and Criminal Evidence Act 1984 c.60
in an attempt to create a balance between the powers of the police and the rights
of citizens.

8 See diagram of the assessment framework from *Working Together* guidance in: HM Government (2015) *Working Together to Safeguard Children*, TSO, London, p. 22.

9 Police and Criminal Evidence Act 1984 c.60.

10 S.47 Children Act 1989 c.41 states *inter alia* that where a local authority 'has reasonable cause to suspect that a child who lives, or is found, in their area is suffering, or is likely to suffer, significant harm, the authority shall make, or cause to be made, such enquiries as they consider necessary to enable them to decide whether they should take any action to safeguard or promote the child's welfare'.

11 HM Government (2015) (n. 8), p. 22.

12 See explanation of the stages of Smith's schema in Chapter 5: Smith, D. (1990) *Facts, Texts and Femininity: Exploring the Relations of Ruling*, Routledge, London, published previously as Smith, D. (1978) 'K is Mentally Ill: The Anatomy of a Factual Account', *Sociology* 12(1): 23–53.

13 Devine, L. and Parker, S. (2015) *Rethinking Child Protection Strategy: Learning from Trends*, Working Paper, Centre for Legal Research, Bristol Law School, UWE, Bristol, Online at: http://eprints.uwe.ac.uk/25258/ (Accessed 28 February 2016).

14 Lord Laming (2003) *The Victoria Climbié Inquiry Report*, HC 570, 24 June. Online at: www.publications.parliament.uk/pa/cm200203/cmselect/cmhealth/570/570.pdf (Accessed 1 January 2016). Lord Laming (2009) *The Protection of Children in England: A Progress Report*, HC 330, TSO, London.

Index